DYNAMICS OF RURAL DEVELOPMENT IN TRIBAL AREAS

About the Author

S.K. Pachauri is a serving officer of the Indian Administrative Service. His educational background includes a B.A. (Hons), and M.A. in History from St. Stephens College, Delhi. He holds a Ph.D. in Public Administration from the Osmania University. Dr Pachauri has extensive experience in the administration of rural development and tribal development programmes in the State of Andhra Pradesh. He is currently involved in the development of the weaker sections of society, in his position as Director in the Ministry of Home Affairs.

Dr. Pachauri has participated in several seminars and conferences and has number of published and unpublished articles to his credit. He has also undergone training at the Institute of Local Government Studies at the University of Birmingham, U.K.

DYNAMICS OF RURAL DEVELOPMENT IN TRIBAL AREAS

A Study of Srikakulam District, Andhra Pradesh

S.K. PACHAURI

CONCEPT PUBLISHING COMPANY PVT. LTD.
NEW DELHI-110059

ISBN: 978-81-7022-155-5

First Published 1984

Published and Printed by

Concept Since 1974

Concept Publishing Company Pvt. Ltd.
A/15-16, Commercial Block, Mohan Garden,
New Delhi-110059 (India)
T: 91-11-41101460
E: publishing@conceptpub.com, *W*: www.conceptpub.com

Preface

TRIBAL uprisings have been numerous down the centuries, but the uprising in Srikakulam during 1968 to 1972 was unique because it was for the first time that Marxist and Leninist principles were tested in tribal areas. It also proved the point that the tribal belts in India are neglected and need an overhaul of their administrative bodies. A study of public agencies, central, state, local and corporate, give a better appreciation of the organisation and functions of the Central Development Agencies, which are under focus in this book.

The Girijan Development Agency, a centrally sponsored scheme was launched in the tribal areas of Srikakulam in January 1972. The main thrust of the Girijan Development Agency was on a family and area-based approach to tribal development. This angle was not developed by most other agencies, perhaps this being their detracting element. Further, the GDA is unique not merely in its approach and focus, but also in its organisation. The Agency offers an interesting example of partnership among central, state, local agencies involving an integrated approach on the part of different levels of government in various spheres of action—a contribution to development administration.

Hence this study will be of great interest both to the academic and to practitioners of public administration.

New Delhi

S.K. PACHAURI

Acknowledgements

My gratitude goes out to my parents, Atma Ram Pachauri and Sumitra Pachauri, my brother R.K. Pachauri and his family, my wife Swaraj and daughter Nayantara, my guide and Professor Dr M.A. Muttalib.

I am indebted to Dr D.R. Pratap, Director, and Mr A. Somasekhar, Deputy Director, Tribal Cultural Research and Training Institute for their generous help in providing library facilities and rare manuscripts and other papers connected with the work. I must express my gratitude to my two Personal Assistants, Sri G. Seetha Ramulu and Sri B.G. Ranganatham who were always readily available to provide their excellent secretarial assistance.

S.K. Pachauri

Contents

List of Tables

List of Charts

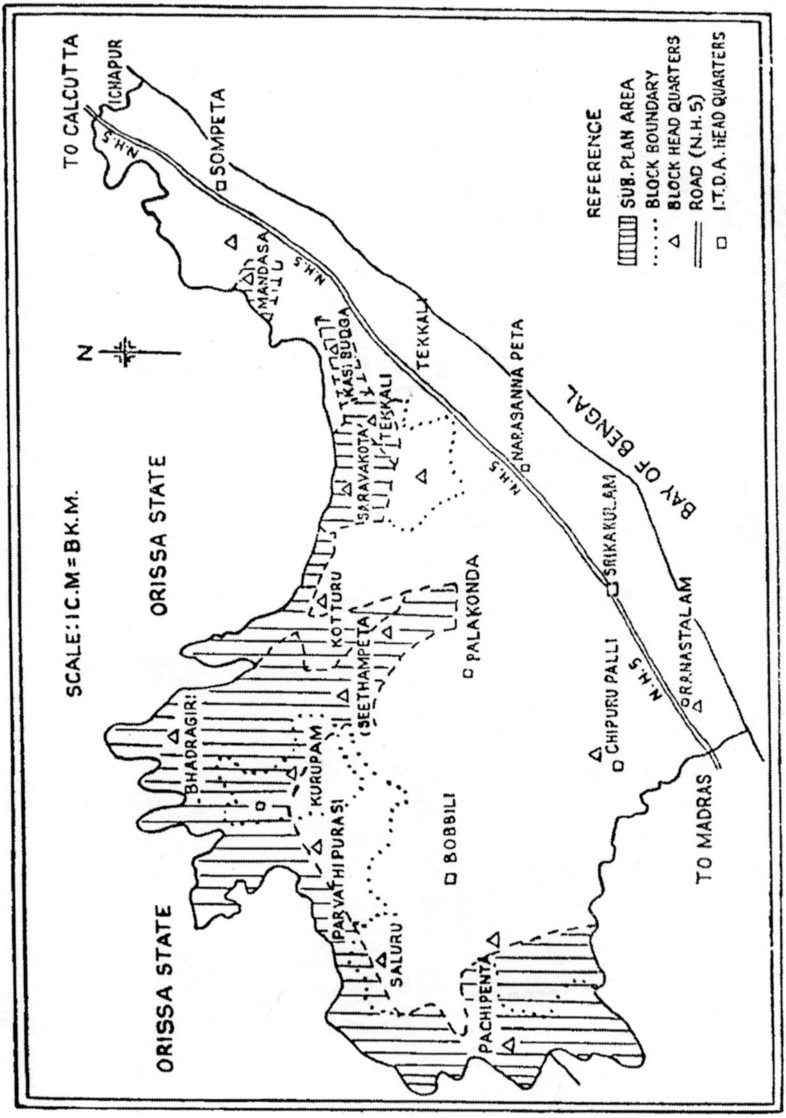

Map : Integrated Tribal Development Agency, Srikakulam

1

INTRODUCTION
Tribal Development

> Believe nothing, O Monks, merely because you have been told it...or because it is traditional, or because you yourselves have imagined it. Do not believe what your teacher tells you merely out of respect for the teacher. But whatsoever, after due examination and analysis, you find to be conducive to the good, the benefit, the welfare of all beings—that doctrine believe and cling to, and take it as your guide.
>
> —*Lord Buddha*

MAN from the very beginning has always struggled to achieve better living conditions and the well-being of his family. As a social being it is also his concern to look after the needs and welfare of those around him. At this point of time it is seen that one-half of the world is highly developed, whereas the other half is underdeveloped and is still struggling with the problem of development, poverty, illiteracy, disease and all the other afflictions which continue to pester mankind. With the rise of the modern democratic state and the emergence of the Industrial Revolution, man's insight into the issues regarding welfare has become more sharp. Rural development as a concept has assumed importance. Very often, policy is shaped because of a particular problem and by solving that problem a new policy emerges. It is here that we come across the problem of interpretation of facts according to an individual style of functioning. Sometimes it is the bureaucrat, sometimes it is the politician and of course the specialist who has his own way of looking at things and interpreting them. During the past thirty years, errors are bound to have cropped up and it happens that policy is made without the problem having been clearly defined.

TRIBAL DEVELOPMENT POLICY

The importance of policy-making cannot be underestimated or over-emphasised in public administration. It is policy which determines the course of action and events of major importance. According to Lasswell,[1,2] the two most important aspects of policy are the intelligence and the appraisal functions. For working purposes the intelligence functions can be understood to include gathering, processing and dissemination of information to participants in the decision process of a body politic. Appraisal is concerned with characterising the degree to which policy objectives have been achieved and to assign responsibility to those who effectively condition the results and are formally responsible for them. It will, however, be noticed that policy is always liable to shift and change according to the circumstances and conditions prevalent in a given situation. In our country, for instance, developmental policy has been translated into action by means of the Five Year Plans. This has been particularly the case after independence. In addition the problems are so vast and diverse that it is but natural that all sections in a democratic system would like to have a 'say' in policy makings. Therefore, problems and demands are constantly being defined and re-defined in the policy process. In our policy towards tribal development there is a bias in favour of the tribals which reflects the attitudes and feelings of the makers of the Constitution and great political stalwarts like Mahatma Gandhi and Pandit Jawaharlal Nehru.

Since independence, Pandit Jawaharlal Nehru took a great deal of interest in tribal development. He was the chief architect of planning in free India and it was his vision and genius which contributed to the formulation of Five Year Plans. Pandit Nehru's views on tribal development were as follows:[3]

1. People should develop along lines of their own genius and we should avoid imposing anything on them.
2. Tribal right in land and forest should be protected.
3. We should try to train and build up a team of their own people to do the work of administration and development.
4. We should not over-administer these areas or overwhelm them with a multiplicity of schemes. We should rather work through and not in rivalry to their own social and cultural institutions.
5. We should judge results not by statistics or the amount of money spent, but by the quality of human life that is evolved.

In more concrete terms the Constitution made provision for promotion of the welfare of scheduled tribes and for raising the level of administration of scheduled and tribal areas to the state level. Article 275 of the Constitution provides for grants-in-aid from the Consolidated Fund of India to states for implementation of developmental programmes. In addition, article 46 lays down as a directive principle of state policy that the state should promote with special care the education and economic interests of weaker sections. Special funds have thus been provided in each plan for welfare of scheduled tribes in the sector of welfare of backward classes.

Plan programmes—A review

There is generally an impression that investments have been made for tribal welfare since the First Plan.[4] These investments, however, are only identifiable under the welfare of backward classes sector. The latter is supplementary to whatever provision is available for development of tribal and scheduled areas under general sectors. Under the welfare of backward classes, it is true that larger expenditures have been incurred for the scheduled tribes, but compared to the total size of the plans, the proportionate expenditure for this purpose has diminished. This will be clear from Table 1.1.

TABLE 1.1 : **Plan programme review**

(Rs. in crores)

Plan Period	Total Plan	Scheduled Tribes	Percentage
First Plan	1960	19.93	1.0
Second Plan	4672	42.92	0.9
Third Plan	8577	50.53	0.5
1966-69	6756	32.32	0.5
Fourth Plan	15902.2 (outlay)	75.00	0.04

In the special sector for welfare of backward classes, the schemes under centre and states can be categorised as those relating to education, economic upliftment, health, housing and other schemes. Progress of expenditure from plan to plan under each category is given in Table 1.2.

TABLE 1.2 : **Progress of expenditure from Plan to Plan under each category**

Group of schemes	Expdr. in First Plan	Expdr. in Second Plan	Expdr. in Third Plan	Expdr. in 1966-69 Plan
Education	5.10	7.84	13.51	9.32
Economic development	4.59	20.00	30.71	24.07
Health, housing & others.	10.14	15.08	6.31	1.93
Total	19.83	42.92	50.53	35.32

The pattern of spending for scheduled tribes except for the First Plan shows emphasis on economic development. This is on account of establishment of tribal development blocks in the Second Plan period. The highest expenditure for economic development of Rs. 30.71 crores in the Third Plan includes not only tribal development blocks but also some major road construction in Assam, Andhra Pradesh and Madhya Pradesh. Major communication schemes after the Third Plan were not debted to plan outlays in tribal welfare sector. This decision taken after the Third Plan, reflects lower expenditure in 1966-69 and in the Fourth Plan. Similarly, there was decrease in expenditure on health, housing and other schemes since the Second Plan, because of inclusion of more tribal areas under tribal block schemes for health, drinking water supply and similar items.

The Fourth Plan

At this juncture, it would be appropriate to discuss certain other events that influenced policy-making. With the commencement of the Fourth Plan, objectives for development of weaker sections and priorities for welfare underwent a change. At about the time of the formulation of the Fourth Plan, Mrs. Gandhi, the then Prime Minister raised the slogan *garibi hatao*. The use of extremism owing to the Naxalite movement also had an impact on the policy-makers. An outstanding feature of the Fourth Plan is that it devotes a very conspicuous and oft-repeated emphasis on "the common man, the weaker sections and less privileged." Reference was made continuously to articles 41, 45 and 46 of the Constitution and the Commission emphasised "that planning should result in greater equality in income and wealth and that benefits of development should accrue more and more to the relatively less privileged classes of society." Hence this was the departure point from the earlier plans and a strong emphasis was placed on solving the problems of the poor. It is from the Fourth Plan onwards that we have special programmes like Small Farmers' Development Agency, Tribal Development projects, Forestry schemes, crash schemes for rural employment.

The Commission indicated a number of measures which it intended to pursue. It wanted, "that in the implementation of the programmes, the weaker are looked after first and the benefits of development are made to flow by plan investment in the under-developed regions and the more backward sections of the community." The development of water resources for the substantial farmers should be financed through their own savings and loans; immediate investment for work which benefit the small farmers should be undertaken through public funds. It could be said with considerable amount of experience that earlier plans had been made under the slogan of socialism during the Nehru era and that is why Professor B.S. Minhas in his book, *Planning for the Poor* said that there was no proper policy frame up to the Fourth Plan.[5] For the first time, planning priorities shifted from establishing a "socialistic pattern of society". But the objectives of planning defined in the Fourth Plan are as follows: "The broad objectives of planning could thus be defined as rapid economic development accompanied by continuous progress towards equality and social justice and the establishment of the social and economic democracy." So the object of a socialistic pattern of society has been substituted by the expression social and economic democracy. Professor Gadgil, noted defects in Indian planning in 1966, viz., (1) The failure of the tax system as a means of restraining consumption and of promoting equality; (2) The failure of real industrialisation and the consequent accentuation of the employment problem; (3) The complete failure to evolve of properly structured overall regulatory framework for the private sector in which graded policy, new investments and expenses, import and export policy, fiscal policy and cost and price policies could be integrated for achieving the plan results. It was this "total absence of policy frame which was the most outstanding feature of the planned Indian economy". The net result of all this according to Professor Gadgil was that in the aggregate the economy operates as almost "a *laissez-faire* economy, in part modified by the operation of particular controls". It is also significant to note that from the Fourth Plan period onwards the area development approach was introduced to implement development projects in backward areas.

New strategy in the Fifth Plan

In the Fifth Plan the programmes prepared for the welfare of scheduled castes and scheduled tribes all together proposed an amount of five hundred crores.[6] The proposals include besides continuation of the existing programmes some entirely new ones. An additional amount of Rs. 500 crores has been proposed for the uplift of hilly and tribal areas. During the Fifth

Plan period the concept of integrated tribal development and preparation of sub-plans was first introduced.

From Table 1.3, it will be seen that there is a continuous decrease in the percentage spending for the development of tribal people. In the Fifth Plan, however, the additional allotment of Rs. 500 crores has changed the picture to some extent which is a healthy sign. The total per capita expenditure till the Fifth Plan comes to Rs. 221.25 only. Looking towards the state-wise figures it is found that Meghalaya where four-fifths of the population is tribal, is spending about Rs. 800 per head in the Fifth Plan.

Policy in Hyderabad State

In Andhra Pradesh, policy towards tribal welfare has always been dynamic and in keeping with the guidelines issued by the Central Government. Prior to 1956, when Andhra Pradesh was formed the Government of Hyderabad had initiated a series of measures which went a long way to ameliorate the conditions of tribals in the Nizam Dominion.[7] Special emphasis was laid on aboriginal welfare and education. Special rules were framed for protecting the tribals from exploitation by outsiders and tribal panchayats were formed which had the backing of law. "The main object of these Panchayats is to simplify the administration of justice to settle most disputes and punish minor offences speedily and without recourse to distinct course of law and to allow the tribals to lead their social life according to their ideas and the values of their traditions." In Andhra area, tribal tracks were always administered according to rules and regulation and generally justice was administered very effectively.

Recent efforts

In the statements of outlays (see Appendices) the various allocations from plan to plan were divided sectorally in recent times. From the Fourth Plan onwards a number of area development schemes have been initiated all over the state. They have found their logical conclusion in the Fifth Five Year Plan where all the agency areas are covered by I.T.D.A. A word may also be mentioned that in successive budgets over the last few years in Andhra Pradesh, an increasing emphasis has been

TABLE 1.3 : **Plan expenditure and the tribals**

(In crores of Rupees)

Plan period	Total Expenditure	Expenditure for S.Ts.	% of total Expenditure	S.T. population	Per capita Expenditure
First Plan: 1951-56	1,960	17.47	0.83	2.25	7.76
Second Plan: 1956-61	4,672	48.86	0.87	2:62*	18.65
Third Plan: 1961-66	8,577	52.55	0.61	2.99	17.57
Annual Plan: 1966-69	6,756	34.64	0.51	3.36*	10.31
Fourth Plan: 1969-74	15,902	75.00	0.47	3.80	19.74
Fifth Plan: 1974-79	54,411	105.00	0.22	4.11*	25.57
		500.00**	0.92	4.11*	121.65

*The increase being 32.73 in five years for 1956, 32.73 in five years for 1966 and 27.09 in three years for 1974.

**This amount of Rs. 500 crores has been allotted as an additional fund for the development of hilly and tribal areas in the country.

laid on the welfare of weaker sections. Particularly during the Emergency, the 20-point programme was implemented very vigorously in Andhra Pradesh; bonded labour being the high priority item. Another very significant aspect of tribal welfare policy in Andhra Pradesh is that most of the backward areas have been brought under the fold of nationalised banks. This has fulfilled an old urge and has pumped in much needed short-term, medium-term and long-term credit in the credit-starved backward area. Even since March 1978, when the Chenna Reddy government assumed office, a major emphasis has been laid on the welfare of weaker sections which is reflected in the state budgets.

CONTENT OF RURAL DEVELOPMENT

Rural Development has been variously defined, but for all purposes here it would mean reaching and helping those who live below the poverty line. In our country about seventy per cent of the people are dependent on agriculture, out of which about fifty per cent are still below the poverty line. Reaching and grasping those below the poverty line is the task of rural development and several strategies have been designed to accomplish this objective. Rural development broadly envisages :

1. Improvement of infrastructure at the micro-level,
2. Grass-roots planning,
3. Provision of better services to the economically backward areas, and
4. Boosting of existing income levels including providing means of livelihood which will be self-sustaining and which should bring about change so that the poor can come up to the margin of viability

It is also essential that in a democratic country, the administrative set-up conducts itself in such a way as not to coerce people into submission, but rather to bring about their active participation in all such rural welfare programmes. So, it is of the utmost importance that there should be a healthy interaction between the administration and the people. It should be emphasised that administration constitutes an input in the development processes.

Indicators of development

For measuring rural development and the success of welfare programmes, there are always certain indicators which can be utilised for measuring changes in a rural economy. Firstly, we will have to take the problem of agriculture, which is very intimately linked with the problem of land holdings. If the farmer is independent and fearless regarding his possession and title over land, most of the other problems diminish logically. It would be seen that agriculture constitutes the most important activity in the life of the rural poor. Here, we refer to the green revolution and its impact on beneficiaries and on rural society as a whole. Side by side, it has generated change in attitudes and belief. The green revolution has directly brought about an increase in the per capita income and also changed the outlook of the farmer which was till recently traditional and sunk in superstition. The improvements in minor irrigation, high-yielding varieties of seeds, pesticides, fertilisers and the application of diesel engines and electric pump-sets for improving irrigation facilities made great contributions. Apart from agriculture two other important activities which can be treated as indicators are health and education facilities.

AREA DEVELOPMENT PLANNING

An aspect which deserves attention is the concept of "area development planning". Area development planning is directly linked up with the concept of micro-level planning which envisages integration of services and also integration of socio-economic programmes. Almost all rural development programmes are based on this concept. The area selected for the purpose of development has to be thoroughly surveyed and the ideas of inducing growth has to be tackled. Hence it is very important that the location of places selected, and places where resources are to be deployed takes precedence over other factors. In a nutshell, it may be said that creation of an infrastructure depends to a large extent on the location and place of the area to be developed. Here it is also to be seen that macro-level planning and micro-level planning must coincide. Accordingly, the administrative machinery has to be geared up and suitably designed to achieve the objectives of special programmes. In such a case, it becomes necessary to integrate the functions of administration at the Central government level, state government level and the district and block level.

The Directive Principles of State Policy clearly provide for the promotion of economic betterment of the weaker sections of our society. There is more specific mention about the protection of the interests of the tribals, and article 244 and 244(a) have laid down clear guidelines for tribal administration. In general, the Directive Principles of State Policy are that facet of the Constitution in which is enshrined the welfare aspect of our society. At this point, it would be very interesting to note that administration of tribal areas was a very important subject during British times. To preserve the integrity of tribal culture and identity, the habitats of the tribals were known as "Scheduled Areas" and were under the direct control of the magistracy. The Collector was designated as the Agent to government for Scheduled Tribal areas. Certain laws and acts were enunciated for protecting the landed interests of the tribals, namely, A.P. Land Transfer Act, 1917 and A.P. Land Transfer Act of 1959. But, in effect, the administration was found wanting in not having implemented these acts sincerely which led to a political upheaval in Srikakulam (Andhra Pradesh). It sowed the seeds of conflict between the tribals and non-tribals for the acquisition of land in Srikakulam. Primarily, the Naxalite movement of 1969 to 1972 was agrarian in character and was a struggle between the rich landlords and money-lenders, the 'haves' and the poor tribal 'have-nots'.

Till recent years no systematic studies have been made about this area and by and large the people were at the mercy of the local administration. As early as 1947, a study was conducted under the chairmanship of Mr. Ayyappan, who went into the causes of backwardness in the tribal areas of Madras Presidency. One of the recommendations of the Ayyappan Committee was the setting up of an agency which could buy and sell the tribal produce and also ensure a fair price to the tribals. This resulted in the setting up of the Girijan Cooperative Corporation. The Girijan Cooperative Corporation has played a pioneering role in bringing about the upliftment and amelioration of the condition of the tribals. Subsequently, another Committee known as the Malayappan Committee was set up. This Committee went into the problem of integrated development of the tribal areas and the question of how to exploit the natural resources and irrigation potential of the areas. However, no sustained follow-up measures as suggested by this Committee were taken up.

Insofar as this particular area is concerned, very few studies are available and there is no systematic effort to probe the cause of backwardness. It is only after the Naxalite movement of 1969 to 1972 that the resources were mobilised to start development efforts in this area. In this work, an attempt will be made to trace the steps taken to develop the area as a result of the political upheaval of 1969 to 1972. It is proposed to illuminate the relationship between political upheaval and economic development. Administration is a vital input in the developmental process to bring about change in rural development and we will see how far the administration has been successful in tackling the situation and help in bringing about a real transformation.

It would be important to evaluate the outlook and psychology of the tribals of the area, and how close they have been brought to modernity and whether they have mingled well with the mainstream of life. The tribal as we know, is free and happy, living in a small and remote world. It would be relevant to examine whether we have any justification in bringing about a change and feeding him with new ideas. It would also be interesting to evaluate whether the new system is an improvement over the past, and whether the feudalist elements continue to dominate the area or not.

We have heard of many tribal uprising down the centuries but the uprising in Srikakulam was unique because it was for the first time that Marxist and Leninist principles were tested in tribal areas. It is indeed surprising to note that the tribal who was supposed to be ignorant of his rights suddenly become aware of his environment and clamoured for change. It is at this point that the administration stepped in, and brought about a change in the outlook of the tribals from a state of hostility, to a position of positive neutrality. Once again the tribal was convinced that the state around him was interested in his welfare, that violence is unproductive and that he had a secure future.

In view of the fact that this area was a disturbed area, there was no contact with outside agencies. Further it is also a scheduled area so the entire developmental effort has been that of the government and administration. Hence this is a useful case for study of government programmes and plans which have proved to be a success.

ROLE OF INFRASTRUCTURE DEVELOPMENT

To begin with, the area lacked in infrastructure facilities at the micro-level. Here again, the government stepped in, in a very big way to create an infrastructure to inject life into the economy of the area so that the tribals may reap the benefits of modern technological development. An integrated programme of action was designed under the aegis of the Girijan Development Agency. This was a central government sponsored programme and started functioning from 1972. It would be worthwhile to evaluate the role of this Agency as the premier agent of development of the tribal areas. It is for the first time that the central government took a very direct interest in this area and keenly implemented developmental programmes. There was no dearth of availability of funds and the programmes moved ahead at a very good pace. However, any developmental effort must have a credit structure which was also provided during the later half of the project period in the shape of Grameen Banks. Earlier, the Girijan Cooperative Corporation had concentrated on short term loans only. But with the coming of the Grameen Bank short term and long term loans also became possible. Another unique feature was the addition of Animal Husbandry programmes and their success. In recent years it is felt that agriculture also includes certain other allied activities like poultry farming, dairy farming and sheep breeding. These programmes also provide a means of livelihood to the farmer and helps in raising incomes.

Personnel problems

No development effort can ever succeed without proper personnel. Several papers and documents have been written on staff and personnel policies but very little has been done to provide a cure for this problem in the tribal areas. It is a very common sight to see a hospital with all medicines and all equipment available, but no doctor to diagnose and prescribe. Similarly, in schools the teacher resides elsewhere and is mostly absent leading to discouragement and frustration for students and parents. Normally, officers are believed to be posted to tribal areas as punishment or on probation. Even if a person is posted on promotion he never really enjoys his stay there due to unattractive working conditions and from the very first day his aim is to seek a transfer. It is, therefore, important to examine personnel policy problems.

Development agency

The Girijan Development Agency has also undergone a lot of change in its personnel policies, procedures, and functioning, the concept of a single line agency of administration has been introduced instead of a multiple line agency. At this point, it would be relevant to mention that till June 1979, Srikakulam was one district. It was then split into two different districts : one is Srikakulam and the other is Vizianagaram.

REASONS FOR SELECTION OF SPECIFIC AREAS FOR STUDY

In Srikakulam during 1969 to 1972, the Naxalite movement was spread all over the district but it was in its most intense and acute form in the agency blocks. There were three agency blocks, namely, Pachipenta, Bhadragiri and Seethampet. Out of these three, Pachipenta was unaffected by the Naxalite movement, and it was only in Pachipenta, Seethampet and Bhadragiri that development activities were stepped up in a big way. Hence, these three blocks have been selected for evaluating the impact of rural development programmes. Although Bhadragiri and Pachipenta after the reorganisation lie in Vizianagaram district, and Seethampet in Srikakulam district the development effort of the last decade and the role of the administration in it is evaluated. An attempt is made to show that the administration has succeeded in spite of many hurdles and impediments.

Tribal welfare policy has passed through various phases from dormancy to dynamism. Amidst the vast plethora of problems which our policy-makers are faced with is being increasingly realised that the tribals cannot be ignored. In order to diffuse tension in society it is essential that a policy which is rational and sympathetic should be pursued for promoting tribal welfare aims and objectives. Another interesting aspect is that tribal welfare is almost devoid of voluntary agency work in the tribal areas. Besides the Bharatiya Adimjati Sangh, there are very few others who have taken any interest in this field. In Andhra Pradesh, policy has undergone a lot of shifts and changes especially in view of the Naxalite uprising from 1968 to 1972. One of the most disturbing features was that tribals were getting politicized by extremist philosophies and this could lead to uneven development. However, the situation has been more than rectified and now we can look forward to an era of prosperity and balanced development. The policy-makers particularly in the field of tribal welfare have not relied on chance but have as Lasswell put it, "been constantly performing the intelligence functions and appraisal functions" meticulously. Since the middle of the 1960s tribal welfare policy has ceased to be slip-shod and given to fancies and ideas of any particular individual or group of individuals. Indeed, even intellectuals have been associated in the process of policy-making and this speaks well of the state.

REFERENCES

1. Nelson, W Polsby, *Policies and Policy Making*, ed. by Fred I. Greenstein, Addision-Wesley Publishing Company.
2. IRA Sharkansky, *Public Administration: Policy-Making in Government Agencies*, Fourth Edition, Rand McNally College Publishing Company, Chicago.
3. Sahay, B.N., *Pragmatism in Development: Application of Anthropology*, Booklive Publishers, New Delhi.
4. Planning Commission, New Delhi, *Report of the Task Force on Development of Tribal Areas*, Govt. of India, New Delhi, 1972.
5. Minhas, B.S., *Planning for the Poor*, S. Chand & Company, New Delhi, First published 1974, pp. 4, 9 & 34.

6. Planning Commission, New Delhi, *Study Team on Tribal Development Programmes: Committee on Plan Projects*, Govt. of India, New Delhi, 1969.
7. Khaja Abdul Gafoor, *Social Service among the Tribes and Backward Classes in Hyderabad*, Krishnavan International Printers & Publishers, Malakpet, Hyderabad-Deccan.

2

TRIBAL DEVELOPMENT
A Comparative Analysis

The first step in raising India, even spiritually, was to destroy her abject poverty. Remove the evils of poverty and hunger.

—*Swami Vivekananda*

THE ENTIRE philosophy and purpose of the State of the Republic of India was enshrined in the Constitution. The Constitution-makers realised the importance of improving the lot of the poverty-stricken masses who had suffered under colonial rule. It was in keeping with the ethos that the purpose of the state was to promote the welfare of the people. Hence separate provisions for this were made in the Constitution by enunciating the Directive Principles of State Policy. In addition, there were specific provisions in the Constitution for the protection and welfare of the tribals. The administration had, therefore, to be geared up to achieve the goals set up by the Constitution-makers.

The solution was found by taking up a massive programme for community development. It was also realised that the administration alone could be utilised for delivering the goods.

The existing machinery at the district level, state level and central level had to be tailored and structured for achieving the desired results. It is necessary to emphasise that for achieving economic betterment and economic uplift of the weaker sections the administration is an indispensable input. Gunnar Myrdal has stated in his work, *The Challenge of World Poverty* (a World Anti-poverty programme in outline) that economic development is just not a matter of considering certain theories and economic terminologies but that development is a "human problem" and that "planning means changing men". Therefore, in a more rationalistic approach institutional development cannot be disregarded, but is an indistinguishable part of the whole, and administration is a companion of the vast array of complex developmental problems, programmes and policies.

To achieve the goals of developmental administration, a certain degree of decentralisation is necessary. Specific provisions for this has been made in our Constitution, where subjects are divided as Central Subjects, State Subjects and Concurrent Subjects. In the development of rural communities, agricultural development takes the foremost place and importance. Similarly, health, education and communications which are part of our package deal must also be viewed as priority items in rural development. To achieve this initially community development programmes were introduced. This constituted the first step towards decentralisation of developmental administration in independent India. It was also felt that people's participation at grass-roots level should be more intensive and hence Panchayat Raj as envisaged by the Balwantrai Mehta Committee was established all over the country. However, in the years to come, there were many inadequacies that were pointed out in Panchayat Raj, and the Government of India also took up various other schemes like Small Farmers' Development Agency, Marginal Farmers and Agricultural Labourers Development Agency, G.D.A., Drought Prone Areas Programme, Tribal Hill Development Area, etc. While agriculture is given a place in the state list it is, however, seen that the centre has always assumed a leadership role in the matter of guidance and advice to the states.* However, Government of India controls items like supply and distribution of inputs because it involves industries partly because of interest in trade and commerce.[1] As Dr. M.A. Muttalib, has rightly pointed out, "Agricultural production is a cooperative enterprise of the central and state governments on one hand and the cultivators on the other. The Constitution of India has visualised promotion of agricultural production as basic responsibility of the state governments. It has also caused a number of responsibilities on the centre with direct or indirect basing on agriculture". Thus from the above statement it appears as though the role of the centre is that of a coordinator on whose benign and cordial relationship the vast network of Agricultural production programme is dependent upon. The state government is, therefore, the real implementor of all such schemes and acts as a direct buffer between districts and the central government.

At the state level, coordination between various departmental agencies and review of plans is taken up regularly. The funds are of the central government routed through the state government to the project level. Another important aspect of the functioning of the state government is that it acts as a liaisoning body between central government and the project level. At the Government of India level, regular meetings are held to review the progress of work in the projects in different states. It is quite frequent that availiability of funds is discussed in these meetings and also whether the budgetary situation provides for adhering to the original outlays. The central government often advises on practical feasibility of new schemes and plans that have to be taken up and also acts as a coordinator.

In India, 38 million persons (6.9%) of the total population belong to the Scheduled Tribes (1971 Census). There are nine states in the Union with a population of more than one million each. The states are Andhra Pradesh, Assam, Bihar,

*Agriculture figures in List-II (State List) of the Seventh Schedule of the Constitution of India, Item 14, entry being "Agriculture, including Agricultural education and research, protection against pests, prevention of plant diseases".

Maharashtra, Gujarat, Madhya Pradesh, Orissa, Rajasthan and West Bengal. In seven states and Union territories the Scheduled Tribes are in majority. These are Megalaya, Nagaland, Arunachal Pradesh, Assam, Mizoram, Manipur and Tripura.

THE NORTH EASTERN STATES

In most of the states the tribal population is only a segment of the total population, hence the total effort is not geared in favour of tribal development. The hopes and aspirations of many other communities are also at stake and hence the various state governments have to be circumspect in discharging their special responsibilities towards the tribals. However, in states like Nagaland, Meghalaya, Arunachal Pradesh and Mizoram, the government caters almost exclusively to protecting and preserving the interests of tribals alone as they constitute a major chunk of the population. Another distinguishing feature of these north-eastern states is that from the very beginning they were looked upon with a paternalistic attitude by the British. One direct consequence was that the area was cut off from the rest of the country and a vast maze of missionaries and other Christian organisations took an active part in developing this area. It is illuminating that even though this is predominantly a tribal area the rate of literacy amongst the tribals is much higher and far exceeds the literacy rates in the larger states. The entire administration is tailored and geared to meet the needs of the tribal people in the north-eastern states, whereas it is not so in the larger states.

GROWTH OF PANCHAYAT RAJ INSTITUTIONS

In the early years after independence, Panchayat Raj schemes were introduced in all states, with varying degrees of success. In Andhra Pradesh, Panchayat Raj was introduced with a great deal of enthusiasm. It helped the poorer and backward communities to realise the benefits of development and gave them a more meaningful role in society. But the Shilu Ao Committee report, 1969 points out that even though in Andhra

Pradesh it was provided that the Samiti President is to be a tribal, in actual practice it was found that non-tribals constitute a major part of the Samiti and even head some of the more important sub-committees of the Panchayat Samiti. With these defects in view and the growth of unrest in tribal areas it was decided by the Government of India to try a new experiment in tribal development which led to the setting up of six Tribal Development Agencies all over the country. It is in this context, we have to view the special efforts made by the Government of India and the programme contained was common to all the agencies. There may have been differences in approach because of varying local conditions and perhaps difference in expectations also. But by and large the targets set up for achievement were implemented successfully.

In the broad structure that has emerged at the district level after the introduction of Panchayat Raj in the various states, the District Collector's association with the emergent system and the roles assigned to him under it vary from state to state. The following patterns are noticed :

(i) In Maharashtra and Gujarat, the District Collector is kept out of the Zilla Parishad.

(ii) in U.P. and Bihar, he is entitled to attend the meeting of the Zilla Parishad and participate in the discussions, but has no voting right. In Bihar, he may also attend the meetings of the Panchayat Samitis and its Standing Committees but without a right to vote.

(iii) in Assam, Orissa, Haryana, Punjab and Rajasthan, the collector is a non-voting member of the Zilla Parishad with which he is associated in purely advisory capacity. Thus, he has no involvement in the decision making process in rural democracy.

(iv) in both Karnataka and Tamilnadu, the Collector is the Chairman of the District Development Council.

(v) at the other end of the scale stands Andhra Pradesh where the Collector is not only a member of the Zilla Parishad but also the Chairman of all the standing Committees in whom is vested executive authority in most matters.

There is, thus a wide variation in the Collector's powers and functions in relation to the Panchayat Raj institutions. Leaving aside Maharashtra and Gujarat, even in the other states, there is no happy union of the administrative system with the political system. The role of the Collector as a coordinator has not been precisely and clearly defined. The Collector continues to have under him, the district level functionaries of all the technical departments, although the latter, in technical matters, deal directly with their respective heads of departments at the state headquarters. There is thus some dual supervision which may occasionally prove to be a source of friction; thus while seeking horizontal coordination at the area level the Collector has often to face the problems of departmental verticalism.

NEW STRATEGY FOR TRIBAL DEVELOPMENT

During the Fourth Plan period a special attempt was made by the Government of India to accelerate the pace of development in tribal areas. The programmes were initiated under the Tribal Development Agency (T.D.A.) set up in the states of Andhra Pradesh, Orissa, Bihar and Madhya Pradesh. In Andhra Pradesh, a pilot project was set up in Srikakulam which started functioning in 1972. In Orissa, they were set up in two phases: first, they were set up in 1971-72 and then later on two more projects were set up in 1973-74; in all, there were eight such projects that were sanctioned up to 31 March, 1979.

The Tribal Development Agencies coursed through seven years from 1972-73 up to 1978-79. These projects were initiated by the Ministry of Agriculture towards the last part of the Fourth Plan, which continued during the Fifth Plan and about one year or so during the Sixth Plan, after which these got merged the Integrated Tribal Development Projects (I.T.D.Ps.) being taken up by the Ministry of Home Affairs (in the tribal sub-plan areas in 1979) (June).

At the time of taking up the T.D.A. projects during the Fourth Plan, there were certain administrative as well as economic compulsions in selecting and launching these projects in the selected tribal areas. The tribal population of India constituted about 7 per cent of the total population of the country. In spite of decades of developmental efforts most of

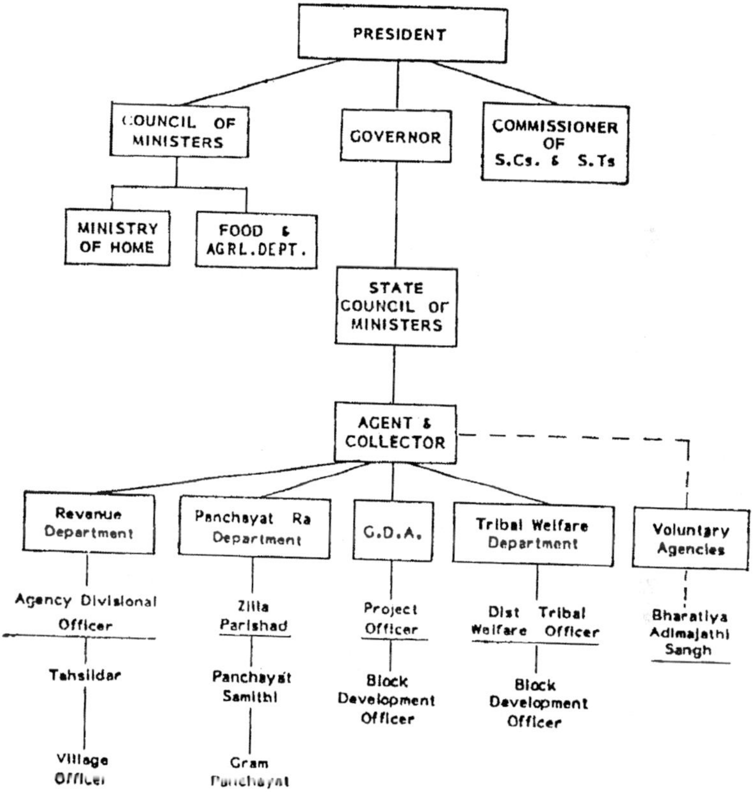

CHART 2.1

This chart illustrates the various tiers of Tribal Welfare Administration and their functional relationship rather than their hierarchic position.

the tribals continued to remain much below the poverty line. The tribal areas continued to remain remote and far away from the mainstream of the national life. The slow pace of economic development and continued exploitation of the tribals by certain categories of non-tribals had also resulted in acute social tension in some of these areas, giving rise to certain epicentres of extremist activities.

Accordingly, the T.D.A. projects were taken up in some of the representative tribal areas of Srikakulam in Andhra Pradesh; Ganjam, Koraput and Phulbani in south Orissa; Dantewada and Konta of Bastar in Madhya Pradesh; Keonjhar in north Orissa; and Singhbhum in Bihar.

The two projects in Singhbhum and Keonjhar, located in the north-east of the Central Indian tract, catered to the needs of the Santhals, the Bhuyans and Juang tribes, while the remaining six projects in Srikakulam, Ganjam, Koraput, Phulbani, Dantewada and Konta in Bastar, established in the south-east of the Central Indian tract, catered to the needs of the Kondhs, Gonds, Sauras, Parajas, Marias, Bhattras, and the like.

Originally, it was conceived that the T.D.A. projects would take care of three aspects of development of the selected tribal areas—economic, social and protective. Problems relating to the core programme of economic development would be looked after by the Ministry of Agriculture, problems relating to the development of social services involving drinking water, health and education would be taken care of by the Union Department of Social Welfare, and problems relating to law and order, enforcement of the protective legislations and development of communications would be the responsibility of the Ministry of Home Affairs.

But for one reason or the other, the T.D.S. projects remained confined to the implementation of the core programme of economic development and construction of certain arterial roads in the inaccessible tribal areas. The contemplated three-pronged coordinated approach to tribal development—economic, social and protective—got somehow truncated and confined to only economic development through agriculture and the allied sector activities. The tripod composite project as originally contemplated never actually got off the ground.

Tribal agriculture was characterised by small holdings and low yields. It was being practised mostly in undulated highlands suffering from problems of soil erosion and lack of soil fertility. The records of right over the lands which the tribals cultivated, were hardly up-to-date; and in fact the land records remained back-dated by periods over decades, as a result of which access to institutional finance remained far away from the reach of the average tribals. Agricultural operations in the tribal areas, both the settled and the shifting types, mostly depended on rains and unpredictable nature. Lack of practice of soil and water conservation measures, lack of exposure to and knowledge of improved agricultural techniques, low investments despite crippling indebtedness, made the tribal agriculture to remain mostly precarious and at subsistence levels. No wonder, the tribal areas, by and large, remained bereft of the fruits of the green revolution and the white floods, which were mostly enjoyed in the plains.

The economic programmes of the tribal development agencies were, therefore, directed towards ensuring an immediate boost to the agricultural and horticultural production in the tribal areas, to improve the economic conditions of the landless among the tribals by providing them with land and inputs, to reorganise the cooperative and marketing structure through setting up of FSS/LAMPS; construction of strategic godowns and arterial roads, and to provide employment and increased income to the tribals through animal keeping, agro- and forest-based cottage industries and the like.

In order to make a dent in the economic situation of the tribals, the programmes of the T.D.As. had to be both family-based as well as area-based. The family-based economic programmes included land reclamation, land development and soil conservation measures, supply of agricultural inputs, agricultural demonstration on various cropping patterns and cropping programmes, popularisation of root crops and improvement of local crops like ginger and turmeric, backyard orcharding, animal and bird-keeping, construction of dug wells where possible, giving legal aid to the tribals in order to safeguard their land rights, and the like.

The area-based economic programmes included construction of arterial roads, building up strategic godowns, execution of minor irrigation and lift irrigation schemes, construction of water-harvesting structures, raising of horticultural plantations in and around the tribal villages, setting up of animal upgradation centres, establishing fruit-processing units in a modest scale and the like.

MACHINERY FOR IMPLEMENTATION

At the state level there is a functional coordination-cum-implementation committee responsible for reviewing the administration of the programmes. A suitable state government department looks after the programme in the different states.

In Andhra Pradesh, the Revenue (TW) Department and, at present, the Employment and Social Welfare Department which is the administrative department to look after the tribal welfare in the state is also administering these special programmes. There is a state level Coordination Committee for tribal welfare with the First Member, Board of Revenue-cum-Commissioner for Tribal Welfare as Chairman. Secretary, Revenue Department and other officers concerned both at the Secretariat level and the Heads of Departments level are members of the Committee. There is a Director, Tribal Welfare who is also ex-officio Joint Secretary of the Board of Revenue. He functions as Member-Secretary of this Committee.

In Bihar State, the Department of Agriculture is administering the special programme. There is a state level Coordination Committee headed by the State Minister of Agriculture to supervise, guide and coordinate the different activities under these programmes. The Agricultural Production Commissioner of the state is its Vice-Chairman. The Director, Tribal Welfare-cum-Joint Secretary is its ex-officio member-secretary, representatives of other concerned department including Home, Education, Health, Public Works, Irrigation, etc., are its members.

In Madhya Pradesh, the Tribal and Harijan Welfare Department was originally looking after the programmes. It was then transferred to the charge of the department of agriculture. The state level Coordination Committee headed by the Chief Secretary is looking after these special programmes and supervises, guides and coordinates the activities in these projects. Representatives of the Department of Home, Education, P.W.D., Irrigation, Health, etc., are co-opted members of this Committee. The Director, Tribal and Harijan Welfare is the ex-officio secretary of this Committee.

In Orissa, the projects are being administered by the Tribal and Rural Welfare Department. State level coordination meetings are being held by the Development Commissioner and the Commissioner of Special Projects who are looking after the special programmes in the tribal development projects. The Director, Tribal and Rural Welfare is the ex-officio Secretary of this Committee. The Secretary of Works, Home, Education and Health Department are its coopted members.

Andhra and Orissa patterns

In Andhra Pradesh the government regarded the project in Srikakulam as very important because it was set up in the wake of the Naxalite movement. In addition to the normal development programmes for agriculture there was also a component for construction of roads. The projects served a dual purpose; one of restoring confidence amongst the tribals; and secondly, to bring them in closer contact with the outside world. In this respect, the road construction programme played an important role. It also provided labour and employment and helped in earning daily wages. The other project in Orissa is that of Keonjhar district. There was no special reason for choosing Keonjhar, unlike the case of Srikakulam except for its backwardness and predominant tribal population there was no other special reason why it was chosen for the purpose of setting up of a tribal development agency.

It is difficult to compare and contrast the success of each of the projects because very few evaluation reports are available. However, in the case of these two projects, one mid-term appraisal of the Srikakulam project was conducted by the Agro-Economic Research Centre, Andhra University, Waltair. In the case of Keonjhar, Orissa an evaluation was carried out by the National Institute of Rural Development, Rajendranagar, Hyderabad. From both these studies it is found that funds were spent as targeted by the Government of India, although the methods for spending and the impact of various schemes on the beneficiaries is dissimilar.

In Andhra Pradesh, as mentioned earlier, the government and the district administration took the objectives of the projects very seriously. An I.A.S. Officer was posted as Project Officer from October 1971 and he was transferred only in the second-half of 1974. So in the very first instance he was associated with all the planning formulation, methodology and implementation of programmes. The District Collector was very closely associated in planning and execution of programmes. In Orissa, correspondingly, an officer was posted and transfers at the Project Officer's level were carried out frequently. There was practically no fixity of tenure and in the absence of that it is difficult to successfully launch any programme which is biased in favour of the poor and can be regarded as an anti-poverty programme.

In Andhra Pradesh non-officials were also very closely associated with the progress and development of tribal welfare programmes because they were not only made members of the governing body but tribal programmes were seriously discussed and deliberated upon in the Zilla Parishad. There were also frequent meetings at the state government level to review the progress of these programmes. Very often the Chief Minister who used to tour the district (the then Chief Minister Sri J. Vengala Rao) would himself enquire from the Collector and Project Officer regarding the progress of programmes. As a matter of fact, during the Emergency period there was more vigorous implementation of tribal programmes than ever before. A massive effort was made to implement the 20-point programme of the then Prime Minister. No evidence seems to have been let in about such activities in Orissa.

A major difference between programme implementation of Andhra Pradesh and Orissa appears to be in the matter of coordinations.[2] In Orissa, funds were distributed to all the district officers and they were asked to treat them as departmental programmes in the project area, whereas in Andhra Pradesh the concept of single line agency was introduced (discussed in other chapters) where the Project Officer was made responsible for implementing all programmes at the block level and had complete control and command of all funds.

Responsibility was fixed on the Collector and Project Officer to deliver the goods rather than to see it as an effort by various departmental agencies.

In Andhra Pradesh, a massive effort was made by setting up Grameen Banks in the tribal areas thereby ensuring the free and easy flow of institutional credit. No such efforts seem to have been made in Keonjhar project area. Supply of inputs like fertilisers, seeds, etc., it was felt that there were delays in timely supply and sometimes the amount supplied was inadequate. This complaint seems to have been voiced in both the projects. However, in Andhra Pradesh a new feature was noticed and that was that sometimes the tribals were keen to utilise inputs like seeds, fertilisers, and so on, without any assistance from the agency. So it can be said that the impact was very positive one.

Another noticeable feature about the Andhra experience was with regard to doing away of the practice of *Podu*. The anti-*podu* committee with Sarpanch, Village Headman, three or four leaders from different tribes and one or two tribal youths, with Block Development Officers as convenors were found to educate the tribals about the evil of *podu* cultivation. Coercion on tribals was given up and in its place extension methods of financing them were adopted to bring down the *podu* cultivation. This appears to have had a good response. Because of the limited sources of information and scanty evaluation reports (except for the two mentioned earlier) an attempt to compare and contrast the achievements of the two agencies will be inhibited.

Agriculture

In the field of agriculture in Srikakulam a massive effort was made to introduce high-yielding varieties and modern practices. A problem that was faced earlier was timely supply of inputs. This deficiency was corrected when the Girijan Development Agency G.D.A. had its own independent staff of agricultural officers responsible for a timely supply of inputs. Their activities were also coordinated with the departmental functionaries at the block and division level to ensure a timely supply. Limited success was achieved because the tribals were not immediately prepared to take to modern practices. However, some of the more receptive farmers themselves started buying inputs without the assistance of the G.D.A. or agriculture departmental officials.[3] Another programme which proved very popular in Srikakulam was the programme of demonstration plots of high-yielding varieties and supply of plough bullock to the farmers. The intensity of supply of plough bullocks increased over the years as it was realised that the plough bullock could also be used for other purposes like drawing the cart and providing labour for other items of work during the non-agricultural season.

In Keonjhar, the high-yielding varieties programme did not have much of an impact because of the inability of the tribals to accept the usage of modern practices. The villagers in Keonjhar felt that they laid more stress on the provision of irrigation facilities. In Keonjhar a timely supply of inputs was not forthcoming as there was not sufficient coordination at lower levels.

Irrigation credit flow

In Srikakulam, lift irrigation schemes proved to be a great boon to the tribal area. The most important reason for its success was that the project had a full-scale engineering division functioning under it. The Project Officer could himself take decisions of sanctioning projects up to Rupees one and a half lakhs and could immediately entrust the scheme to the engineering division for speedy execution.

In Keonjhar, the government did not provide sufficient staff support to the rural engineering organisation and somehow there were considerable delays in the execution of the projects. One advantage which the Keonjhar project enjoyed was that a voluntary organisation, viz., OXFAM was associated in the execution of minor irrigation projects. There were very few new minor irrigation projects in Keonjhar and mostly the funds were expended on improvement of existing projects. About ten minor irrigation projects were completed in Keonjhar.

In Srikakulam, a well-digging programme was also fairly successful. However, a number of wells had to be abandoned because of lack of proper ground water survey in the tribal areas of Srikakulam.

In Keonjhar, the impact of dug-wells was not much and the programme of well construction was not very successful.

Education

In the field of education although it did not form part of the G.D.A. programme, however, the Project Officer had control over the state funds because of the single line agency administrative system. A tremendous enthusiasm prevailed in Srikakulam tribal areas for setting up of Ashram schools, tribal hostels and upper primary schools. In 1977-78 itself about twenty new Ashram schools were set up as I.T.D.A funds were also simultaneously pouring in. In the Ashram schools, children were well fed, and properly clothed and regular medical check-ups were also carried out. The parents of tribal children regarded it as a great symbol of prestige to send children to the Ashram schools. Another reason why education was popular was because of the communist propaganda that gave importance to education to enable people to fight for their rights in times of social and economic distress.

In Keonjhar, education was not very popular as the tribals regarded it as a deterrent to their occupational pattern, which required that their children be at their homes helping their parents in other works. It must be seen here that in Srikakulam regular drives were launched to ensure compulsory attendance and that parents were convinced about the importance of sending their children to school. The schools were also very regularly inspected by higher officials to ensure that teachers were not absenting themselves from duty. No such effort seems to have been made in Keonjhar.

Health

In the field of health in Srikakulam, one very welcome feature has been that tribals have changed their attitude, and have started by going to hospitals for treatment of ailments. In Srikakulam, however, one difficulty which was faced by the administration was that hospitals in tribal areas were not properly staffed and very often the doctors would not join their posts. At the same time the regular health department took up a massive programme for eradication of malaria and certain check-posts were set up in the agency area for detection of cases. Potable drinking water was accorded high priority for commission in the tribal areas although sometimes its success was limited. Particular care was taken by officials to see that A.N.P., and N.S.P. centres function properly.

In Keonjhar there is not much of a change of attitude on the part of tribals and hence modern medicine is not very popular.

Industries

In Srikakulam industries had only limited success although efforts were made in this direction also. In Keonjhar, the bee-keeping programme was very successful in Bansapal Block although there was no proper follow-up. Similarly, Tusser silk was also tried but with limited success. In Srikakulam corresponding efforts were made and mulberry sericulture programmes were introduced in a {big way and had some limited success. The other important achievement in the Girijan area was the setting up of a Khandsari Cooperative Sugar Factory which started functioning from 1978 onwards. The biggest achievement of all was that for the first time sugarcane was grown in the tribal area.

Infrastructure—Roads

Road construction programmes were accorded very high priority because of the law and order problem in Srikakulam tribal areas. The most important road in the area was connecting Seethampet with Bhadragiri road which ran through the heart of the agency areas. The Government of India made adequate provision for road development. The state government also allocated a special engineering division at Parvatipuram for road construction programmes. A very notable feature was that no sooner the road was ready and within a few days the District Collector would grant a permit for plying buses in the area. The roads have definitely connected and opened up the agency area and has been an important catalyst in the development of the area. It has also enabled the administration to have a better control and supervision over all local institutions and developmental programmes.

In Keonjhar the roads were not an item of high priority. The lack of success of road development in Keonjhar can be measured by two factors: first the state government did not provide supporting finance; and secondly, the engineering staff provided by the state government was very inadequate. As such in Keonjhar, road development infrastructure development did not have any serious impact.

Banks

In Keonjhar, a number of credit institutions in the shape of LAMPS were established. In Srikakulam, Grameen Banks and commercial banks penetrated the tribal areas. The immediate impact of Grameen Banks in Srikakulam was that medium-term loaning programmes received a shot in the arm and the Grameen Banks were very popular. Similarly, the Andhra Bank also set up branches in the tribal areas of Seethampet and successfully launched village adoption schemes. Here, it may also be mentioned that in Srikakulam simultaneously the revenue machinery also took action under debt relief regulations and the money-lenders regulation. The old debts were scaled down and money-lenders were penalised for their nefarious activities. Although it cannot be ruled out that in certain pockets the money-lenders may still be operating surreptitiously and clandestinely.

In Keonjhar there was no effort to book money-lenders and no offences were booked under the money-lenders and debt relief regulations. Money-lending by private agencies seems to be still rampant. Money-lenders are still giving loans in kind also in the tribal areas of Keonjhar at exorbitant rates of interest.

Animal husbandry programme

In the sphere of animal husbandry programmes success was not consistent. The tribals in Srikakulam initially resisted keeping cows and buffaloes as they regarded consumption of milk to be the prerogative of calves only. However, this programme picked up with the passage of time. With the coming of Grameen Banks credit was available for purchase of animals. The major problem was of course availability of animals and cost of transport which inhibited the farmer from purchase of animals. But a great deal of enthusiasm was exhibited by the state government and three milk chilling plants were set up near the agency areas namely Ramabharapuram near Salur and Panchipenta near Kurupam and one at Seethampet itself.

In Keonjhar poultry keeping and goat herds were fairly popular and successful. But dairy programmes proved a complete failure. Poultry programmes were popular in Keonjhar because it serves not only their dairy needs, but used for their rites and rituals. Dairy programmes in Srikakulam were popular because good veterinary coverage was provided. Bulls were also supplied in the tribal areas for crossing the cows and improve the breed of the cattle. Similarly, plough bullocks were also very popular because they were used by the tribal farmers for various purposes. In addition, veterinary officers were also posted in the project. In Srikakulam they were able to coordinate their activities with the departmental staff at the block and division level. In Keonjhar even though staff was provided, the area lacked proper veterinary institutions and coverage.

In Srikakulam the milk chilling plants at Ramabarapuram was functioning successfully and Kurupem and Seethampet have also recently started functioning well. This shows that the tribal is able to get a return and increase of income out of the animals supplied to him. The success of goat and poultry programmes in Keonjhar did not give any economic return to the farmers.

Girijan Krishi Kendra

One of the most important achievements in Srikakulam tribal areas was setting up of the Girijan Krishi Kendra. The Krishi Kendra has become a nucleus around which training programmes of tribal farmers in improved agriculture are carried out. Krishi Kendra also gives advice and has its own research and development wing for administrative purpose in the tribal areas. Krishi Kendra has had a major impact in shaping the attitude of tribals by demonstrating modern agricultural practices. The Kendra is directly under the control of Andhra Pradesh Agricultural University and is also funded by the Indian Council of Agricultural Research. Similar effort was not made in Keonjhar.

As mentioned earlier, in the absence of source material it is not very easy to compare and contrast major programmes in two different states. However, in view of the material available with us there are certain conclusions that can be arrived at. Firstly, a strong administrative structure facilitates successful implementation of developmental programmes. Support should be inter-linked and there must be a realisation at both micro and macro levels about the importance of programmes in backward areas. It is not merely enough to spend funds and produce a clean balance-sheet but it is also necessary to learn and be aware of the fact whether the funds provided have achieved their intended purpose. In that sense it can be said that the programmes implementation and monitoring was much more effective in Andhra Pradesh compared to Keonjhar (Orissa). A major difference being that in Andhra Pradesh the involvement and commitment of the state government and district administration was more intense when compared to the same in Orissa. In Orissa the T.D.A. programme was treated like any other ordinary Government of India extension and support programme, whereas in Andhra Pradesh there was a grave sense of urgency and a question of survival of democracy that was at stake. If democracy had to survive in the tribal areas of Srikakulam it had to be effectively demonstrated to them that government, people and the administration were firmly behind them to bring peace and prosperity in the area.

SRIKAKULAM DISTRICT : DEVELOPMENT INDICATORS

Results available after the completion of two bench mark surveys

The availability of qualitative and quantitative information is a fundamental pre-requisite for the assessment of present socio-economic conditions which in turn helps the social engineer to find out the impact of a particular project or programme after a certain period of time. The Bench Mark Survey was primarily aimed to collect bench mark data with a broad time gap extending over 1971-72 to 1977-78.

The first leg Bench Mark Survey was conducted during 1971-72 while the second leg was conducted during 1977-78. The objectives of the survey are as follows:

(1) to study the occupational structure of the tribals in the project area;
(2) to study the existing conditions of agriculture and irrigation facilities;
(3) to find out the magnitude of indebtedness and to study the institutional credit agencies *vis-a-vis* the traditional credit agencies; and
(4) to analyse the prevailing socio-economic conditions of tribals.

The survey is confined to nine blocks, nemely, Bhadragiri, Seethampeta, Pachipenta (T.D. Blocks) Salur, Parvatipuram, Kurupem, Kothuru, Savarakota and Mandasa. The survey was conducted in two stages, viz., villages and households. Altogether, 776 tribal households and 142 villages were selected through stratified proportionate random sampling and surveyed in the project area. Since the same villages and the same households were surveyed, the trends revealed by results of the two surveys (first and second leg) would indicate effects generated during the gestation period of the pilot project named Girijan Development Agency. It is with this intention, the comparison of the results of the two surveys conducted at the beginning of the project and at the end of the project have been made to understand the changes that occurred during the process of implementation.

Average size of the household

The average size of the household is 4.64 persons in the project area as against 4.5 persons of the first leg. The maximum number of households are found in the size group of two to four persons and the Mukadora tribe has the highest average size (5.00) indicating that there is no significant variation in the average aize of the households in the project area.

Earners and non-earners

The earning capacity of the person indicates the economic progress in that particular household. The percentage of earners in the selected villages works out to 60.13 per cent as against 68.3 per cent of the first leg indicating that the earning members of the selected households have decreased. This may be attributed to the factors like seasonal employment in agricultural sector, illiteracy among scheduled tribes, population growth rate, etc. The non-earners account for 39.87 per cent in the project area as against 31.7 per cent during the previous survey results meaning to say that non-earners or dependants increased to a considerable extent. The non-earners include aged persons, children and disabled tribal people who contribute nothing to the economic benefit of the family.

Literacy

The literacy rate in the project is 14.06 per cent as against 9.54 per cent of the first leg showing an improvement in the literacy rate to a great extent. Further, the percentage of primary literates have increased considerably which accounts for 94. 58 per cent during second leg as against 88.9 per cent of the first leg. The percentage of secondary literates is some what lesser during second leg (4.80) when compared to the first leg (6.9%). The reason being that drop-outs from the primary level onwards are high. However, to improve the literacy rate of children living in tribal areas, the government established several Primary schools, Ashram schools and extended several facilities like mid-day meals, special nutrition programmes, supply of slates, books, clothing, etc. It is an admitted fact that some type of incentive is necessary to avoid drop-outs. Therefore, incentives like supply of text-books, note-books, stationery and free scholarships are necessary. This is now being implemented in most of the tribal areas of Srikakulam District.

Land holdings

The average size of the land holding in the project area is 3.5 as against 3.9 in the first leg showing a slight decrease in the size of land holding due to fragmentation of land holdings, population explosion and nucleus family system. Moreover, the percentage of selected households possessing land works out to 76.15 per cent as against 75.7 per cent of the first leg indicating thereby the land-owning class remaining the same in both the surveys. The remaining 23.85 per cent of the selected households in the project area are landless. However, land holdings in the hands of tribal people are limited and the lands should be allotted to the landless tribal households.

Size of holdings

Agricultural production has a direct relationship with the size of holding. It is necessary to understand the distribution of size of holdings in the project area. The maximum number of households that is, 56.58 per cent of the households possess land within three acres as against 45.8 per cent during first leg bench mark survey followed by 21.19 per cent in the size group of 3 to 4.99 acres which is slightly decreased as against first leg. Further 18.61 per cent of the households have land around 1 acre as against 13.7 per cent during first leg revealing that most of the land owners (small farmers) are either labourers or owning *podu* fields in the hills and hillocks. Only 3.62 per cent of the households possess land within 5 acres as against 14.25 per cent during the first leg indicating a drastic decrease. The reason may be due to fragmentation of land holdings and leasing out of portions of land. Thus it can be understood that the limited land holdings available with the cultivators are uneconomic and should be improved by intensive cultivation and adopting new techniques.

Area cultivated and cropping pattern

Mere holdings of land in the possession of tribals is not an important fact but how much of that area is cultivated is the prime function to be considered. Nearly 86.0 per cent of land is cultivated in the project area by the selected households and this is more or less equal to that in first leg (85.9%).

The food crops raised in the project area are *ragi, paddy, bajra, sema, vooda,* besides growing pulses like red gram, green gram, blackgram, etc. The area under food crops account for 90.60 per cent as against 90.5 per cent of the first leg. This rise in the percentage of cultivation of food crops may be due to implementation of various agricultural oriented programmes like supply of S.T. inputs on 50 per cent subsidy basis, land reclamation on 50 per cent subsidy; supply of M.T. inputs on 50 per cent subsidy, etc. Moreover the area covered under commercial crops works out to 9.40 per cent which is slightly lower than 9.50 per cent during the first leg.

The important commercial crops are *mesta*, sugarcane and groundnut. However, the Girijan Development Agency has successfully implemented the agricultural programmes during the period of its operation. A considerable amount of progress has been achieved by changing the attitudes of the tribals and adopting new innovations in the field of agriculture.

Irrigation

Irrigation occupies an important place in the field of agriculture. The area irrigated in the project area accounts for 31.8 per cent as against 30.7 per cent during the first leg showing an acute increase in the irrigation facility. The major source of irrigation for the sample households is hill streams which works out to 72.8 per cent which is more or less equal with the first leg survey results. The project area is bountiful with innumerable hill streams crisscrossing the entire territory. Further, the canals form another source of irrigation which accounts for 9 per cent of the project area which is more or less equal with the first leg survey results (ie., 9.4%) The area irrigated by tanks form 16 per cent in the project area to the total irrigated area as against 15.7 per cent during first leg indicating a slight increase in the irrigated area by tanks. Only a small percentage of the area, i.e., 2.2 per cent is under wells without pump sets. With the introduction of the Girijan Development Agency. Srikakulam, the minor irrigation schemes like check-dams and irrigation wells at 50 per cent subsidy and oil engines, electric motors and maintenance of anicuts and reservoirs in tribal areas and lift irrigation schemes have been streamlined in the project area. The analysis indicates that even though there is an improvement in the irrigation sources with the intervention of Girijan development schemes yet the majority of the area shall be brought under irrigation if the proper irrigation schemes can be planned in the project area.

Income

The average income per household in the project area is Rs. 1108, while in the case of the tribal household as per the first leg it was Rs. 640. The per capita income of the household works out to 230.79 whereas as per the first leg it was only 141.81. The income from agriculture which is a major source accounts for 74.3 per cent as against 61.7 per cent of first leg survey which indicates the greater dependence of tribals on the agricultural sector. The income derived from minor forest produce accounts for 10.29 per cent in the project area when compared to 10.6 per cent during first leg survey results. The income from wages account for 15.44 per cent in the project area as against 26.6 per cent during first leg indicating a strong decrease in the percentage of income from wages because of the seasonal employment.

Expenditure

The average expenditure per household works out to Rs. 1,254 as against Rs. 804 of the first leg indicating a considerable increase to the tune of Rs. 450. The per capita expenditure per household works out to Rs. 274.36. Food is a major item of expenditure which accounts for 61.52 per cent, which is almost equal to the results of the first leg survey. Expenditure on drinks which is a favourite with all tribal people (males, females and children) accounts for 11.3 per cent as against 11.1 per cent of the previous survey results. The expenditure on tobacco is also high and accounts for 9.49 per cent to the total income of the household which is almost equal to the first leg Bench Mark Survey results, i.e., 9.4 per cent. Here, an important observation is that tribals smoke with the burning end in the mouth, and it is called reverse smoking. Rites and ceremonies play an important role in the cultural and social scene of the tribals and generally the expenditure on this item is also high which accounts for 9.11 per cent as against 8.5 per cent of the first leg. Finally the expenditure on clothing is also high. Even though there is a general impression that tribals wear only loin cloth and a shirt on the upper part of the body yet with the cultural and social contact with non-tribals and officials they also learned to wear trousers, pyjamas, shirts, and sarees and blouses. Therefore now-a-days, the expenditure on this item has also increased to a considerable extent which accounts for 8.59 per cent to the total expenditure on household as against 7.4 per cent of the first leg. Today, radios, transistors, cycles, gold and artificial gold ornaments, brasswares, wood articles are found in the tribal households.

The tribals have adapted themselves well and are in tune with the growing needs of society.

Loans

Generally, a tribal household leads a poor life unless some help from governmental agencies is available. The tribals cannot afford to lead a normal economic and social life. This is the reason why government is now granting loans to the poor and needy tribals in the tribal areas of the district. Government agencies like Girijan Development Agency, Tribal Welfare Department, Girijan Cooperative Corporation, TRICOR, Grameen Banks, Land Mortgage Banks, nationalised Banks, Taluk Office, Panchayat Samiti Office, etc., are implementing loan programmes to tribal beneficiaries. The average amount of debt in the project area from money-lenders is Rs. 242 as against Rs. 182 in the previous survey results. This shows that tribals are still borrowing loans from private money-lenders for various purposes. Out of 776 tribal households selected in the study nearly 31.25 per cent of the households have borrowed loans as against 64.1 per cent during the first leg survey indicating that the tribals are gradually withdrawing from borrowing loans from money-lenders due to the functioning of institutional credit agencies. Out of 776 households surveyed 56.7 per cent of the households borrowed from institutional credit agencies as against 38.0 per cent during the first leg. This indicates a welcome increase in granting loans to the tribal people by the institutional credit agencies due to encouragement given by the government to finance them for productive purposes. The average debt per household is Rs. 409 as against Rs. 128 the first leg indicating that borrowing capacity among the tribal people has increased.

In general, the analysis indicates that tribal people are now very much aware of the functioning and the role of institutional credit agencies to a great extent, and they also understand that the private money-lenders are charging exhorbitant rates of interest. They are unable to discharge the debt during their life-time and they also understand that the bonded labour conditions were created by the money-lenders due to non-payment of their loan. The tribals are aware of their constitutional rights and their role in society. The government agencies have helped in uplifting the tribals to a level which has enabled them to raise their standard of living which is on par with the people living in the non-scheduled areas.

TABLE 2.1: **Development indicators**

S. No.	Name of the indicator	I leg project	II leg project
1	2	3	4
	Total number of surveyed households	776	776
1.	Average size of the household	4.5	4.6
2.	*Percentage*		
	(a) earners	68.3	60.13
	(b) non-earners	31.7	39.87
3.	*Literacy (%)*	9.54	14.06
	(a) primary literates	88.9	94.58
	(b) secondary literates	6.9	4.80
	(c) others	4.2	0.62
4.	Average size of holding	3.9	3.5
5.	% of households possessing land	75.77	76.15
6.	*Size of holding (% of distribution) of households*		
	(a) 0 - 0.99	13.7	18.61
	(b) 1—2.99	45.8	56.58
	(c) 3—4.99	26.3	21.19
	(d) +5	14.2	3.62
7.	Percentage of land cultivated	85.9	86.0
8.	*Percentage of area*		
	(a) under food crops	90.5	90.60
	(b) under commercial crops	9.5	9.40
9.	*Percentage of area irrigated*	30.7	31.8
	(a) by canals	9.4	9.00
	(b) by streams	72.7	72.80
	(c) by tanks	15.7	16.00
	(d) by wells without pumpsets	2.2	2.2
10.	*Average income per household (% Income from)*	640	1108
	(a) agriculture	61.7	74.3
	(b) mFP	10.6	10.3
	(c) wages	26.6	15.4
11.	*Average expenditure per household (% Expenditure for)*	804	1254
	(a) food	61.4	61.5
	(b) drinks	11.1	11.3
	(c) tobacco	9.4	9.5

TABLE 2.1—*contd.*

1	2	3	4
	(d) clothing	7.4	8.6
	(e) rites and ceremonies	8.5	9.1
12.	*Average loan per household*		
	(i) *Institutional*		
	(a) amount in Rs.	128	409
	(b) % of households borrowed	38.0	56.7
	(ii) *Traditional* :		
	(a) amount in Rs.	182	247
	(b) % of households borrowed	64.1	31.3

REFERENCES

1. Prof. Muttalib, M.A., *Development Administration in Rural Government for Agricultural Production—An Approach in Comparative Administration*, Dept. of Publications Press, Osmania University, Hyderabad, 1973, p. 69.
2. Tripathy, R.N.; Pradhan, F.M.; Lakshmaiah, T., "Tribal Development Programme in Keonjhar (Orissa)—An Evaluation," National Institute of Rural Development, Hyderabad, August, 1979, p. 400-1.
3. Prof. Sarveswara Rao, B.; Prof. Parthasarathy, G.; Dr. Rao, T.V.S., "Report of the Study of Girijan Development Agency, Srikakulam district," Agro Economic Research Centre, Andhra University, Waltair, April 1977, p. 117.

3

GIRIJAN COOPERATIVE CORPORATION

The Adivasis are the original inhabitants whose material position is perhaps no better than that of Harijans and who have long been victims of neglect on the part of the so-called high classes. They are like the indigenous medicine, of the soil, and their roots lie deep there.

—*Mahatma Gandhi*

THE TRIBAL SITUATION IN ANDHRA PRADESH

ANDHRA PRADESH has a large concentration of tribal population. The total tribal population according to the 1971 census is 16.58 lakhs. Consequent to the inclusion of Yerukulas, Yanadis and Sugalis of Telangana region in the list of scheduled tribes, the scheduled tribes population has gone up by 5.69 lakhs. Now the total scheduled tribes population in Andhra Pradesh is 22.26 lakhs.

The hill tribes are socially and economically very poor. Innocence and illiteracy are significant among them. Collection and sale of minor forest produce forms not only a major source of their sustenance, but also a means of livelihood through trade and barter.

As most of the agency areas lack in proper transport and communication facilities, the tribals could not command a better market for the minor forest produce to their advantage and this deprived them from securing a better price. As a result, the petty traders took advantage of the situation and exploited the tribals. Petty traders supplied tribals their daily requirements which were two or three times deficient in value to the forest produce obtained from them. Underweighment of produce bought by them was a common practice with the petty traders.

Political factors

In the early stages of the formation of Andhra State, Sri Tanguturi Prakasam Pantulu, the then Chief Minister, who was a close follower of Mahatma Gandhi took a lot of interest in tribal development and the economic uplift of the poor. The Constitution already bespoke a special attention to the tribal problem. Therefore, in keeping with the directives of state policy, and protection of tribals in particular, the state government took a keen interest in tribal matters. Moreover, at that point of time there was the Congress government at the centre and in Andhra, both were wedded to the principle laid down by Gandhiji as enshrined in the Constitution.

In order to mitigate the hardships and to protect the tribals from exploitation by the plain-men, the government took substantive steps and passed protective and restrictive legislations. The network of multipurpose cooperative credit societies formed for the promotion of the welfare of the tribals could not work effectively. Based on the recommendations of the Malayappan Committee.[1] The government started "The Andhra Scheduled Tribes Finance and Development Corporation Ltd." for the economic development of the tribals in the agency areas in 1956 vide G.O.Ms. No. 2551, Education and Endowments Department, dated 14 December, 1955. Accordingly, this corporation was originally registered under the Indian Companies Act I of 1956.

The Girijan Cooperative Corporation's main aim is to uplift the hill tribes and protect them from exploitation by the plain traders and money-lenders, by extending agricultural credit facilities. Its mission is to extend the 'healing touch' to those less fortunate people. Marketing of the forest produce, comprising 45 items, such as tamarind, honey and herbs, is one of the activities of the Corporation. More than half of the Corporation employees are Harijans and Girijans. Tribal women are trained in such jobs as leaf-stitching and de-seeding. Financially, the Corporation's budget has gone from Rs. 20 lakhs to Rs. 2 crores. It pays to the state government nearly Rs. 15 lakhs by way of rentals and commerical taxes.

In Andhra Pradesh, the large concentration of scheduled castes and scheduled tribes constitute 4.5 per cent of the state population and are scattered over an agency area of 11,350 sq. miles. In our society, it is not enough (to borrow Galbraith's words) if the comfortable are afflicted. It is more than necessary to comfort the afflicted. That is what the Girijan Cooperative Corporation is seeking to achieve. It is a task being faced by the government. It is also a social responsibility which we can no longer shirk. Added to this are certain subsidiary objectives like strengthening the cooperative structure :

(a) to take shares in the affiliated societies from its own funds;
(b) to provide working capital to the affiliated societies by advancing loans and cash credits;
(c) to borrow funds for issue of loans to Girijans through affiliated societies for agricultural purposes; and
(d) to coordinate, supervise and control the activities of the affiliated societies.

In order to enable carrying on the business of the G.C.C., certain infrastructural facilities were made available to cover long distances and remote areas. Hence for successful trading activity, certain other objectives which are vital for successful fulfilment to the Corporation's activities, namely :

(a) to acquire or take on lease godowns or sales depots for the purpose of storage and sale of agricultural and forest produce;
(b) to undertake activities such as processing and grading

for the benefit of the Corporation and making available necessary machinery; and

(c) to own or hire lorries for transport for carrying produce and other goods.

Further, the G.C.C. has also an educational role in the sense that one of its objectives is :

(a) to encourage self-help; thrift and cooperation among to affiliated societies and their members; and

(b) to undertake generally such other activities as are conducive to the promotion of the socio-economic welfare of the tribals and any other matter which helps in their batterment. Finally, the G.C.C. has acted as the information centre of the government for promoting welfare of the tribals.

The G.C.C. established its headquarters at Visakhapatnam. When the institution first started functioning in 1957, it had only two primary societies one at Donnur of Vishakhapatnam district and the other at G.L. Puram of Srikakulam district (presently in Vizianagaram district) with two D.R. Depots and its annual turnover was just Rs. 4.13 lakhs.

The G.C.C. is a cooperative institution registered under the A.P. Cooperative Societies Act. It is an apex organisation with primary marketing societies as its members functioning in different areas of the state. The organisational pattern of the Corporation follows the usual cooperative structure with primary societies at the operational level; and the Corporation as an apex organisation at the state level. In course of time the Corporation expanded its activity both in Andhra and Telangana regions to cover the entire population of the scheduled tribes in the agency areas.

The objectives of the Corporation as set out above show that the Corporation is bound by a clear-cut social policy with the ultimate aim of passing on to the tribals the maximum price for their produce and to supply them their daily requirements at reasonable rates, and to provide credit to enable them to progressively improve their economic condition. This Corporation is, therefore, a welfare-oriented institution.

However, within three years since its inception a one-man committee under Shri K. Ananta Raman, was appointed to look into the working of the G.C.C. This report was submitted in 1961 and it generally expressed dissatisfaction with the work that was being done by the G.C.C. However, at that particular point of time the organisation was still in an infant stage, and it was too much to expect fantastic results in its nascent stages.

ANANTARAMAN REPORT

In 1961 the Ananta Raman Committee[2] investigated into the working of the Girijan Cooperative Corporation and suggested that the business should be conducted more efficiently and that procedures and activities should be streamlined so that the impact is maximised. It was also recommended that freedom should be given to the managers in disposal of stock perishable commodities. It was also felt that commodities should be displayed in a very attractive manner and there should be proper advertisement.

Regarding the domestic requirement depots it was felt that there was need to intensify the supply of the domestic requirements to all the villagers in the area of operation.

It was felt that the loans and advances to the tribals were extremely inadequate and the number of tribals source were very small. The Corporation had not tackled even the fringe of the problem. The objective of the Corporation would be fulfilled only "when it is able to reach the tribal at home, give him daily requirements at moderate price and furnish him adequate credit and evoke in him unqualified appreciation". This report also emphasised the need for providing irrigation schemes to improve the economic resources of the tribes. It was felt that tribals resorted to *podu* cultivation because they had no other alternative source of income.

However, it was not until 1967, that the G.C.C. was really faced with a challenge. This challenge came in the shape of the Naxalite movement in Srikakulam District. It was suddenly realised that there was a maximum amount of work that remained to be done in the tribal areas and it is here that the

G.C.C took upon itself the job of working into a disturbed area.

EXPANSION OF ACTIVITIES

The Corporation started on a limited scale with two primaries and two domestic requirement depots in the year 1956-57 and had by the end of 1971-72 grown to a gigantic organisation, spreading its area of operation to the entire state with 27 primaries and 247 domestic requirement depots and by the end of 1978, the number of domestic requirement depots has gone up to around 400.

On account of the Naxalite activities and growing unrest in the tribal areas, mostly in Srikakulam and Vishakhapatnam districts, among others, it was considered necessary to streamline the activities of the Corporation and to undertake comprehensive welfare measures for the scheduled tribes in the agency areas and this resulted in a reorientation of the policy of expansion and diversification of the activities of the Corporation. From about 1968, the Corporation underwent a process of expansion in all directions. In terms of jurisdiction its activities were extended to the Telangana Region and the plain pockets of Srikakulam, Nellore, Karimnagar and Rayalaseema Districts. In terms of identification of its functions, a large number of domestic requirement depots were opened. The Corporation also succeeded in its efforts in getting it recognised by the Reserve Bank of India as the sole agency for distribution of short-term credit and medium-term credit to the scheduled tribes in Srikakulam, Khammam and Warangal Districts. Further, the Government of Andhra Pradesh have also placed at the disposal of the Corporation a sum of Rs. 25 lakhs to form a corpus of revolving fund providing agricultural credit to the scheduled tribes from time to time.

Insofar as payment of purchase price to the produce brought by the tribal was concerned, there was then a severe criticism from all quarters. Up to 1969-70, the purchase price policy of the Corporation was to pay a fair price to the tribal for the produce brought by him. This purchase price was being arrived at duly deducting 41 per cent towards overhead charges plus the percentage of permissible driages from the price prevailing in the nearest wholesale market. This 41 per cent overhead charges includes (i) forest rentals, (ii) trade charges, (iii) transport charges, and (iv) establishment charges. This came in for sharp criticism on the obvious ground that the resultant price offered to the tribal was very low. In fact, forest rentals and establishment charges alone accounted for 23 per cent of the deductions from the purchase price payable to the tribals. This caused disincentive to the tribal to sell his produce to the Corporation. Keeping the social unrest of the tribal in view and the need to reconsider the earlier stand, the government ordered the Corporation* to fix purchase price without making any deductions on account of forest rentals and establishment charges. The government also undertook to subsidise the Corporation for its losses on account of non-deduction of these two items. In pursuance of the above orders, the Corporation was restricting its incidental charges, etc., only to 15 per cent.

From the above facts it may be seen that originally the Corporation while arriving at the purchase price to be paid to the tribal was deducting 41 per cent from the nearest wholesale market which would include both establishment charges and forest rentals among others. This deduction on account of establishment charges was made by the Corporation even while getting 12½ per cent as subsidy over the sales turnover towards establishment charges from the government. The revised pricing policy of the Corporation as envisaged in G.O.Ms. No. 1477, Revenue (T.W.I) Department dated 31 December, 1970, prohibits the Corporation to charge anything towards establishment charges on the prices to be passed on to the tribals. This means that if the Corporation were to survive and discharge its duties it should get an appropriate subsidy from the Government in addition to the subsidy of 12½ per cent over the sales turnover which was already committed much prior to the revised pricing policy and was found to be the absolute minimum.

**Vide* G.O.Ms. No. 1477, Revenue (T.W.I.) Department, dated 31 December, 1970.

Staff Structure Committee

Constitution of Staff Structure Committee in 1971 and orders of the government thereon

The Corporation approached the government to enhance the subsidy on establishment charges suitably to meet the changed position. The government after considering the various factors involved in the matter constituted a committee consisting of six members with the Registrar of Co-operative Societies as its Chairman*

The Committee was asked to go into the entire staff structure of the Corporation and suggest measures for its optimum utilisation, ensuring at the same time economy and efficiency and advise the government on a line of policy to be adopted by them to meet the staff costs of the Corporation.

After examining the matter the committee submitted a detailed report to the government not only on the pattern of the staff to be employed but also the broad guidelines on which the Corporation may open societies and [domestic requirement depots, etc. The salient features of the recommendations of the Committee are :

(i) a primary society should be set up for every 50,000 population of the scheduled tribes.

(ii) a domestic requirement depot should be opened for every 2,000 population of scheduled tribes, the location of the depot being determined by considerations of accessibility.

(iii) the Divisional Offices be retained.

(iv) an officer of the rank of Selection Grade Personal Assistant to the Collector should assist the Managing Director in the performance of his duties at Head-quarters.

(v) the managerial staff at the primary should be :

(a) Primaries with a trade turnover over Rs. 12.00 lakhs :	Manager to be of the rank of Tahsildar to be assisted by a Deputy Manager of the rank of Deputy Tahsildar.

*Vide Government Memo No. 1050, TW-II-11-2-73, Revenue Department, dated 22 January, 1971.

(b) Societies with a turnover of Rs. 6.00 lakhs to Rs. 12.00 lakhs.	A Manager of the rank of Deputy Tahsildar assisted by a Senior Inspector.
(c) Societies with a T.O. of less than Rs. 6.00 lakhs.	A Deputy Tahsildar/Manager only.

(vi) the staff could be drawn from Revenue or Cooperative Department.

(vii) no modification in the rest of the staff at the primary level for running the office, maintenance of accounts, etc., is necessary. The staff for the Divisional Offices also does not require any modification.

(viii) there is no need to fix any specific percentage of overheads as the ceiling on staff costs. The government should bear the entire staff cost and make the equi valent reimbursement every year to the Corporation.

The Committee while concluding its report observed that instead of controlling staff cost by a rule-of-the-thumb method of linking to the percentage of turnover, it would be more imaginative and realistic to link up the staff costs to a given pattern of staff for each unit of operation.

The report of the Staff Structure Committee is, however, silent on the issue relating to the staff costs on industrial units like honey plant, sheekakai grinding plant, etc., which were in existence even then.

The government after considering the report of the Staff Structure Committee issued orders with regard to the staff to be employed in the Corporation and the mode of reimbursement of the costs. However, important posts like shandy inspectors, cashiers and typists were not covered by this sanction. These posts were in existence in the Corporation even prior to the recommendations of the Staff Structure Committee. It may be mentioned that without the posts of the shandy inspectors, cashiers and typists it is impossible to run the Primary Societies.

The Staff Structure Committee did not touch the issues in regard to the reimbursement of the costs on the staff employed in industrial units. A decision as to whether the staff costs of industrial units should be subsidised would have to be taken.

As explained earlier, the Corporation has been extending its activities both in terms of jurisdiction and business and thereby there was considerable improvement in turnovers which necessitated creation of some more middle level supervisory posts besides the field staff. By the time the Staff Structure Committee submitted its report (1971-72) the Corporation was having 247 domestic requirement depots and 27 primary societies with a total turnover of Rs. 198 lakhs. By the end of 1977. the number of societies affiliated were 30 with about 400 domestic requirement depots with a total turnover of Rs. 656 lakhs. In terms of quantity of procurement also there was conspicuous improvement in important commodities like gum. In the year 1971-72 the procurement of gum was 1,770 quintals while by the end of 1977 this has gone up to 10,975 quintals. The domestic requirements turnover has also gone up enormously as can be seen from the fact that by the end of 1977 it was about Rs. 498 lakhs as against Rs. 131 lakhs by the end of 1971-72.

G.C.C. COOPERATIVE CHARACTER

The Girijan Cooperative Corporation Limited, is a cooperative institution registered under the Cooperative Societies Act. The organizational pattern follows the usual cooperative structure with primaries at the operational level and an apex organisation at the state level.

There are 30 Primary societies/branches of the Girijan Cooperative Corporation scattered in the tribal areas of Srikakulam, Visakhapatnam, East Godavari, West Godavari, Nellore, Chittoor, Anantapur, Prakasam, Khammam, Warangal, Karimnagar, Mahboobnagar, Nizamabad and Adilabad districts.

For purposes of supervision, control and coordination the entire area of Corporation is divided into two regions, viz.,

Andhra and Telengana. Under each region there are three divisions as shown below :

Telengana region	*Andhra region*
1. Palwancha	4. Srikakulam
2. Warangal	5. Visakhapatnam
3. Adilabad	6. Rajahmundry

Under the control of each division there are four to six societies.

Till the year 1975 there was no regional set-up and the Divisional Managers were directly answerable to the Managing Director. Right from 1972, there was a proposal to create a Regional Office with the headquarters at Hyderabad to effectively supervise and coordinate the activities in Telangana region since the Corporation was intensifying its activities in Telengana region also. This proposal finally materialised in the year 1975 when the Board of Directors of the Corporation resolved to appoint a Regional Manager of the cadre of Special Grade Deputy Collector to supervise the working of the activities in Telangana region. Till 1975, there was a small Marketing Office at Hyderabad and this was upgraded to the status of a Regional Office headed by a Regional Manager.

So far as the Andhra region was concerned all the divisions were then directly under the control of the Managing Director. To have an effective control at the field level and to intensively supervise and coordinate the activities of the Corporation in the Andhra region, the General Manager at Headquarters was designated as Regional Manager for the Andhra region, in the year 1978. Thus the General Manager at Headquarters while discharging his functions as second-in-command at the Headquarters was also entrusted with the responsibility of supervising the three divisions in the Andhra region. Both the Regional Managers were delegated with suitable powers to deal with all matters in their respective regions.

While the Regional Manager at Hyderabad had an independent office with necessary supporting staff, the Regional Manager at the Headquarters had no independent staff. The staff at Corporation Head Office itself is assisting the General

CHART 3.1 : **Corporation Head office**

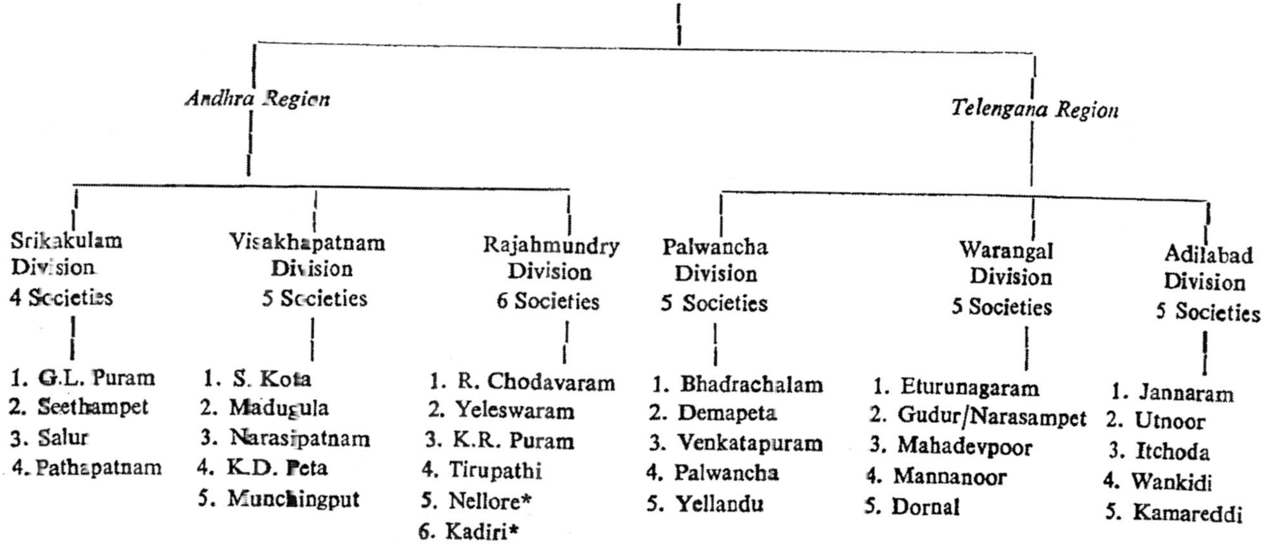

*N.B.—Nellore and Kadiri Societies were ordered to be closed by the government, however, they are covered by stay orders of the High Court.

Manager to discharge his duties as Regional Manager, Andhra. Since the jurisdiction of the Managing Director is vast and the area of operation is scattered and distributed almost over the entire state, this regional set-up was considered essential for effective control and supervision of field-level work.

At the divisional level, the Divisional officers are headed by officers of the cadre of Deputy Collectors/Deputy Registrar of Cooperative Societies with suitable supporting staff.

ORGANISATION CHART

The Office-wise structure and functions are broadly as follows:

Corporation Head Office

1. The Corporation Head Office is broadly divided into three sections, viz., administration, commercial and accounts. The administrative section includes personnel management, secretariat work, vigilance cell, credit, transport and engineering branches. These branches are supervised by the General Manager, who is also ex-officio Regional Manager for Andhra region.

2. The commercial branch is headed by a Commercial Manager assisted by a Deputy Commercial Manager to advise on all technical matters relating to storage, etc. The Commercial Manager has necessary supporting staff. The Commercial Manager is also to supervise the work of the industrial units, viz., honey processing unit, shikakai plant and soap unit.

3. The accounts branch is headed by the Chief Accounts Officer, who is a chartered accountant assisted by a Senior Accounts Officer, Accounts Officer and other supporting staff. The Senior Accounts Officer will function as a second-in-command in the accounts section of the Corporation Head Office. In the absence of Chief Accounts Officer at Headquarters he will attend to all routine work in the accounts branch. Further, the Senior Accounts Officer is attending to important items of work like income-tax, commercial taxes, reconciliation of accounts, budgetary controls, preparation of final accounts and cash credit proposals, etc. Further, in the revised set-up it is proposed to entrust the Senior Accounts Officer with

credit work also. He has to coordinate the work of the two regions. The other supporting staff has got sufficient work load.

4. In the absence of Managing Director at Headquarters, as second-in-command, the General Manager will also be competent to pass orders on the files relating to accounts and commercial branches where there is no statutory obligation.

5. The organisational chart at Corporation Head Office is as follows:

CHART 3.2

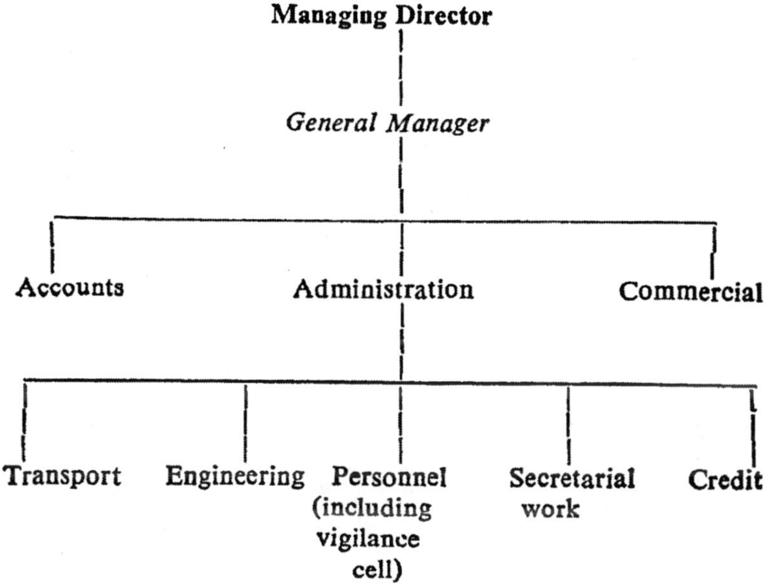

Functions of subordinate offices are:

Regional office

1. The Regional Office at Hyderabad is headed by the Regional Manager of the cadre of Special Grade Deputy Collector, who will, among others, attend to the following major items of work.

(a) conduct of periodic auctions and sale of gum karaya in the raw form or after processing. The Regional

Manager is responsible to pool up gum procured from time to time in different units of Telangana region and arrange for its disposal.

(b) In respect of other commodities procured in Telangana region where the Divisional Managers are not competent to dispose of certain decentralised items of minor forest produce, the Regional Manager was empowered to dispose of them to the best advantage of the Corporation.

(c) The Regional Office can operate on the cash-credit account held with the A.P. State Cooperative Bank, Hyderabad, and distribute funds in the Primary Societies of Telangana region depending on their need and watch for their recoveries and remittances.

(d) In respect of works the Regional Manager is empowered to execute original and maintenance works up to certain limits. For this purpose he is assisted by an Assistant Engineer at the Regional Office, Hyderabad.

(e) He is responsible for proper maintenance of vehicles and he shall arrange for carrying out repair and renewals to the vehicles up to certain limit after scrutiny of estimates, etc., by the Transport Officer.

(f) The Regional Manager shall cause inspection of branches/societies in Telangana region.

(g) The Regional Office shall cause verification of stocks held in several units in Telangana region.

(h) A small internal audit cell is also attached to the Regional Office which shall function under the control of the Regional Manager and he has to arrange for internal audit of the units in Telangana region.

(i) The Regional Office is in sole charge for drawal and distribution of controlled cloth to all the units of the Corporation and for this purpose the Regional Manager has to maintain necessary registers and records.

(j) In regard to legal matters, the Regional Manager shall execute agreements and other legal documents on behalf of the Corporation in so far as operations of the Corporation in his region are concerned and he shall file written statements, affidavits after proper scrutiny and approval by the Managing Director.

(k) In regard to service matters the Regional Manager is appointing authority up to and inclusive of the cadre of senior assistants and he is also the appellate authority on the disciplinary and other orders passed by the Divisional Managers.

2. In the revised set-up, the Regional Manager at Visakhapatnam will also exercise the same powers. Both the Regional Managers will be responsible for the work in their respective regions.

Divisional Office

1. The Divisional Manager is the supervising authority over the field operations by the primary societies in the divisions. In order to make the divisional office more effective, certain powers in regard to the fixing up purchase price of minor forest produce and disposal of decentralised items of minor forest produce and agricultural produce fixing up certain margins were delegated to the Divisional Managers. The Divisional Office is headed by an officer of the cadre of a Deputy Collector with limited supporting staff. The Divisional Office is responsible to supervise and coordinate the activities of the Primaries in the division. Further, the Divisional Managers have to coordinate the work of the Corporation with the District Collectors and other functionaries of the Revenue, Agriculture, Forest, Industries, Civil Supplies, and Cooperative Departments. The Divisional Office is responsible to make all purchases for supply to the domestic requirements depots and it is also responsible for securing the required quantities of essential commodities like rice, kerosine, sugar, and so on. The Divisional Manager at his level is expected to tour intensively and cover all activities of the primary societies. Further, the Divisional Manager is also Ex-officio Chairman of the Primary Societies.

2. The Divisional Manager is primarily assisted by a Junior Manager (Superintendent) of the rank of a Deputy Tahsildar and an Accountant of the cadre of senior assistant.

Primary Societies

As already mentioned the primaries are functional units of the Corporation. It is at this level that the actual procurement of minor forest produce, agricultural produce, and sale of domestic requirements and also provision of credit is done. The Manager of the Primary Society has multifarious duties. Big societies are headed by a Senior Manager of the cadre of Tahsildar assisted by a Junior Manager of the rank of a Deputy Tahsildar whereas small societies are headed by Junior Managers of the cadre of Deputy Tahsildars. Under the control of each primary society there are domestic requirement depots ranging from 5 to 18. The Manager is assisted by an accountant to look after all account matters; shandy inspectors for procurement of minor forest produce and agricultural produce; stores assistants to receive, deliver and to safeguard stocks; and salesman to man the domestic requirement depot sales to the tribals. In the societies where there is credit work, the Manager is assisted by Credit Assistants.

Besides the above offices at the Regional, Divisional and Society levels, there are small industrial units at the following places:

(a) Honey Processing Unit, Narsipatnam.
(b) Shikakai Grinding Plant, Narsipatnam.
(c) Niger Oil Extraction Plant, Paderu.
(d) Soap Making Unit, Paderu.
(e) Gum Processing Unit, Nirmal.

SITUATION IN OTHER STATES—CONTRAST

It would be appropriate to compare and contrast the method and disposal of minor forest produce prevailing in Andhra Pradesh and other neighbouring states. It is, therefore, proposed to compare and contrast the procedures and policies followed in Andhra Pradesh, Orissa, Madhya Pradesh and Bihar. A study was conducted by the Consulting and Applied Research Division of Administrative Staff College of India in 1977-78.[3] (This study of *Management of Tribal Development Programmes; Study of Minor Forest Produce* was commissioned by the Government of India, Ministry of Home Affairs.) The object of the study was to examine certain issues in the economies of collection, marketing and appropriation of gains out of the minor forest produce to the tribals. Here it may be mentioned that the G.C.C. is the first institution of its kind that was established anywhere in the country after independence. The distinguishing feature about the G.C.C. is that it has been given monopoly rights over the minor forest produce of the tribal areas in Andhra Pradesh; so in fact it becomes an organisation not only for the Girijans but also by the Girijans. The M.F.P. procured from the tribals are disposed of in various ways and for various purposes.

It is seen in other states that the G.C.Cs. and its corresponding organisations in Orissa, Bihar and Madhya Pradesh have not been vested with the monopoly rights over the forest produce as has been the case in Andhra Pradesh. Secondly, various procurements are effected by a single agency in Andhra Pradesh, that is, Girijan, Cooperative Corporation. Various agencies are at work in these other states including middlemen; state trading agencies and the forest department. In Madhya Pradesh, Orissa and Bihar, the forest department obtains the returns in the shape of profits by the sale of M.F.P. This has reduced the tribal from being a natural owner of M.F.P. he collects; to the level of a wage-earner. In all the states and to a greater degree in Bihar, Madhya Pradesh and Orissa, all the commercially important items of M.F.P. like *sal* seeds, *kendu* leaves, and so on, are taken up by the forest departments as nationalised items of collection and trading. Neither the tribal for whose benefits the M.F.P. items are supposed to be exploited, nor the apex cooperative bodies which came into existence and carry out these functions are anywhere in the picture. In fact, the object of such nationalisation or monopoly state trading turned out to be to earn more revenue by the forest departments and through them to the states. Thirdly, the apex cooperative organisations which were supposed to be promoting agencies created for tribal development utilising amongst other means; the M.F.P. are very ineffective particularly in Madhya Pradesh and Bihar. However, all the four states suffer from one common element and that is the apex cooperative bodies are faced with financial problems. Whenever they suffer losses, they look to the government for subsidies. The 'royalty' they have to pay to the forest department for handling M.F.P. and their ineffective operations have compounded their problems. Fourthly, there is no proper inventory of resources about the availability of M.F.P. items—how much is available, how much is consumed, and how much would be surplus (it would be the quantity available for procurement). Briefly, some of the conditions prevailing in these states are stated below. Out of these after an overall view it is found that the system prevailing in Andhra Pradesh is the best and should be followed by other states of the Indian Union.

Madhya Pradesh

1. All minor forest produce is treated as property of the forest department. Hence in this state the tribal is not treated as an owner of the minor forest produce.

2. Some items are not nationalised and hence are open to private trading.

3. The revenue from M.F.P. is not considered as a revenue for the tribal but for the forest department or for the Madhya Pradesh State Tribal Cooperative Development Federation. The non-nationalised or non-specified items are collected by the tribals on their own and procured by the T.C.D.F.

4. No marketing or processing of the M.F.P. is possible or is undertaken to add value to the M.F.P. to benefit the tribals. All the marketing and processing is done after the sale to the wholesale traders.

5. There is no concerted plan between the agencies involved in developing the M.F.P. transactions into an instrument of tribal development.

Bihar

By and large conditions prevalent in Madhya Pradesh hold good here also. However, the following additional points are relevant.

1. The objectives of the T.C.D.C. are defined by them as follows :

> "The Corporation plays essentially a promotional role and its main object includes provision of financial, technical and

managerial assistance as well as marketing facilities to the scheduled castes and scheduled tribes organised co-operatively. The Corporation helps the cooperative societies in obtaining settlement of forest coupes and minor produce."

This falls short of what is needed—an organisation to completely take up work by itself, effectively organise collection, procurement, processing and marketing of all quantities of all M.F.P.

2. The following items of M.F.P. are handled by the state agencies :

(a) *Kendu* leaves, (b) *Sal* seeds, (c) Lac, (d) *Myro balans*, (e) *Siyaly* leaves, (f) *Tasar* ccoons, (g) *Chirongi* seeds, (h) *Kusum* seeds, (i) *Mahua* flowers, (j) *Mahua* seeds and (k) *Pala* seeds.

Of these there are two items the *kendu* leaves, *sal* leaves which are monopoly items of state procurement. Some items are collected by the tribals on their own and procured by the Bihar Tribal Development Corporation in competition with the private trader.

3. The staff of the T.C.D.C. have no background of forestry or tribal affairs.

4. The work done presently by the forest department should be done by the T.C.D.C., the Forest Development Corporation should be for planning developmental activities of forests and not for trading in tribal produce.

Orissa

1. Here again the Orissa Forest Department plays a leading role and the tribal far from being the owner of the M.F.P. entitled to the intrinsic value of the material, is reduced to a mere labourer getting only a wage. This is particularly true in the case of nationalised items.

2. Some items are not even nationalised and hence are open to private trading even in the case of nationalised items the private trader is the contractor employed for collection.

3. The revenue from the M.F.P. is not considered as a

revenue for the tribal, but for the forest department or for the T.C.D.C.

Andhra Pradesh

In Andhra Pradesh as is well known all items of M.F.P. are monopoly items of procurement, that is only state procurement from tribals is permissible. The Girijan Cooperative Corporation is the only body involved in procurement work. Girijan Cooperative Corporation pays a royalty to the forest department, there is no other liaison.

1. There are however, some items which perhaps go through the private trading channel which has to be checked effectively.
2. Liaison between forest department and G.C.C. should be improved in particular by preventing leakage to private channels.
3. Foresters who have close knowledge of and rapport with tribals should be employed by the G.C.C. and its various primary collection centres.
4. G.C.C. is well organised to take up processing of minor forest produce (M.F.P.) items at various stages (at the level of primary collection centres or at the level of a cluster of such centres, or at the level of the apex body); to initiate systematic marketing arrangements and to arrange for research and development efforts wherever needed.

A BUREAUCRATIC ORGANIZATION

Having discussed the situation prevailing in other states and seen the methods of operation similar to G.C.C. in its purpose and goal attainment; it would be appropriate at this point to suggest any changes for improved functioning and efficient management. As is known, while discussing internal structural differentiation, three factors come into play: (a) division of labour within an organisation; (b) nature and complexity of technology used; and (c) nature of the skill structure. By and large, the personnel managing the affairs of the G.C.C. are drawn from the Revenue and Cooperative Departments. Hence the culture of the organisation is by and large a bureaucratic one. The gravitational flow and chain of command is vertical and most of the policies are formulated in the top-most echelons of the organisation. As yet, the G.C.C. is not comparable to an organisation which has a culture where modern management practices are given due attention. It is a fact that at lower levels organisational control and coordination is severely lacking. This point has been emphasised by the Report of the Committee of the House to enquire into matters relating to deficits and misappropriations in the Girijan Cooperative Corporation, etc.[4]

Misappropriations

This report was discussed in the A.P. Legislative Assembly and in fact the Assembly took a very serious note of recurrence of misappropriations in the G.C.C. which was found to be a regular feature and the delay in taking effective steps for the recovery of balances from all the concerned; in as much as the amount so far recovered was reported to be Rs. 1.56 lakhs out of a total amount of Rs. 6.20 lakhs leaving a balance of Rs. 4.64 lakhs. It was also emphasised that legal action had only been taken in 23 cases out of 180 cases. It was felt that the Managing Director had not persued action vigorously to check misappropriation to institute necessary proceedings against all delinquent subordinates and ensuring speedy recovery from them. It was after an investigation into the causes of misappropriation it was felt that there are two points at which leaks and misappropriation occur.

(1) Salesmen in the D.R. depots who were kept in charge of nearly about Rs. 10,000 to 15,000 worth of stocks, though they are practically semi-literates; and
(2) Shandy inspectors in shandies who deal at every shandy to the extent of about Rs. 50,000 to Rs. 60,000.

Weak links

It was further felt that it is difficult to curtail the malpractices in the Corporation unless the basic organisation is strengthened. In the areas under operation by the Girijan Cooperative Corporation there are integrated tribal development agencies.

In these areas, there are tribal blocks with a full complement of staff in the field.

Better coordination

To illustrate, in Visakhapatnam district there are seven tribal blocks. Each block has got one Block Development Officer, seven Extension Officers besides other technical officers and Village level workers. In Visakhapatnam district the Corporation has got five societies managing 78 D.R. depots. All these D.R. depots are controlled and supervised by these five managers, though they are dispersed in the interior and forest hilly areas. Though much hard work is put forth, there cannot be effective supervision by five Managers and one Divisional Manager in this district. There are seven B.D.Os. and 50 Extension Officers going up and down in the same area. At present they do not seem to feel that they have the responsibility for checking these D.R. depots and shandies.

There are no instructions from the government that they should be involved in the operations of the Girijan Cooperative Corporation and the G.C.C. also by tradition has a feeling that they should not be interfered with. It was suggested that the integrated tribal development agencies, Department of Tribal Welfare and the Girijan Cooperative Corporation are all for the tribal welfare and that if these three organisations are brought into one stream, there will be better supervision as also greater cooperation. The present Divisional Manager posts may be abolished and the entire Corporation could be placed under the administrative control of the Project Officers of integrated tribal development agencies by dovetailing the tribal blocks and the Girijan Cooperative Corporation societies. The societies of the Corporation retaining their independent existence can be fitted into a pattern under the administrative control of the Project Officer and under the immediate guidance and supervision of the B.D.Os. and Extension Officers who have good local knowledge and stature. Instead of one Divisional Manager and five Managers struggling for supervision as is being done now in Visakhapatnam district, the whole tribal welfare operations can be supervised by seven B.D.Os., five Managers and with the District Tribal Welfare Officer in Visakhapatnam district also to supervise. The

Managing Director of Girijan Cooperative Corporation may be made in-charge of the entire tribal welfare work.

If these changes could be carried out, they would bring about better integration of functions; coordination of tasks; improved feedback to the Head Office and contribute to the good health of the organisation. It may also be necessary to have regular review of the activities of the G.C.C. by the legislature as it concerns the welfare of the poorest and most backward sections of the society and whether the organisation is effective in delivering the goods.

The Girijan Cooperative Corporation over the years has earned a great deal of appreciation from all quarters. It is significant to note the change in consumer patterns and consumer behaviour among the Girijans. As a matter of fact it has helped in acting as a catalyst in bringing the Girijans into the cash nexus and has also helped in social integration. There is perhaps a need to tailor its personnel policies so that personnel with specialist background in marketing techniques could be inducted into the organisation. There is also a necessity for commodities planning so that the performance of domestic requirement depots could be improved. Forecasting of commodities required and sold has not been attempted. There is also a necessity for employing tribals in various rungs of the organisation. For the G.C.C. should become more efficient as a credit agency, a role which is only partially fulfilled.

The Girijan Cooperative Corporation has over the years come to be regarded as an important institution in the lives of the Girijans. It has served not only to increase the tribals confidence in government agencies, but also acts as an important socio-economic institution. In this sense, it is an unique institution because it always comes to the rescue of the tribals meeting their needs and requirements in times of distress and crisis. It also has helped considerably in stimulating growth in the area and has been largely responsible as an agent of change and rural development. It is also one of the unique institutions of its kind in the world. In an age where there is increasing inflation and the risk of "stagnation" G.C.C. still manages to offer a fair price, and hope amidst adversity.

GIRIJAN COOPERATIVE CORPORATION AT WORK

The Girijan Cooperative Corporation was set up in 1956 and an examination of its functioning would be incomplete without knowing how the tribals themselves feel about this organisation. Hence a few case studies were conducted in Bhadragiri, Pachipenta, and Seethampet blocks of Srikakulam District.

The primary data for the study was derived from an interview with the two tribals in each of the blocks Pachipenta, Bhadragiri and Seethampet. It was also noted that all the tribals interviewed possessed lands and were dependent on agricultural activity. The interviews were held on the basis of carefully constructed schedules or questionnaires. They had been standardised on the basis of observations of conditions and problems. Discussions of these problems was also held with officials of the Tribal Research Institute.

The study was designed to find out the perception and awareness of the tribal about the G.C.C. Secondly, how was the G.C.C. a better organisation in the matter of offering fair price; and to what extent the dependence of the tribal on the middleman has been reduced. The consumer behaviour of the tribal was also investigated and how he reacted to the domestic supply depots and the choice he had in the matter of preferring goods and services offered by the G.C.C. It was also decided to find out how valuable it is for the tribal to conduct business in the shandies and how the shandy acts as an important medium of social intercourse and lastly it was decided to find out whether the G.C.C. had brought about any increase in the income of the tribals.

The case studies were analysed from two viewpoints. Firstly, to survey the interaction between G.C.C. and the tribal; secondly, how important a role the G.C.C. plays in the day-to-day life of the tribals.

Findings

It was found that in the average annual income of the tribal minor forest produce (M.F.P.) and its sale constituted an important part of the earning.

About 10 per cent of the annual income came from the sale of minor forest produce. Incidentally it is interesting to know that in the last ten years there has been a steady rise in the income derived from M.F.P. This reveals that M.F.P. is becoming an important source of income. The case study also reveals that this income from M.F.P. helped the tribals in purchase of items like domestic vessels and even fancy items like watches, transistors. The case study reveals that the tribals were unanimous in their confidence and faith in the institution of G.C.C. There may be occasions when the tribal goes to the shandy and purchases some items of daily consumption in the open market, but he would generally prefer to make his domestic requirements available from the domestic requirement depots.

What enables the tribal to renew his faith in the G.C.C. is the fact that payments are quick and a fair price is offered. Another factor which can be attributed for this confidence is that procurement agencies of the G.C.C. are available at important shandy points. Here also prices paid are fair by the G.C.C. and payment is prompt. In this sense the G.C.C. while encouraging the purchase at shandy points also helps the tribal to renew his social contacts and helps him to communicate more effectively with other tribals and acts as a medium of social intercourse. Generally the loads of M.F.P. are carried by head and the burden is shared by other family members. Perhaps the G.C.C. could also help in providing the tribal with a cheap mode of transport for carrying the M.F.P. to the shandy point.

Impact of Girijan Cooperative Corporation on tribal economy

To know the impact of Girijan Cooperative Corporation on tribal economy, three tribal development blocks, i.e., Bhadragiri, Seethampet and Pachipenta have been selected. Among these three tribal development blocks, six tribals were selected (i.e., two from each Panchayat Samiti) to interview about the role played by G.C.C. on their economy. Time at our disposal being limited, only the neighbouring villagers were picked up for case study analysis.

The impact of Girijan Cooperative Corporation can be gauged on the following heads :

(a) Economic conditions,
(b) Purchasing power of tribals,

(c) Marketing activities of tribals, and
(d) Barter system.

Economic conditions

Before the G.C.C. started its operation in these Samitis, merchants used to cheat innocent tribals by way of barter system. It is observed that many merchants from plains area settled in the agency area by extending their business activities. It is a fact that they used to supply cloth, rice, oil, jaggery and other requirements which are not available to tribals by way of barter system. They used to get exorbitant profit by this trade. Like this, many merchants earned and owned more than 25 to 50 acres of landed property in the agency parts. Presently, some of them have lost their lands by Special Acts. Tribals developed good faith in G.C.C. They are being benefited and getting a maximum rate for their produce as G.C.C. have opened purchasing centres all over the agency with a view to serve tribals. Tribals are offered a maximum rate for their produce as well as they are getting their daily needs at very cheap rate. G.C.C. is selling Kerosine oil, rice, wheat, sugar, cloth on control rate prescribed by government. Most of the D.R. depots are incurring loss on D.R. business to serve the tribals for whom the organisation is designed.

Purchasing power

Previously before G.C.C. took active role in the tribal economy in these tribal development blocks tribals had to face much trouble because petty merchants used to cheat them to the maximum extent possible for their selfish ends. By their intrusion into their economic activity the purchasing power of the tribal was very low. Even one year of their whole effort by collecting M.F.P. like tamarind, *myra bolams*, mahuwa seed, *nux vomica*, etc., could not fetch them their minimum needs for survival. As G.C.C. is paying competitive price they are in a position to save something for their future needs as well as leading a better life than previously what they were used to be.

Marketing activity

Tribals are very enthusiastic to sell their produce to G.C.C. Even they prefer to wait for some time to hand over their produce to G.C.C. only. They are well aware that they would be benefited, offered better price if their produce is sold to G.C.C.

Barter system

Some time produce like mondseed, cleaning nuts collection of each tribal may be very less. They may starve till they hand over the produce to shady inspectors at shady points on a shady day. To reduce such difficulties to the tribals, the G.C.C. extended the facility of barter system by exchanging M.F.P. to domestic requirements like rice, sugar, *dhall*, etc., Presently they are not adopting such procedures.

Inter-variations among case studies

The per capita income ranges from Rs. 289 to Rs. 465. It depends on various factors like (a) Number of earners in the family, (b) Extent of land possessed, and (c) Number of days engaged in M.F.P. collection, etc.

In case study No. (1) there are three earners and all of them are engaged in M.F.P. collections as well as agricultural operations. Among the earners two are male and one female. They spent nearly 230 man hours on collection of M.F.P. and the remaining time they are devoting for agricultural operations and other allied activities. Therefore, mostly they derive maximum amount from agriculture and allied activities and only 32.5 per cent received from M.F.P. They are receiving 67.5 per cent from agriculture and allied activity.

In case study No. (2) the total income is reduced as they are only 2 earners. He has only 2 acres of wet land thereby he receives a comparatively lesser amount. He resides in Seethampeta proper and he is devoid of M.F.P. thereby his annual income is reduced to a great extent.

In case study No. (3) also the individual is able to receive maximum income that is 79.47 per cent from agriculture. He receives only 11.25 per cent from M.F.P. This shows that his family is devoted mostly to agriculture and allied activity. He and his family members are spending only 80 manhours on collection of M.F.P. thereby he receives very lesser amount.

In Case Study No. (4) there are 3 earners and possessing 2 acres of wet and 2 acres of dry land. There are 3 earners of

TABLE 3.1 : **Variations of income**

Name of the individual in case study	Land		Income Rs	No. of persons engaged in MFP	% of income through agri.	% of income through MFP	% of income through wages	% of income through other sources	Per capita income Rs
	Wet (acres)	Dry (acres)							
(1)	(2)	(3)	(4)	(5)	(6)	(7)	(8)	(9)	(10)
Age.									
1. Nimaka Ramaswamy, 40 years Jatapu, 3-earners, 2 Non-earners, Seethampet (v)	2.00	1.00	1750	$\frac{2M+1F}{3}$	65	23	12	—	350
2. Arika Dandasi, 30 years Jatapu, 2 earners, 1 non-earner, Seethampeta (v)	2.00	—	1274	$\frac{1M+1F}{2}$	70.64	—	14.91	14.44	425
3. K. Tata, 44 years, Konda Dora, 2 earners, 3 non-earners, Gogadevalasa (v) Pachipenta Block.	2.00	2.00	1510	$\frac{1M+1F}{2}$	79.47	11.25	9.27	—	302
4. K. Narasaiah, 40 years, Konda Dora, 3 earners, 2 non-earners, Gogadevalasa (v) Pachipenta block.	2.00	2.00	1650	$\frac{1M+2F}{3}$	66.66	21.22	12.12	—	330

5. B. Ramulu, 40 years Jatapu 3 earners, 1 non-earners, Rastakuntu Bai (v) Badragiri Block.	2.00	—	1862	1M+2F / 3	53.70	19.44	16.11	10.75	465
6. S. Krishna, 50 years, Konda Dora, 2 earners, 4 non-earners G. L. Puram (v) Bhadragiri block	2.00	—	1732	1M+2F / 3	51.96	20.90	15.58	11.32	289
			9778		62.00	17.30	13.43	5.9	350

which only one male and the remaining are females. They derive a maximum income, i.e., 66.66 per cent from agriculture. They receive one-fifth of their total income from collection of M.F.P.

In Case Study No. (5) he receives only 53.70 per cent from agriculture and 19.44 per cent from M.F.P. collection. In this particular case, it finds marked variation even though there are 3 earners spending 240 man hours and it is attributed to the family members, that is, only one male member and 2 female members.

REFERENCES

1. Malayappan Committee Report, 1952.
2. Anantaraman Committee Report, 1961.
3. Report of the Administrative Staff College of India, 1977-78.
4. House Committee Report on Deficits and misappropriations in the Girijan Cooperative Corporation" of the A.P. Legislative Assembly, 1976.

4

ROLE OF PANCHAYAT RAJ BODIES

PANCHAYAT Raj is a synonym for democratic decentralisation. The process of development started with the Community Development (C.D.) Programme and was followed up by panchayat raj. In conceptional terms, this institution has assumed the mantle of 'developmental mechanism'. The process of democratic decentralisation was completed with the formation of Panchayat Samitis for all the existing blocks in the scheduled areas in the year 1962. As recommended by Balwantrai Mehta Committee, devolution of power and responsibility was made among the three tiers of panchayat raj, namely, the gram panchayat at village level; the panchayat samiti at block level; and zilla parishad at district level.

The panchayat samiti occupies the intermediary level in the three-tier organisational set-up of democratic decentralisation. According to Section 18 of the Andhra Pradesh Panchayat Samiti and Zilla Parishad Act, 1959, "the administration of the Block shall rest in the Panchayat Samiti. Every Panchayat Samiti shall endeavour to install among the people within its jurisdiction a spirit of self-help and initiative and harness their enthusiasm for raising the standard of living". Broadly

TABLE 4.1 : **The location of Tribal Development Blocks in Srikakulam District**

S. No.	T.D. Block	Year of starting	Year of conversion into T.D. Block	Area in square metres	Population		
					Tribal	Non-tribal	Total
1	2	3	4	5	6	7	8
1.	Bhadragiri	1958	1961	684.21	34,866	6,259	41,125
2.	Pachipenta	1963	1965	421.66	22,319	11,188	33,507
3.	Seethampeta	1962	1964	498.56	31,994	2,254	34,248
					89,179	19,701	1,08,880

speaking, the implementation of the entire development programme is the responsibility of the Panchayat Samiti.

Administrative infrastructure

The Tribal Development Blocks were started during the Third Five Year Plan.

The size, population and the ethnic composition have a bearing on the functioning of Tribal Development (T.D.) Blocks due to the following reasons.

1. Funds were allocated by the state government on the basis of population. Blocks with small population were placed at a disadvantageous position compared to blocks with large population.
2. Non-tribal population used to get a lion's share in programme benefits.
3. Backwardness of the blocks was not taken into account while allotting funds.

FUNDS

The investment pattern of government was changed in tribal areas from time to time with the increasing responsibility of developing local resources. Every block was provided with a schematic budget pre-determined at the central government level. It was Rs. 7.5 lakhs for National Extension Service block; the budget provided for a C.D. Block was Rs. 15 lakhs for a programme period of five years. The ceilings were again revised as follows by staging the blocks as intensive and post-intensive. In stage one, (intensive period) Rs. 12 lakhs for five years (Rs. 8 lakhs non-loan; Rs. 4 lakhs loan) were provided; and for stage two, Rs. 5 lakhs were provided for five years. This was intended to provide a continued monetary assistance for a period of ten years.

During the Second Plan period, the multipurpose projects in tribal areas functioned with Rs. 12 lakhs as the share of the Ministry of Community Development; Rs. 15 lakhs were made available by the Government of India (Ministry of Home Affairs) in order to supplement the C.D. grants for intensive development. Due to the recommendations of the Elwin Committee and Dhebar Commission, the additional financial assistance of the Government of India was later fixed at Rs. 10 lakhs. Thus while the budget of M.P.P. was Rs. 27 lakhs, that of the T.D. Block established during the Third Plan was Rs. 22 lakhs for a period of five years. The allocation, however, remained unchanged for the post-intensive phase.

At the first instance, those blocks were provided with schematic budgeting, with fixed ceilings for each head of development. The Elwin Committee rightly pointed out that the monetary ceilings tend to limit the scope of the programme and leave no discretion on the part of the local authorities to adopt the programme to the conditions peculiar to each area. Acting upon the advice of the Committee, the state government were vested with the discretion of diverting the amounts from one head to another on the basis of local needs. However, a model programme was provided for the blocks and broad objectives to be achieved were clearly defined.

The High Powered Committee appointed by the Government of Andhra Pradesh brought about a radical change in the pattern of financial assistance for the blocks. The distinction between stage one and two was recommended to be eliminated and it suggested that all the blocks in the state could be categorised as advanced, ordinary, backward and tribal. A ratio was fixed according to which grants could be provided to each block on the basis of population. In this pattern, advanced blocks get 3/4; the share of the tribal blocks would be 2X. (X representing the financial assistance).

According to Government Order of Madras (G.O.Ms.) No. 922, Public Relations Department dated October 31, 1966, the T.D. Blocks are vested with full powers to utilise the T.D. and C.D. funds as per the felt needs. The only ceiling is on cooperation which is fixed at Rs. 1.60 lakhs. Thus the recommendations reiterated by various study teams have been implemented.

A field study was carried out in the Agency Blocks of Bhadragiri, Seethampeta and Pachipenta to assess the functioning of panchayat raj institutions in these areas. Some of the conditions prevalent in the field are discussed hereafter.

PERSONNEL

A well-knit and efficient organisation need not be emphasised in the task of developing the scheduled areas. In the words of Prof. Tailor, "the personnel of administrative mechinery at all levels should not merely be equipped with administrative and other technical skill but must be fairly well versed in skills, skills based on the knowledge of social laws about voluntary association and community participation".

Frequent changes of personnel should be avoided. The duration of stay of personnel in tribal areas is of the utmost importance. In order to assess the situation, the data regarding the number of persons posted in each category of post of the

TABLE 4.2 : **The organisation chart of Tribal Panchayat Samiti**

Block Development Officer

Administration	Extension
Manager—1	Extension Officers—6
U.D.Cs —2	(Agriculture, Animal husbandry, Panchayat, Education, Coops., Women & Child Welfare)
L.D.Cs —4	Engineering supervisor—1
Typist —1	Engineering supervisor—1
Attenders—3	Loans Inspector—1
Sahayaks—5	Progress Assistant—1
Night Watcher—1	V.D.O. (M)—10
	V.D.O. (W)—2
	Teachers

Samiti is recorded for a period of five years. The position is shown block-wise in Table 4.3.

TABLE 4.3 : **Frequency of transfers**

Block	Category of post	No. of persons posted during the last 5 years
1. Seethampet :	1. B.D.O.	1
	2. Extension Officer	10
	3. V.D.Os. (M)	15
	4. V.D.Os. (W)	2
	5. Ministerial	10
2. Bhadragiri :	1. B.D.O.	1
	2. Extension Officer	8
	3. V.D.Os. (M)	15
	4. V.D.Os. (W)	2
3. Pachipenta :	N.R.	

The frequency of transfers in key posts such as Block Development Officers (B.D.Os.) and Extension Officers (E.Os.) is not found to be abnormal. However, the key personnel should not be disturbed at least for a period of five years. If the personnel are changed often; programmes are bound to be disjointed and haphazard since the tribals rarely respond to persons not intimate to them. The main problem of personnel is lack of adequate number of staff quarters. In Seethampet Panchayat Samiti, it is reported that the staff members of the Samiti are not getting their salaries regularly due to the lack of funds.

The progress of any scheme is bound to be retarded not only by the frequency of transfers but also by keeping the posts vacant for a long period. The vacancy position as on date of visit, categorywise in three T.D. Blocks of Srikakulam District is given in Table 4.4.

TABLE 4.4 : **Vacancy position—categorywise**

Block	Category of vacant post	No. of posts vacant
1. Bhadragiri	E.O. (W)	1
	L.D.Cs.	2
2. Seethampet	E.O. (W & CW)	1
	V.D.Os.	3
3. Pachipenta	V.D.Os.	3

It is ascertained that three posts of Village Development Officers (V.D.Os.) in Pachipenta Block have been vacant since 1 November, 1979.

The jurisdiction of a low-level key functionary, the V.D.O. is most important since he has to cater to the needs of tribals. The jurisdiction of each V.D.O. in terms of number of vIllages of each block is shown in Table 4.5

TABLE 4.5 : **Jurisdiction of each V.D.O.**

S. No.	Block	No. of villages	No. of VDO circles	V.D.Os Jurisdiction (No. of villages) Minimum	Maximum	Average
1.	Bhadragiri	200	15	10	21	13.3
2.	Seethampet	199	15	5	16	13.2
3.	Pachipenta	96	10	5	19	9.6
		495	40	20	56	12.2

The average jurisdiction of each V.D.O. works out to 12 villages. This is above the normal jurisdiction of a V.D.O. The village tribal blocks are interior and the distance from village to village is more due to hills and rugged terraln. It ls, therefore necessary that the overall number of villages covered by each V.D.O. should be reduced to the extent possible.

The intensity of extension work of V.D.O. can be measured by the size of the Village Level Worker (V.L.W.) circle and its population. The details of area and population served by each Village Development Officer is shown in Table 4.6.

TABLE 4.6 : **Area and population served by each V.D.O.**

S. No.	Particulars	Blocks		
		Bhadragiri	Seethampet	Pachipenta
1.	Area (sq. km.)	684.21	498.56	421.66
2.	No. of V.D.Os/Circles	15	15	10
3.	Average Area (sq. km.) served	45.61	33.24	42.16
4.	Population	41125	34248	33507
5.	Average Population served	2742	2283	3351

The average area served by each V.D.O. varies from 33.24 km in Seethampet block to 45.61 km in Bhadragiri block and the population served on average comes to 2,792. On comparison the position in tribal blocks appears to be satisfactory.

TRIBALS AND ADMINISTRATION

Tribal employees in these three Panchayat Samitis are deficient in number. The Block Development Officer of Seethampet Panchayat Samiti (Sri S. Gopal Rao) belongs to a scheduled tribe community. One Village Development Officer of this Samiti also belongs to a scheduled tribe. It is said that the President of this Samiti wants to interfere in allotment of works to contractors, and transfers of personnel. In Salur Samiti there was one Assistant Agricultural Officer, a tribal who worked from July 1976 to July 1979. He earned a good name among tribals and he took interest in Samiti administration.

The general impression of tribals towards administration is that the tribals feel happy since they are being benefited by several developmental activities and schemes of the block. They are of the opinion that the administration is meant for their upliftment. At the same time, they do not feel responsible to utilise them properly. Though they are not aware of the concept of administration, they know that the benefits accrued to them are the net result of administration.

After the Naxalite movement in tribal areas of Srikakulam District, the tribals are coming to the administrators to solve their problems. They are actively participating in the Samiti meetings and taking decisions about the developmental programmes. The tribal members are fighting for the development of their villages especially in the case of laying of roads, repairs to tanks, supply of seeds, fertilisers and cultivation of drinking water and wells. Whenever the tribals approach the Samiti authorities for fertilisers, pesticides, etc., they behave in a polite way. There are instances in Bhadragiri block where the tribal people demanded implementation of certain programmes as a matter of right. Further whenever the B.D.O., or E.O., visits the village, they gather around him and express their problems. This situation indicates that the tribals are aware of administration, and they try to be benefited under different developmental programmes. The literate tribal youth are also playing a vital role in explaining the problems to officers and in getting the work done. Of late, there is a tendency among some of the tribals to think that the officers are thriving at their cost and they are exploiting the tribals. This negative trend towards administration should be controlled.

TRIBALS AND DEVELOPMENT

The financial allocations in the case of T.D. Blocks are relatively higher than in the case of C.D. Blocks. In essence, the tribal development programme is community development without the element of people's monetary contribution. The activities of tribal development blocks cover almost all the facets of development. The main achievements under important development programmes are discussed hereunder.

Agriculture

Agriculture has been the traditional occupation for the tribals of Srikakulam district. The agricultural practices of various tribes living in each region are conditioned by the ecological factors obtaining in those areas. They practise both settled and shifting cultivation. Savaras of Seethampet area are famous for terrace cultivation.

An analysis of land use pattern of tribal areas indicates that the percentage of net areas sown to the total area is 17.64; while land under forests constitutes 62.25 per cent. Similarly, barren and uncultivable land constitutes 11.38 per cent; fallows 3.22 per cent, cultivable waste 4.75 per cent; miscellaneous tree crops and groves 0.76 per cent.

The major crops grown in the scheduled areas of this district are paddy, ragi, sama, and ginger. The T.D. Block-wise cropping pattern is shown in Table 4.7.

Paddy, jowar, bajra, ragi and groundnut are the common crops in the three T.D. Blocks. Tobacco is found only in Pachipenta block. Most of the crops like mesta, sugarcane, sama, tobacco, niger are not grown. Vegetables are raised by tribals in Bhadragiri and Seethampet T.D. Blocks. The total area under food crops and commercial crops constitute 87.25 per cent and 12.72 per cent respectively.

The yield per acre of certain important crops is given in Table 4.8.

TABLE 4.7 : **Block-wise cropping pattern**

S. No.	Crop	Bhadragiri (Hects)	Seethampet (Hects)	Pachipenta (Hects)	Total (Hects)
1	2	3	4	5	6
1.	Paddy	1,660	1,680	1,482	4,822
2.	Jowar	210	140	512	862
3.	Bajra	184	300	2,088	2,572
4.	Ragi	1,056	2,300	1,456	4,812
5.	Gram	260	—	686	946
6.	Other pulses	20	—	24	44
7.	Mesta	76	—	134	210
8.	Groundnut	208	72	580	860
9.	Sugarcane	100	—	10	1 0

TABLE 4.7—*contd.*

1	2	3	4	5	6
10.	Tobacco	—	—	430	430
11.	Sama	600	—	—	600
12.	Niger	200	—	—	200
13.	Ginger	300	—	—	300
14.	Turmeric	180	162	—	342
15.	Vegetables	264	326	—	592
	Total	5,318	4,982	7,402	17,702

TABLE 4.8 : **Yield per acre of certain crops**

S. No.	Crop	Yield per acre		
		Bhadragiri	Seethampet	Pachipenta
1.	Paddy (kg)	800	1,500	1,500
2.	Ragi (kg)	300	300	400
3.	Sama (kg)	200	—	—
4.	Jowar (kg)	250	—	—
5.	Bajra (kg)	300	—	600
6.	Udalu (kg)	300	—	—

The yield per acre varies from region to region. The yield of paddy per acre is more in Seethampet and Paohipenta when compared to Bhadragiri block.

Minor irrigation

The details of irrigation in each T.D. Block are given in Table 4.9.

TABLE 4.9 : **Irrigation in each T.D. Block**

S. No.	Block	No. of M.I. works	Area under irrigation (acres)
1.	Bhadragiri	132	3,520
2.	Seethampet	190	4,200
3.	Pachipenta	151	2,530
		473	10,250

Further 13 bore-wells are functioning in Pachipenta T.D. Block.

Communications

The details of major and minor roads length-wise are furnished in Table 4.10.

TABLE 4.10 : **Major and minor roads**

S. No.	Type of Road	Bhadragiri	Seethampet (Length in km)	Pachipenta
1.	Major Roads	83.40	148.6	14.0
2.	Minor Roads	10.00	30.0	25.0
3.	Approach Roads & Intra- & Inter-village Road	54.70	22.7	20.0
4.	Post Offices	21	25	8
5.	Telegraph Offices	1	1	—

Major Roads—R & B; Minor Roads—P.R.;
Approach Roads—Samiti.

Electricity

Block-wise electrified villages are shown in Table 4.11.

TABLE 4.11 : **Block-wise electrified village**

S. No.	Block	No. of villages electrified
1.	Bhadragiri	9
2.	Seethampet	11
3.	Pachipenta	8
	Total	28

Education

Due emphasis on education of scheduled tribes has been laid during the previous plans. The education programme covers some of the following fields.

(a) Expansion of education facilities;
(b) Opening of Ashram schools;
(c) Construction of school buildings and teacher quarters and running of hostels; and
(d) Opening of mid-day meal centres.

The number of Primary schools and Aṣhram schools in each T.D. Block is given in Table 4.12.

TABLE 4.12 : **Educational Facilities (Block-wise)**

S. No.	Items	Pachipenta	Seethampet	Bhadragiri
1.	No. of High Schools	1	1	—
2.	No. of Elementary Schools	63	52	—
3.	No. of Upper Primary Schools	2	2	—
4.	No. of Ashram Schools	7	12	12
5.	Tribal Welfare Hostels	2	14	5
6.	Social Welfare Hostels	2	—	—
7.	Mid-day meal centres	10	28	—
8.	S.N.P.	39	81	74
9.	Construction of school buildings	7	—	—

Medical and health

The aims and objectives of the health programmes are : (1) To eradicate the endemic diseases; (2) To provide medical facilities; and (3) To provide drinking water supply. The medical and health infrastructure constitute hospitals, dispensaries, primary health centres, mobile medical units, family planning units and special nutrition programme centres, etc. The distribution of medical and health institutions in each T.D. Block is given in Table 4.13.

TABLE 4.13 : Distribution of medical and health institutions

S. No.	Types of institution	Bhadragiri	Seethampet	Pachipenta
1.	Govt. Hospitals	1	1	1 (Dispensary)
2.	Primary Health Centres	1	1	1
3.	M.H. Units	1	1	—
4.	F.P. Centres	1	1	—
5.	NMEP Units	1	4	—
6.	Leprosy Units	1	2	—
7.	S.N.P. Centres	74	81	39

Panchayat raj institutions have acquired a status and have become an indispensable part of national life. Even though panchayat raj has helped in setting up an apparatus at the grassroots level for accelerating infrastructural development, it has its shortcomings. Panchayat raj institutions in tribal areas helped in creating awareness of day-to-day problems, but the benefits of the developmental process could not filter down to the poorest of the poor. Instead, it helped the rural elites to consolidate their position and get a grip over funds, men and material to serve their own selfish ends. In Srikakulam particularly, void was visible, and panchayat raj institutions did not help to bring about prosperity in the tribal areas. It is only after the G.D.A. came into existence that rapid economic and social development of the area could take place. However, the infrastructure created by panchayat raj institutions can be utilised in a better way by training and motivating the panchayat raj personnel working in the tribal areas. Ultimately, the test of all developmental schemes is whether the goods have been delivered and whether there is a qualitative change in the life of the people inhabiting the area.

5

GIRIJAN UPHEAVAL IN SRIKAKULAM

You ask us to improve our agriculture. How can we do so unless we have land to improve? You tell us to use better implements. How can we make them unless we have the teak which alone is suitable? You call our boys for training in cottage industries. But what is the use if they cannot get wood to make doors and windows, or bamboo to make mats and baskets, or grass to make ropes? You teach us to build better houses and of course we would like to, but how can we if we cannot get timber for the framework, or bamboo and poles for the roof, or even wood for fencing? And how can we live happily so long as we have no *pattas* or rights in our land, and all the time we are being threatened and abused, and have no say in what should be done with the country which once was ours?

—Girijans explaining their difficulties quoted in the *Report of the Committee on Special Multipurpose Tribal Blocks*: March 1960.

SRIKAKULAM District is bound on the north and the west by the State of Orissa; on the east by the Bay of Bengal and on the south by Visakhapatnam District. It is located between the northern latitude of 18° 20′ and 19° 10′ and between the eastern longitude of 83° 25′ and 84° 53′. The district may roughly be divided into two geographical divisions—the hilly region, and the plains. The hilly region consists of parts of Palakonda, Parvatipuram and Salur taluks which lies in the north-west part of the district. The hilly areas of these taluks are known as agency tracts. The portions of Pathapatnam, Tekkali and Sompeta taluks are also hilly but they are not declared as ageny tracts. The taluks of Ichapuram, Narasannapet, Srikakulam and Cheepurupalli and portions of Tekkali and Sompeta taluks are on the coast. The eastern ghats run roughly partly to the sea from the north-east to the south-west and, therefore, this district trends from the Ghats to the sea. Most of the hill tops and hilly areas of the district are populated by the tribals. The main concentration of the tribal population is in the agency tracts of Salur, Parvatipuram and Palakonda taluks (Salur and Parvatipuram has since been transferred to Vizianagaram district in June, 1979). The hill tracts are also thickly populated with forests which occur in the north-west portion of the district, namely, Salur, Parvatipuram and Palakonda taluks. Till 1948, most of the forests of this district were in the hands of the zamindars. As a result of the A.P. (Andhra Area) Estates Abolition and Conversion into Ryotwari Act of 1948, these forests were handed over to the government and the process of taking them over was completed in this district in a period of ten years. Prior to this period these projects were subjected to massive abuse, ruthless destruction and exploitation. It may be mentioned here that reservation of forests and tribal life are inextricably linked and the forest is the home and shelter of the tribals.

The total geographical area of the district is 3,901 sq miles and according to the 1971 census with a population of 25,89,991, of which the tribal population is 2,13,928. The notified agency areas like in Parvatipuram, Palakonda and Salur taluks extend over an area of 1,310 sq km, where 74,470 tribals are residing; while the rest of the population of 1,39,458 resides in the plain areas extending over an area of 8,344.7 sq km in the district. The tribals in the scheduled areas enjoy the benefits of the protective leglslations while the benefits are not extended to the tribals living in the plain areas. The following protective regulations are in force in the scheduled areas: (a) A.P.L.T. Regulation I of 1959, (b) A.P. Money Lenders Regulation, 1960, and (c) A.P. Debt Relief Regulation of 1970.

Survey and settlement

The agency portion of Srikakulam District lies in Parvatipuram, Palakonda and Salur taluks consisting of 503 villages. Out of these villages 104 villages of Palakonda taluk was settled in the year 1941. There remained four Mukhasa villages of Palakonda taluk; 141 villages of Salur taluk and 254 villages of Parvatipuram taluk unsurveyed. The 141 villages of Salur taluk were covered by the stay orders issued by the Supreme Court in connection with the dispute regarding the ownership of the areas between Andhra Pradesh and Orissa States. Therefore, survey operations were taken up in the year 1969, 254 agency villages of Rapur taluk and in the four Mukhasa villages of Palakonda taluk covering a total area of 198.01 sq km. The survey operations in all these villages were completed in the year 1972. This, therefore, is the general background regarding the position and status of the tribals in the district of Srikakulam.

THE DIAGNOSIS

In the 1960s there was unrest amongst the tribals. This can be attributed to many factors. The problem may be examined from four aspects: (a) deficiencies in the institutional set-up and the ill-effects of feudal systems; (b) the bureaucracy and its functioning and the implementation of tribal welfare and Panchayat Raj programmes; (c) organisation which was responsible for galvanising and bringing together the tribals with a common goal and aims; (d) development of infrastructure and deficiencies.

Deficiencies in the institutional set-up and the ill-effects of feudal systems

The Malayappan Report, 1952 highlighted four problems facing the tribals[1]: (a) An immediate improvement of their economic conditions so that they may free themselves from the clutches of sowkars and feudal institutions to stand on their own legs; (b) The opening up of communications so that they could carry their produce to the shandies or to the place with comfort and ease and realise better prices for them; (c) Eradication of chronic diseases like yaws and malaria to which they are constant victims and provision of some immediate medical aid; and (d) Education to enable them to know the outside world and civilisation. As pointed out earlier, even though the Zamindari Abolition Act had been passed, the hangover from the past feudal practices outlived the legislative enactments.

The muttadari sytem

The Malayappan Report pointed out that most of the agency areas were governed in the matter of revenue collections by the *muttadari* system. It is a feudal form of organisation and is very archaic. In some areas there was *mukhasedars* who had been granted land by government on feasible terms for services rendered. A *mutta* is an estate held on services tenure of watch and ward. The *muttadari* system came into existence many centuries ago and existed in the tribal areas of Visakhapatnam, Srikakulam, East and West Godavari and parts of Khammam. The *muttadari* system functioned under the estate areas of Golugonda, Madhgol, Vizianagaram and Pachipenta which were all parts of Visakhapatnam agency during the rule of the British. The agency portions of these states were divided into groups of villages called *muttas* and the management of the *muttas* appears to have been entrusted in the distant past to influential individuals called *muttadors*. There is no record of the conditions on which these *muttas* were originally granted. The conditions can only be inferred from the existing customs and from the genuine old documents which have survived. The main conditions were payment of *kist*, partly in cash and partly in kind, presentation of *mamuls* in the shape of fruit, vegetables and forest produce, and attendance at *durbar* during Desara and Sankaramanam. The *muttadars* originally held their *muttas* on the condition (among others) of assisting the *zamindar* to keep peace. They were bound to capture and hand over to the *zamindar*, any offender or bad characters and were also bound to give immediate information whenever any offence or *fituri* (disturbance) occurred or was under contemplation. The *muttadars* were thus in a sense feudatories responsible for the good management of their *muttas* and bound to render military and police services to the *zamindars*.

The *muttadars* commanded considerable respect from the hill tribes and wielded very great influence over them. They received tribute in various forms from the villagers, who rendered *vetti* service (unpaid labour) to them. The *muttadars* collected all money and produce due to the estate through the *pattandar* (headman) in-charge of villages or group of villages within their *muttas* and remitted to the *zamindar* his dues, retaining a portion of the collection for themselves as their remuneration for collecting the amounts and for the service, both personal, police and military, rendered to the *zamindar* whenever they were called upon to do so. The two main duties of a *muttadar* were therefore : (i) keeping the peace in the *mutta* or rendering military assistance in case of need, and (ii) collection of revenue.

With the advent of the British Government, the duty of maintaining peace devolved on government and the *muttadar* became responsible to the government for maintaining law and order in his *mutta* and continued to be responsible to the *zamindar* for collection of the revenue due to the estates. The system of dual control over the *muttadar* by the government and the *zamindar* thus came into vogue. The *muttadars* in *zamindari* areas had, therefore, two overlords.

The *muttadars* by virtue of their social status exert influence on the *ryots*. They interfered in all the affairs of the inhabitants. In Padenu and other *muttas* all the best cultivable land is owned by *muttadars*. They harass people in several ways by making illegal encroachment of the lands, etc. The *muttdars* in several cases did not issue receipts for the *kist* collected. At the time of the marriage he has to be paid *katnams* ranging from Rupees 5 to 50 according to the status of the party. In Dr. Aiyappan's report the following facts are revealed.[2]

Raja *lanchanams* are given in the shape of vegetables. They (*muttadars*) compel the *ryots* to plough their lands free. They also exact *jaati* work, i.e., carrying loads without wages. Every *ryot* has to work for the *muttadar* for about a week or 10 days in the year, 'both men and women'. Only meals are given but the wages are not paid.

In the areas where the system prevails, two forms of

labour are in vague, i.e., *gothi* and *vetti*. These two are forms of forced labour. At the time this was the best suited form of labour for the agency as the population was dense and procurement of labour in the above two forms became necessary.

Gotti labour is the system whereby a man is bound to work under the creditor as agricultural labourer in lieu of a loan taken. It is the same as the *namatia* system of Bihar and '*paleru*' or *kamatem* system of Andhra Pradesh. The employer will pay the debtor inadequately and extracts work from him until the debt is cleared off.

Vetti labour is the most inhuman form of labour. It is labour done freely but compulsorily. The *muttadars*, as a matter of right are entitled to *vetti* from the village folk at the rate of one person from each hut.

The *muttadari* system was abolished as late as 1969 by the Muttadari Abolition Act, 1969. Apart from the *muttadari* system, the land was taxed on a very unscientific basis; only plough tax was collected at the rate of Re. 1 to Rs. 1.50 per plough. Sometimes uniform tax was levied according to the quantity of seed sown. The tribal is fond of his surroundings and the land. But he was not the land-owner—the land belonged to the *zamindars* or *muttadars*. The *ryots* have only occupancy rights. There was another problem of indebtedness of the tribals. Indebtedness drove the tribals to a position of starvation—landlessness and migration. The money-lenders from the plains area visited the agency areas and rendered financial assistance in small amounts. The trust worthy behaviour of the tribals and their ignorance of conditions of the outside world were used by the plainmen. The *sowcar*, the traders and money-lenders are known as always having aimed at capturing tribal produce or land in lieu of repayment of loans. The rate of interest was never stipulated in terms of money despite the working of the Act I of 1970. Exploitation of the poor folk went on endlessly. The Malayappan mentioned that in some cases the rate of interest charged by money-lenders ranged from 25 per cent to 75 per cent and even more.

In Seethampet agency the debts was borrowed under the *faida* system. *Faida* means instalment. Usually for each rupee the debtor has to pay in each instalment a sum varying from Re. 0.75 to Re. 1. The amount was always collected in kind at the rate of three or four *addas* grown each time in the land, per rupee.

Nearabout Makkuva in Salur agency the money-lenders advanced grain in times of need. For evey putti lent, the borrower has to pay in the second years two *putties*. If he failed to do so, in the third year he had to pay four *putties*. In this way, debt, increases until the tribal in order to pay off the debt had to sell away his cattle and crop. By this ceaseless process of exploitation *sowcars* in all the villages and towns adjoining the agency tracts became good land-holders and also they raised buildings after buildings, while the tribals were reduced to the status of serfs and paupers.

Shandies or the weekly markets, were the only centres in the agency, where the tribals had to fulfil the economic undertakings and complete monetary transactions. In the absence of proper vigilance, the petty traders sold away things like piece clothes, rice, salt, and other commodities, for high prices. It was not uncommon to find that these businessmen used false weighing-rods and measures. They took the hill produce in one weight and gave their goods in an other weight. This corrupt transactions need to be stopped. The contract system where by Rella bark was peeled out and *Adda* leaf was gathered needs to be regulated and systematized.

The home-economics of the tribals also warrant the immediate attention of the concerned authorities. The crop of the tribals was taken away by the *sowcar* and the money-lender; the little he had, was spent on food, there was no proper dressing for the inmates, their health was shattered by malaria and other diseases, and their housing conditions were lamentable. They did not even possess bullocks to till the land. There were no proper agricultural implements. The headman of the village and the *muttadar*—these have been *de facto* rulers of the hill villages. The hill-men were exploited by them also. The Revenue, Police and Forest Departments, the only influential governmental agencies in these areas, did not provide a sympathetic approach to their problems. Often it was said that some of the officials connived with the influential *muttadars* and involved the poor tribals in trouble. It was really pathetic that for each court trial the poor tribal had to walk miles after miles, through the midst of thick jungles wherein roam wild beasts dreaded by the hillmen.

Protective regulations

The first Act to protect the interests of the tribals is known as the Agency Tracts Interests and Land Transfer Act, 1917. The object of this Act was to regulate the rate of interest and transfer of land in the tracts of Ganjem, Visakhapatnam and Godavari districts. The transfer of immovable property made without previous consent of agent or any prescribed officer, has been made absolutely null and void unless it is in favour of another hill tribe. The provision of Act No. 1 of 1917 were in force till the promulgation of the A.P. Scheduled Areas Land Transfer Regulation, 1959 by which the said Act was repealed.

The important features of the A.P. Land Transfer Act of 1959 are :

(i) in the agency tracts any transfer of immovable property by the member of a scheduled tribe without prior sanction of competent authority is null and void;

(ii) where the transfer of immovable property made by the member other than a scheduled tribe, the agent or the Agency Divisional Officer on application by any interested person can restore the property to the transferor or his heir; and

(iii) no immovable property situated in agency tracts owned by member of a scheduled tribe is liable to be attached and sold in execution of money decree (vide Sec. 3 of Regulation 1).

Under the Act I of 1917, the transfer of immovable property between other communities who were not scheduled tribes but were residents of scheduled areas were not prohibited (vide Sec. 4 of the Act). But under Regulation 1 of 1959 even such transactions were prohibited.

It is pertinent to note that the word scheduled tribe used in the Regulation 1 of 1959 has been defined as meaning any tribe or tribal community as specified in the notification by the

President of India, under clause I of Article 342; whereas under Act I of 1917, the transfer of immovable property by a member of a hill tribe is prohibited unless made in favour of a hill tribe [Sec. 4 (1) of the Act]. The words 'hill tribe' have been defined under Act I of 1917 as meaning anybody or class of persons resident in the agency tracts, but excluding the land-holder as defined under the Estate Land Act of 1908 that may be notified from time to time under the Estate Land Act 1908 [Sec. 2, clause (c) of the Act]. Therefore, it follows under the Act I of 1917 the transfer of immovable property between other communities who are not scheduled tribes, but are residents of scheduled areas is not prohibited. But under Regulation I of 1959, such transactions are prohibited. Under Regulation I of 1959, where the transfer of immovable properties made in contravention of subsection (1) of Sec. 3, any person in possession of the property claiming under such transfer may be evicted by the prescribed officer after due notice and restore the same to the transferor of his heirs. If the transferor or his heirs were not willing to take back the property, or their whereabouts were not known, the prescribed officer may assign or sell the property to any other member of the scheduled tribe or a cooperative society of the tribals, or otherwise dispose of the same as if it is a property of the government [Sec. 3 clause (2) of the Act]. The validity of Regulation I of 1959 has been challenged in the High Court and it was upheld in W.P. 4931/68 dated 17-9-1969.

The bureaucracy and its functioning in the implementation of tribal welfare and panchayat raj programmes

During the years prior to the outbreak of violence in the tribal areas of Srikakulam District, the impression is given that tribal welfare was not a high priority item in the eyes of the district administration. Representative samples of the concern for tribal administration are available. By studying the administration report of Srikakulam Agency, prepared by the Collector, Srikakulam an Agent to government for Agency Administration; as early as 1955, evidence is available to suggest, "Agency interests in land transfer Act I of 1917 in force in the Agency area. Permission was granted in two cases to sell their lands in favour of plain-men."[3] Similarly, the Agency administration report for 1957 speaks of the inability of the Taluk level officers to devote more time for Agency areas. "The duties of the Taluk Officers being multifarious, they are not able to devote more time for work in the Agency."[4] Similarly, even though efforts made to abolish the *muttadari* system the report of the Collector speaks of the inability of the administration to curb this evil practice. "The Muttadars and Mustajars in the former Zamindari areas in Parvatipuram and Salur agencies have ceased to function as agents for the collection of land revenue and consequently all the revenue in these agency estate villages is being collected by the Revenue Inspectors direct from the hill-tribes as there are no Village Officers appointed for the agency villages of these two Taluks. This system is not working well in the agency area mainly on account of the fact that there can be no proper and effective supervision over the work of the Revenue Inspector because of the vastness of the area and lack of communication facilities. This is not a workable method but it could not be helped in the absence of regular village establishment. Proposals were submitted long before for the appointment of Village Officers for the agency areas of Parvatipuram and Salur Taluks and orders are awaited. For want of village officers the extent of land owned and the proportionate assessment payable could not be correctly worked out. The *muttadars* still hold their sway over the ignorant tribals in parts of the interior agency and this can be effectively checked only by the appointment of Village Officers".[5]

As late as 1964, there was no proper Village Officers establishment as is evident from the report of the Special Agent. "Land Revenue Establishment: There is village establishment for running village administration in Palakonda Agency which is surveyed and settled. There is no village establishment in agency tracts of Salur and Parvatipuram taluks."[6] Similarly, the work of providing debt relief to tribals under the Agency Debt Relief Act no work was produced. "Agency Debt Relief: The post of the Special Deputy Tahsildar for debt relief work was disbanded on 29.2.1963 on the expiration of sanction. No cases for scaling down debts were filed for adjudication during the year."[7] The Agent also spoke of the enormity of the problem of debt relief. "The indebtedness of the tribals is the primary reason for their perpetual poverty. The money lenders

Regulation I of 1960 and Debt Relief Regulation II of 1960 aim at eradicating the indebtedness of the Tribals. A socio-economic Survey of Tribals for scaling down debts has been undertaken and it is almost completed. The indebtedness of tribals so far is estimated to be Rs. 1,07,986 in cash, and 1,450 imperial maunds in grains. The next stage in the process is to file applications under Section II of the Regulation II of 1960 for scaling down debts before the Agency District Munsiffs for adjudication. The bottleneck in this regard is that the information furnished by the tribals has to be supplemented by the information from the records of the money-lenders and to get at the records necessary powers have not been vested in the Enquiry Officers. Mere scaling down of the debts of the tribals will not improve the economic condition of the tribals. Since the tribals are not accustomed to save for their future, it is necessary that advance should be made to them to redeem their debts to the plains people as well as to provide them with some funds to meet their daily demands of life. The cooperative Rules and Regulations are so rigid as not to allow adequate credit to them. Security is the primary factor on which a cooperative loan is based. Personal surety of tribals is not considered good enough for advancing loans for the reasons that they are nomadic and have no economic status. The rules of cooperative societies in this regard require a radical change and the government have to stand as surety for the loans to be advanced to the Tribal Cooperative Credit Societies. If tribals fail to pay back the loans, the land offered by them as security cannot be sold to plain-men unless permission of the Agent is obtained. If this permission is granted, the land in the Agency may pass into the hands of plain-men. These hurdles come in the way of successful elimination of the money-lenders from the tribal area. It is necessary to find a solution is this regard. The primary marketing societies of the Andhra Scheduled Tribes Cooperative Finance and Development Corporation have not been granting enough credit. They should not only purchase the minor forest produce from the tribals at reasonable rates but should also advance weekly or fortnightly loans in the shape of kind or cash to meet their daily needs."[8]

The Shilu Ao Committee Report of 1969 spoke of their impressions regarding the implementation of tribal welfare programmes in Andhra Pradesh.[9] During the course of its tour of the various states, the Study Team noticed certain weaknesses in the set-up of the tribal welfare departments. In Andhra Pradesh, no separate field staff had been given to the Director of Tribal Welfare. The District Social Welfare Officers, who were under the administrative control of the Zilla Parishads, were also the field personnel of the Directorate of Tribal Welfare. This arrangement could not be considered satisfactory for the effective working of schemes for tribal welfare. Separate District Officers for tribal welfare should be appointed to work under the Director of Tribal Welfare in the state.

Regarding tribal development blocks, the Shilu Ao Committee was critical of the way in which the programmes were functioning. In their financial pattern, the tribal development blocks deviated considerably from the C.D. Blocks or even from the old special multipurpose tribal blocks. A tribal development block gets Rs. 10 lakhs in Stage I and Rs. 5 lakhs in Stage II from the Department of Social Welfare and also Rs. 12 lakhs in Stage I and Rs. 5 lakhs in Stage II from the Ministry of Food, Agriculture, Community Development and Cooperation (Department of Community Development). While drawing up development schemes, the block agencies are guided by what is called the "schematic budget", earmarking specific percentage of funds for programmes under different heads. The "schematic budget" of a tribal block was intended to be a flexible one and in theory, could be varied according to the local conditions. In practice, however, the budget tended to follow a rigid pattern regardless of the special needs of the people of the area. The Study Team felt that the budget should be sufficiently flexible to enable schemes to be reoriented to suit the wishes and felt needs of the people.

It was brought to the notice of the Team that salaries of the staff to T.D. Blocks tend to absorb a considerable proportion and in some cases, the bulk of the development provision. For instance, in one of the states out of a sum of Rs. 100,000, sanctioned for a T.D. Block nearly Rs. 73,000 or nearly three-fourths of the entire provision had been spent on staff and out of a sum of Rs. 20,000 sanctioned for a sub-block, the salaries of staff alone accounted for Rs. 16,000.

Although the schematic budget provides for a ceiling on the expenditure on personnel, the pattern of expenditure is liable to be and in practice has been distorted very considerably as it has not been possible for the state to effect a reduction in staff to correspond with the savage cuts imposed on the tribal provision in recent years.

It would be idle to expect any significant progress in the development of T.D. Blocks if the bulk of the provision meant for development is absorbed by way of expenditure on staff. The Team at one stage was inclined to suggest that expenditure on staff should not exceed 10 per cent of the available provision. On a provision of one lakh of rupees the expenditure on staff would have to be limited on this basis to ten thousand rupees—a sum barely sufficient to meet the salaries of a couple of officers and their ancillary staff. Considering that the development work in tribal areas needs the services of men who have specialised in a number of disciplines, an upper limit of 10 per cent may in practice prove to be completely unrealistic. After a careful consideration of the question, the Study Team felt that it would be reasonable to shift the burden of expenditure on staff,—other than clerical and lower categories of staff appointed to implement development programmes in T.D. Blocks on to the general provision. Thus the salary of an Agricultural Officer employed in a T.D. Block could be debited to the general agricultural budget and not to the T.D. Budget, the salary of an Engineer to the P.W.D. Budget, of a Medical Officer to the budget of the Medical Department and so on. Such a procedure would be in consonance with the suggestion repeatedly made by the government and the Planning Commission that the special provision made for tribal development should be regarded as a supplement to the general provision which at present does not but in fairness should bear a reasonable proportion of the financial burden in the administration and development of the tribal areas.

The danger of confusing the tribals by introducing a large number of programmes has been pointed out by the expert committees who have reviewed the working of the tribal development programmes. The Team suggested that in any programme drawn up, agriculture should ordinarily be given the highest priority. The areas covered by the T.D.Blocks have not yet reached the stage of development envisaged for them and the benefits which have already accrued are likely to be nullified if schemes are given up while they are only half-way through.

With the introduction of the scheme of democratic decentralisation, the implementation of the T.D. Blocks programme has increasingly come to rest with Panchayat Raj institutions. As implementing agencies, these institutions have not proved to be effective.

Special provisions in the Constitution

The Constitution of India provides for a number of measures for ameliorating tribals living standards and problems. The following are the special provisions in the Constitution regarding tribal problems.

1. Articlo 46 regarding promotion of education and economic interests of the scheduled tribes.

2. Article 275 regarding grants from the Union to certain states for promoting the welfare of the scheduled tribes or raising the level of administration of the scheduled areas in accordance with the provisions of the Fifth Schedule.

3. Article 275 regarding grants from the Union to certain states for promoting the welfare of the scheduled tribes or raising the level of administration of the scheduled areas in state.

4. Article 330 and 332 regarding reservation of seats for the scheduled tribes in the Lower Houses of the Union and State Legislatures.

5. Article 334 regarding reservation of seats for the schedled tribes to be in force for a period of thirty years for the commencement of the Constitution.

6. Article 335 regarding consideration for claims of the scheduled tribes in making appointments to services and posts in the union.

7. Article 339 regarding provisions for the appointment of a Commission by the President of India to report on the administration of Scheduled Areas.

The scheme of administration of scheduled areas under the Fifth Schedule of the Constitution visualises a division of responsibility between the state governments and Union

Government[10]. The state government has the duty of screening legislation unsuitable for extension to the tribal areas and of framing the regulations of peace and good government, with particular reference to the protection of tribal land, allotment of waste land and protection from exploitation by money-lenders. It has also to implement special schemes for the welfare and general development of the scheduled tribes living within its boundaries. The Union Government has the responsibility to provide guidance in regard to the administration of the scheduled areas and additional funds required to raise the level of administration and the standard of life of the tribal communities. It can also give directions to the state government regarding the implementation of particular schemes, laying down priorities in their implementation and in regard to the general administration of tribal areas.

The responsibilities of the state government in regard to tribal administration have to be looked after specially by the Governor of the state. The Governor has to submit to the President of India an Annual Report or reports at intervals required by the Union Government regarding administration of the scheduled area in the state.

All these provisions are intended to assist the tribals in enjoying their existing rights without any obstruction by others. No less important than the protection of tribal rights is the need for developing the scheduled areas and securing the economic, educational and social progress of the scheduled tribes. But in regard to both protection and development, the Scheduled Areas and Scheduled Tribes (Dhebar) Commission came to the conclusion that there were obvious failures leading to hardship and loss and anticipated results did not materialise. It found the remedy for this state of affairs in working the Constitution in a manner calculated to secure its original objectives.[11]

Organisation which was responsible for galvanising and bringing together the tribals with a common goal and aim

It has been pointed out "that politics is the study of 'who gets what, when and how' . . it suggests that politics is the authoritative allocation of scarce resources.[12] It has also been pointed out that in politics there are certain underlying factors which play an important role in the allocation of resources and formulation of politics. All human societies are faced with the problem of scarce resources and there is a constant struggle with regard to whether it is wealth, status, or power between the demand and supply of these scarce resources. Secondly, in the working of a government to prevent uprisings and conflicts resulting from distribution of scarce resources; dominant groups always manage to get what they want by suitably encouraging and devising decisions in their favour. Such being the case, because of the constant struggle for allocation of scarce resources there are always 'haves' and 'have-nots' in any system and the latter mount up constant pressure and try to articulate their demands as effectively as possible. This is more or less a permissible form of protest in a democracy whereas under a dictatorship it would not be possible. The 'haves' always try to maintain the status quo and try to guard the privileges they have been able to win at the expense of alienating the 'have-nots'. And hence the system of government if they are able to convince the masses of their legitimacy and that it is serving the masses better than before when there is even a greater attempt to justify their privileges and maintenance of status quo.

Politics is the constant interplay between the rulers (elite) and the ruled. It is also a pervasive conflict among competing elites for the right to rule. Formal political institutions, such as parliaments, politbureaus, and tribal leaderships, are the institutionalised focal point of this struggle. For the elite, formal institutions are one means of controlling the masses and of securing their position against competitive elites. For the masses, formal institutions symbolize the status quo and are the primary target of change.[13]

It may be seen that even though as mentioned earlier several provisions were made in the Constitution for ensuring a good standard of living for tribals; nothing much was achieved as seen from their standard of living. There was no dynamism in their political and social life. In addition, they were subservient to a feudalistic system of society and their personal means of livelihood was entirely dependent on it. There was very limited political penetration by the Congress leaders in the tribal areas. It must be remembered that the

Congress was the dominant ruling party in the post-independence years. Their apathy and a lack of awareness of the problems of tribals gave rise to frustration amongst the tribals, which led to a revolutionary upsurge led by the Communist Party in this area.

Another factor which also played an important role was that tribals as an ethnic group felt that their identity was being threatened and would face extinction very soon owing to economic hardship. This was fostered by the land grab and selfish attitude of the big landlords and money-lenders. In the case of Srikakulam, even though the illiteracy rate amongst the tribals was not very high; there was a group of middle class leaders who grew to influence and change their thinking after losing their own lands. Loss of land also meant losing their dignity and self-respect and this gave birth to a renewed sense of solidarity amongst the tribals. This was the seed of the tribal revolt in Srikakulam.

The main grievances of the tribals were: (a) the imposition of forest land by the forest department. This meant that movement of tribals was restricted and curbed their instinct for living a free life. The tribals always regarded the forests as their homes and have also been sometimes referred to as *vanavasis*; (b) emphatic declaration of the forest as property of the government; (c) land revenue demands were too much of a burden on the already over-exploited tribal; (d) pclitical and economic system which imposed too much of psychological pressure on the tribal which was beyond his comprehension; which was in turn taken advantage of by feudal landlords and money-lenders who were able to squeeze the tribals into a state of submission and swallow their lands for non-payment of loans. The money-lenders in turn got (a) labour to work on the agriculture and forest contract work; and (b) also held the land on which the tribal worked as a farmer servant.[14] Thus almost all tribals in the areas were depressed and their spirits were very low. Though the government made efforts to pass new legislations in favour of the tribals; tribal welfare activities did not appear to be a high priority item in state politics and district administration. The elites successfully managed to manoeuvre and manage things in their favour by taking advantage of the ignorance and lack of will and poverty of the tribals. Therefore, the elites were able to preserve their rights better than those of the tribals.

Since 1957, in Srikakulam agency areas tribals were organised into Sanghams by two communist school teachers; Vempatapu Satyanarayana and Adibhatla Kailasam. Through constant meetings and living closely with the tribals they were able to expose the injustice that had overcome them and thus were able to gain the confidence of the tribals. The Sanghams used to meet regularly and they started to agitate on issues like better labour wages; against the lower bureaucracy, that is, block and taluk level downwards; forced occupation of forest lands; and inadequacies of the legal system, and hate campaigns against village revenue officials for exorbitant and unfair revenue collections. Such a campaign led to an increase of confidence amongst tribals and the creation of a sense of hope and longing for a better future. There was also an air of militancy in their demands. An illustration would be necessary at this point to show how and why the popularity of the Sangham rose. Reading of a deposition contained in the judgment of the famous Parvatipuram conspiracy case will provide the best possible evidence to illustrate the point.

At this stage, a passage from the evidence of P.W. 41 is absolutely necessary. It need not be stated again that P.W. 41 is a tribal Sarpanch of Pottivada within the Parvatipuram agency areas. He says that:

> I know Vempatapu Satyanarayana. He was originally a teacher in Kondabaridi. He left the job and shifted himself to Mondemkhallu about fifteen years back. I know Adibhatla Kailasam, I heard that he was originally a school teacher. Our area is an agency area with Savaras and Jatapus. There are Girijan cadres. We, the Girijans of the area used to live on cultivation. We raise all crops. We have to purchase cloth, salt and chillies only. We used to borrow monies from the landlords of Mondemkhal. The money-lenders used to charge exorbitant interest say, we had to pay two kunchams of grain and cereals for rupee. We used to adjust our produce towards the monies we borrowed. Still, the money-lender used to take away

our lands or livestock stating that the money which we borrowed still remained undischarged. When we wanted to cultivate the land on the hills the Forest Department used to obstruct us. In that way, we became short of necessities of life like food and clothing. Vempatapu Satyam used to tell us that because there was nobody to look to for help, we had to organise Girijan Sanghams and agitate against the injustice done to us by the landlords. Accordingly, we formed Girijan Sanghams in our agency area. Vempatapu Satyanarayana submitted, on our behalf petitions and applications to the government for the redressal of our grievances. This sort of petitioning went on for some time, but nothing came out of it. On behalf of the Girijan Sangham led by Vempatapu Satyanarayana we observed Satyagrahas also to attract the attention of the government at Mondemkhal, in 1967. Vempatapu Satyanarayana told us that only by defying the government we could save our lands and thereby we would be in a position to maintain ourselves. Besides Vempatapu Satyanarayana, Kolla Venkeyya attended the meeting at Mondemkhal, Kolla Venkayya comes from Guntur District. The landlords of Gummalaxmipuram scolded and beat some of the Girijans at Levidi while they were going to attend the meeting. At the meeting we came to know about the assault. We immediately proceeded to Levidi from Mondemkhal and found that two Girijans were killed by the landlords of Levidi and Gummalaxmipuram. In that connection, there was a murder case and the said case ended in acquittal. Vempatapu Satyanarayana exhorted us in a meeting that because the government was not doing justice even when some Girijans were killed by the landlords and because the landlords were out to grab our lands and because the courts also were not doing justice to the Girijans when they were murdered by the landlords, the only alternative honourable course left open to us was to lead an armed a struggle against the government. We were all convinced about the correctness of the method suggested by Vempatapu Satyanarayana and commenced armed revolt against the government. Vempatapu Satyanarayana in order to make the fight effect, formed Dalams, and through Dalams we began our revolt, Vempatapu Satyanarayana left Mondemkhal and shifted himself to the hills along with his family and was moving with us on the hills. His family consists of himself and his wife, Santhamma and his daughter Bharathi. The place where Vempatapu Satyanarayana was moving about was known as 'centre' while he was moving on the hills there used to come some persons from plains and we all used to sit and discuss and take decisions and we accordingly used to translate them into action.

In the cross-examination, he says that

After the armed revolt was started, I myself entered the movement of my own accord though the Sangham people did not invite me. It is not true that after my removal from the Sangham I had nothing to do with the activities of the Sangham or the Communist Party. I was attached personally to Vempatapu Satyanarayana. We used to purchase cloth, chillies and salt at high rates and we used to part with our forest produce and grains at lesser rates. The landlords used to occupy our lands and take away our livestock forcibly. Before Vempatapu Satyanarayana came to Mondemkhal we were not able to represent our grievances to the police and after his shifting himself to Mondemkhal, though representations were made to the Police, no action was taken on the representation. The Jatapu and Savaras used to go for cooly also. The cooly rates were very low. We used to be paid from half a rupee to twelve annas per day for our work from day dawn to day dusk. Under the leadership of Vempatapu Satyanarayana we observed strikes to enhance the wages. In spite of Satyagrahas the cooly rate was not raised. When we asked for higher wages the landlords used to get coolies from outside areas. When we were objecting to the outside coolies working in our area, the landlords used to threaten us with dire consequences in case we prevented the outside coolies from working under them. Though we made representations in this regard to the government officials nothing was done for us.

Again he says in the cross-examination that :

> During the pendency of the Levidi murder case, the landlords used to hold out threats to witnesses and thus they used to prevent the witnesses from deposing without fear. In spite of our reports to the police in that regard nothing was done to us.

The cross-examination by Sri P.L. Naidu, he said :

> Manganna and Koranna are the two persons who were murdered by the landlords in Levidi. In the beginning, after the two murders, the only rupees six for cutting the crop, and carrying it on head loads to the threshing floor. In average, the wage used to come to four annas per head per day. Because of the struggle led by Vempatpu Satyanarayana the cooly rates were raised to two rupees fifty paise a day to three rupees per day. Before the establishment of our Sanghams a farm servant used to be paid five or six *Putties* per year, whereas, it became twenty-five to thirty putties per year by 1967. The landlords used to be at the workers of the Girijan Sangham with a view to completely annihilate them. The landlords with the same end in view used to foist false cases against the workers of the Girijan Sangham. The landlords of the Agency area formed a Sangham under the leadership of Medida Satyanarayana, Gudla Satyanarayana and Labala Ramamurthy and others by 1967. The landlords collected funds to the tune of rupees one lakh and employed *gundas* to beat the workers of the Girijan Sangham and to murder Vempatapu Satyanarayana and others. When the *gundas*, employed by Medida Satyanarayana and other landlords, fell upon some Girijan workers and villagers they deserted the village and took shelter on the hills. In order to give a stiff fight to the *gundas* employed by the landlords, Vempatapu Satyanarayana formed Dalams.

Development of infrastructure and deficiencies

Being cloistered in the interiors due to lack of communications, the tribals did not get all the benefits of economic development.

Moreover, their means of livelihood were primitive, hence a lot needed to be done to ameliorate the living conditions of tribals. The Agency Administration Report of Srikakulam District for the year 1962-63 also says that "the standard of living of these people is generally below average. The main occupation of the tribe's men in agency areas in cultivation and collection and sale of minor forest produce such as tamarind, *mahuwa* flower, honey, etc. They sell the produce in the shandies to the agents of Andhra Scheduled Tribes Finance & Development Corporation, Visakhapatnam".

One of the reasons why this backwardness was still prevalent was owing to the fact of lack of necessary inputs in infrastructure for speedy and rapid development. There were hardly any roads which could help in stimulating economic activity in the tribal areas. Even to market their agricultural and forest produce the tribals had to walk long distances for selling them. If there were more roads, the G.C.C. could perhaps organise shandies in the deep and remote areas. In the absence of roads there was no scope of communication with the outside world and the tribals were thus left entirely at the mercy of the local money-lenders. This must have added to the frustration of tribal life. Secondly, other than the aspect of development of tribal areas was that there were no drinking water facilities and the area was constantly affected by diseases like malaria and yaws. Due to the unhealthy conditions people remain reluctant to work in tribal areas. Nothing much was done besides establishing a few Primary Health Centres to improve the lot of the tribals. Most of the time, the staff was not available, there was virtually no cure for complicated diseases as the tribal could not afford expensive medicines. Another related aspect is that nutrition for children and expectant mothers was not of a high level and much was left to be desired. Lastly, another factor was the very slow pace of development of the educational infrastructure. More schools like the Ashram schools should have been established; but not many were sanctioned. However, the number of primary schools was quite high. In 1962-63, there were 137 elementary schools in the agency area. There was the permanent problem of dropouts and this problem remains unsolved. Another shortfall was the development of agricultural infrastructure. *Podu* was very popular and not much effort was made to introduce modern practices of agriculture in the agency area. In the absence of irrigation facilities very little could be done to convince the tribals about the need for taking up modern agricultural practices.

The struggle in Srikakulam as we have seen was primarily agrarian in character; a set-up outside elements infiltered into the area and aroused the hostile feelings of Girijans by exposing the injustices prevalent in their society. The main target of attack was the rural elites-cum-landlords and money-lenders, forest department officials and the bureaucracy in general. Due to ineffective administration in the tribal areas, the law of the jungle prevailed and this led to a state of anarchy where violent methods held sway over democratic means. It may be seen that such conditions were fostered because of the existence of political vacuum where the party in power and its machinery were not able to penetrate the backward areas and provide relief to the frustration of the tribals. In the absence of any political conduit, an organisation dominated by Communist elements mushroomed in the tribal areas which was able to fan the flames of discontent and led the banner of revolt. Such a crisis had never been witnessed in the tribal areas of Andhra Pradesh or any other part of India where for the first time tribals had become politicised and infected by Communist elements.

In retrospect, it may be said that the government has achieved a fair measure of success in rectifying the imbalance that had been created by setting up new developmental programmes like the G.D.A. and its successor the I.T.D.A. The experience of Srikakulam can be regarded as an objective lesson in history and we must remind ourselves that even the most ignorant and backward people in a democratic framework should be regarded as important, and all human values which are cherished by freedom lovers should be given proper expression, and each should get his share of what is due to him. In effect, our search for better methods and ways and means for evolving an egalitarian society should not be content with the mere tinkering with the problem of poverty, but should be more subjective and we should put our best efforts to find better solutions.

REFERENCES

1. Malayappan Committee Report, 1952.
2. Aiyappan Committee Report, 1946.
3. Administration Report of Srikakulam Agency, 1955, p. 5.
4. Administration Report of Srikakulam Agency, 1957, p. 12.
5. Ibid., p. 2.
6. Administration Report of Srikakulam Agency, 1962-63, p. 12.
7. Ibid, p 11.
8. Ibid, p. 13-14.
9. Shilu Ao Committee Report, 1969.
10. Report of Scheduled Area and Scheduled Tribes Commission, Government of India, 1961, p. 31.
11. Ibid, p. 40 and 41.
12. Palmer Monte & Thomson William, R., *The Comparative Analysis of Politics*, F.E. Peacock Publishers, INC, Itasca-Illinois—60143, 1978, p. 7.
13. Ibid, p. 6.
14. Ram Reddy, G. & Sharma B.A.V., *State Government and Politics : Andhra Pradesh*, Sterling Publishers Pvt. Ltd., Delhi, 1979, p. 532 and 533.

6

GIRIJAN DEVELOPMENT AGENCY
Organisation and Functions

IT is also realised that 80 per cent of the population live in rural areas and hence concern for the uplift of the rural poor is a major concern of the central leadership. By and large these activities were looked after by the Union Ministry of Agriculture whose main objectives were (i) achievement of rapid development of agriculture; and (ii) amelioration of the lot of weaker sections of the agricultural community.

AGRICULTURE AND PLANNING

In this context, it may be mentioned that a very high priority was accorded to agriculture in the programmes of development launched immediately after independence and in the successive five-year plans.

In the early sixties, in certain selected districts pilot projects namely Intensive Agriculture Development Programme (IADP) were taken up for achieving increased production by using the latest technology and yielding the quickest possible results. Already ground work in the form of the panchayat raj had been initiated by setting up developmental blocks all over the

TABLE 6.1 : **Public sector outlay for agricultural sector**

(Rs. in crores)

Public Sector Outlay	Agriculture (including irrigation and flood control)	Total all sectors
1. First Plan (Actual)	724	1,960
2. Second Plan (Actual)	949	4,600
3. Third Plan (Actual)	1,754	8,573
4. Annual Plans (Actuals) 1966-67 to 1968-69	1,578	6,625
5. Fourth Plan (Anticipated)	3,466	16,774
6. Fifth Plan (Outlay)	7,616	37,250

country. Food production assumed new importance in terms of the corresponding growth of population. Similarly, efforts were also made to better the lot of the weaker sections, i.e., scheduled castes and scheduled tribes.

Agriculture in tribal areas

In spite of decades of developmental efforts and substantial investment for the development of agriculture in tribal areas, the agriculture production in tribal belts has not been able to catch with the production level in the plains. The tribal areas, by and large, have remained untouched by the green revolution. The uneven sharing of gains from modernising agriculture and the yawning gulf of disparity has resulted in acute social tension and has also created some epicentres of extremist activities. Dissatisfaction due to the slow pace of agricultural development, deteriorating conditions of law and order and the alleged continuing exploitation of the tribals by certain categories of non-tribals has been causing the Government of India considerable concern, and the need for a well directed development efforts was keenly felt.

The Central Coordination Committee for Rural Development and Employment at its fourth meeting held on the 14

August, 1970 recognised the need for intensive development of the tribal areas all over the country and considered the problems of development facing the backward tribes and the tribal areas and decided that a number of pilot projects for their economic development should be formulated for finding a solution to the problems confronting the tribals. The matter was further discussed at the special meeting of the Central Co-ordination Committee held on 17 August, 1970 and it was decided that to start with some pilot projects namely Intensive Agricultural Development Programme may be located in the states of Andhra Pradesh, Bihar, Madhya Pradesh and Orissa, and executed as a central sector scheme during the fourth plan. Accordingly, six pilot tribal development projects for the economic development of the selected tribal areas were sanctioned by the Government of India during the later part of 1971-72. These projects were located in (i) Srikakulam District of Andhra Pradesh, (ii) Singhbhum District of Bihar, (iii) Dentewada and (iv) Konta tahsils of Bastar District of Madhya Pradesh, and (v) Ganjam and Koraput districts of Orissa State.

Components of pilot projects

The Central Coordination Committee identified three important components of these pilot projects. Problems relating to law and order, communications, police and administrative matters for which the Ministry of Home Affairs was assigned to oversee other problems relating economic development which are the core programmes of projects were entrusted to the Ministry of Agriculture.

Problems relating to supporting facilities of social services like drinking water, health and education, etc., came under the purview of the Department of Social Welfare.[1]

At this point of time it was felt that there were a large number of farmers in the countryside, whose holdings were very small and uneconomic, and hence efforts to identify this group and bring them on par with others were initiated. At about the same time a number of Small Farmers' Development Agencies and Marginal Farmers' Development Agencies were also established by the central government. Another factor of significance was that there was Congress government at the state as well as at the centre; hence it was but natural that the problems of Andhra Pradesh would receive a certain amount of consideration by the central leadership. Normally, the Constitution provides for a central leadership to assume more powers whenever there is an internal disturbance effecting the tranquillity and peace of any area or state in the country. Such a situation did exist in Srikakulam District. To counter the law and order situation the state government declared the Agency areas in Srikakulam district as 'disturbed' in June 1969 and in the plains area in August 1969.[2] (Under Sec. 3 of A.P. Separation of Disturbance Act of 1948 : Government, order No. 371 of G.A.D.), Implications of this order was that the Police were allowed to shoot at sight and to prevent more than five people from gathering together. It must be mentioned that with the existence of such a situation, the centre was perturbed. The Naxalite movement in Srikakulam was part of an All India strategy to achieve revolution along Marxian line; hence it had all-India implications. The state government invoked the assistance of the centre and as a matter of fact C.R.P. units were rushed in to bring stability to the area. Here it may also be relevant to add that even though tribal welfare is a state subject, there is a specific responsibility cast upon the central government in this Constitution to oversee tribal development all over the country. It was also around 1969-70 that the then Prime Minister, Mrs. Indira Gandhi popularised *Garibi Hatao* slogans which the executive attempted to implement by ameliorating the lot of the poor. The state government was also anxious to obtain funds from the centre for its developmental programmes.

MALADY-REMEDY ANALYSIS OF PANCHAYAT RAJ INSTITUTIONS

The twenty first Report of Commissioner for Scheduled Castes and Sheduled Tribes (1971-72 and 1972-73) speaks of the failure of tribal development block programme and note with concern that "this programme has fallen short of expectations although it has brought in a change in outlook of tribals, particularly, in the field of education and agriculture. However, other tribal welfare programmes did not receive any significant support from general development provisions. The main reason for the shortcomings of the programme appears to be the small geographical entity of tribal blocks which cannot take schemes like soil conservation, major and medium irrigation schemes, education at secondary level, and technical education. These schemes should have perhaps formed part of the area development programmes."[3]

Some findings in the studies by the Tribal Research Institute show that tribal development block programmes succeeded in making only a limited impact due to certain inherent problems such as the subsistent level of living, undeveloped infrastructure and high percentage of illiteracy among them. It was also noted that the land alienation problem and shifting cultivation as practised by tribals hampered development of these blocks. Further, other problems like dearth of trained personnel to work among the people and frequent transfers of block level officials hampered development. The programme has also been adversely commented upon for the following reasons :

(i) A large number of standardised schemes in vogue among advanced communities have been applied to tribal areas;
(ii) employment aspect of development has not been attended to;
(iii) settlement of land disputes at pre-extension stage was not taken up ;
(iv) 60 to 70 per cent of the funds are spent on "brick and mortar" schemes ; and
(v) in many cases co-operatives have been started by block officers without much education or preparation of the tribal people.

One of the problems retarding widespread development has been that more advanced sections of the tribal population are able to take away the lion's share of benefits of various schemes undertaken in blocks. There was also a tendency on the part of the block authorities to start schemes in the areas which were easily accessible and it was rarely that schemes were started after ascertaining the real needs of the people inhabiting that area.

CENTRAL LEAD IN DEVELOPMENT PROCESS

Besides, agriculture as seen from our Constitution is a concurrent subject and in all matters of agricultural innovations and research, the centre has always taken the lead. It has always assumed the role of a grand coordinator and oversees all agricultural programmes for production throughout the length and breadth of the country. It may be relevant to point out that state governments have never exercised enough initiative in devising new programmes for increased agricultural efficiency and productivity. Be it Panchayat Raj or I.A.D.P. or S.F.D.A , M.F.A.L. or Tribal Development projects; the lead has always come from the centre. The Report of the Commissioner of Scheduled Castes and Scheduled Tribes (1971-72 and 1972-73) has also admitted, "In view of the political unrest in certain tribal areas, it was decided to set up a few pilot projects with an aim to develop these areas by integrating various programmes implemented under general sectors and tribal welfare and pooling all resources for the the project areas.[4]

The salient features of the programme

The tribal projects sanctioned by the Government of India in the latter part of 1971-72 were for a period of five years. The outlay of each of the projects was fixed at Rs. 1.50 crores for a programme of economic development and Rs. 0.50 crore for the construction of arterial roads, i.e., Rs. 2 crores in each case due to enhanced period of operation by two years. During 1976-77, the project was increased by Rs. 80 lakhs in the case of T.D.A. Srikakulam. The approach to the economic problems of tribals would as far as possible be comprehensive and integrated. The programme was related to the specific needs of the areas, since project uniformity in programmes in different areas was not insisted upon in view of the diverse socio-economic and physio-geographic conditions. The agencies were also promoted to benefit the tribal development like T.D. Cooperatives, Land Development Banks, central and ancestral cooperative banks with risk cover fund contribution and managerial subsidies. Another interesting aspect of the programme was taking care of tribal labour and offering them employment under various construction programmes relating to irrigation projects, rail roads, arterial roads, etc. The Agency was instructed to take care that the labourers employed in such work get a fair wage. The project was completed through society registered under the Societies Registration Act, 1860 called the Girijan Development Agency with the District Collector as the Chairman and other connected District level officers and M.L.As./M.Ps. as members. The grants were directly released by the Government of India to the chairman of the Agency and each project had a whole time Project Officer of the rank of Joint Collector or District Revenue Officer to ensure coordination and effective implementation of the various programmes. In Srikakulam District, even though the project comprises of nine blocks, for the purpose of study, however, we have taken up only three blocks which are tribal development blocks and the other are non-tribal development blocks, although there is tribal population in those areas. The projects were additive in their nature and were not intended to replace the normal flow of financial allocation for the on-going schemes under the general community development and tribal development programmes.

Administration

At the national level the planning Commission and the Ministry of Agriculture and Irrigation had the responsibility of guiding and reviewing the implementation of these projects. The Central Coordination Committee on Rural Development and Employment gives the necessary policy guidance. At the Ministry's level the Secretaries/Committee (sanctioning) was constituted for the purpose of sanctioning and reviewing these projects. In the department of rural development a small officer-oriented unit headed by a Director and assisted by an Under Secretary and minimum complement staff was created to guide, coordinate and supervise these projects. The economic development programme implemented in the pilot projects was based on Action Plans formulated and duly approved by sanctioning committee. In respect of 4 T.D.As. namely Srikakulam, Singhbhum, Ganjam and Koraput, revised action plans were also formulated and approved by sanctioning committee for the extended period beyond 31 March, 1977. In order that the work in the projects could proceed quickly, grants-in-aid out of the schematic provision for each project were directly released by the Government of India to the Chairman (Collector) of each tribal development agency.

At the state level there was a functional coordination-cum-implementation committee responsible for reviewing the administration of the programme. A suitable state government department looks after the programme in different states.

In Andhra Pradesh at present, the Employment and Social Welfare Department which was the administrative department to look after the tribal welfare in the state is also administering these special programmes. There is a state-level coordination committee for tribal welfare with the First Member, Board of Revenue-cum-Commissioner for Tribal Welfare as Chairman, Secretary : Revenue Department and other officers concerned both at the Secretariat level and the Heads of Department level are members of this Committee. There is a Director, Tribal Welfare who is also ex-officio Joint Secretary of the Board of Revenue. He functions as Member-Secretary of this Committee.

The Administrative set-up

Before proceeding further it would be appropriate to discuss the various agencies at work for the welfare of tribals in the district. The premier institution is the Girijan Corporation which looks after marketing of tribal produce and supply of domestic requirements in the tribal areas. As such it can be said that the G.C.C. by its very nature being a Corporation does not form an integral part of the district administration.

Prior to the setting up of the G.D.A., the other agencies in the field were the regular tribal welfare department which was in charge of looking after the smooth running of tribal development blocks. Thus the tribal welfare department looked after the developmental aspect of tribal welfare and culture. The regulatory administration was headed by the Collector who in turn was assisted by the field staff. The Collector is also the special agent to government and he is supposed to

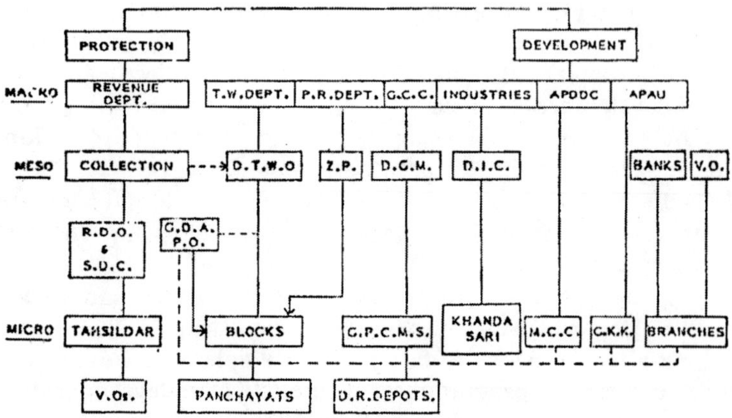

CHART 6.1

Rural Development

KEY

MACRO=State Level, MESO=District Level, MICRO=Field Level.
Indicates Hierarchy
Indicates Functional Coordination.
R.D.O.=Revenue Divisional Officer.
&
S.D.C.
V.Os.=Village Officer.
G.D.A.=Girijan Development Agency.
P.O.=Project Officer.
T.W. Dept.=Tribal Welfare Department.
D.T.W.O.=District Tribal Welfare Officer.
G.C.C.=Girijain Co-operative Corporation.
D.G.M.=Divisional General Manager.
G.P.C.M.S.=Girijan Primary Co-operative Marketing Societies.
D.R. Depots=Domestic Requirement Depots.
P.R. Dept =Panchayat Raj Department.
Z.P.=Zilla Parishad.
D.I.C.=District Industries Centre.
A.P.D.D.C.=Anohra Pradesh Dairy Development Corporation.
M.C.C.—Milk Chilling Centre.
A.P.A.U.=Andhra Pradesh Agricultural University.
G.K.K=Girijan Krishi Kendra.
V.O.=Voluntary Organisation.

prepare a report on tribal administration every year and submit it to the Governor through the government. In Srikakulam district, the Sub-Collector, Parvatipuram was designated as the Assistant Agent to Government and Divisional Agency Officer. The main function of the Sub-Collector, Parvatipuram was to properly implement the Land Transfer Regulation Act, the Money Lenders Regulation Act, and the Debt Relief Act. The Sub-Collector is also in his capacity as Sub-divisional Magistrate, the Criminal and Civil Sub-Judge of the Agency area. Apart from this, the Sub-Collector can also convene divisional coordination committees of the B.D.Os. functioning in his jurisdiction and review the implementation of developmental programmes.

The tribal welfare grants were being channelled through the Zila Parishad which was headed by the Collector for administrative purposes. Up to 1973, there was no post of District Tribal Welfare Officer, it was only the District Social Welfare Officer who was looking after the implementation of tribal welfare programmes. As a matter of fact as far back as 1966, the Study Team on Tribal Development programmes, 1966* had observed, "Separate District Offices for tribal welfare should be appointed to work under the Director of Tribal Welfare in Andhra Pradesh".[5] However in 1970, at the height of the Naxalite movement one post of Special Deputy Collector for Land Transfer regulations was sanctioned and he was stationed at Elwinpet in Bhadragiri block of Parvatipuram taluk which was the centre of all extremist activity. There was also one Special First Class Magistrate stationed at Elwinpet who was of the rank of Tahsildar and whose main work was to expedite the disposal of criminal cases that were instituted against the Girijans who were arrested for crimes and involvement in extremist activity. This was done because the normal jurisdiction of judicial administration does not extend to the scheduled agency areas of the district.

At this point it would be worthwhile considering the advantages of establishing the G.D.A. and how it is more

*Report on All India, New Delhi : Planning Commission Committee on Plan Projects.

superior for better implementation of tribal welfare programmes than the normal tribal welfare department.

TABLE 6.2 : **Tribal welfare programmes than the normal tribal welfare department**

G.D.A.	Tribal Welfare Dept. at District level
1. Subject matter specialists in the fields of Agriculture, Irrigation, Animal Husbandry have been functioning under the control of the Project Officer.	No field staff for implementation of schemes except the post of D.T.W.O. which was created during 1972-73.
2. Direct implementation of schemes.	Coordination of programmes.
3. Flexibility in financial administration.	No flexibility.
4. Step towards single line of administration.	Steps were taken to create the post of D.T.W.O.
5. Step towards administration integration.	T.D. Blocks were kept under the control of Tribal Welfare Department.
6. Central sector scheme implemented by State Government for intensive economic development.	New programmes such as Village officers training, masonry training etc., were taken up.
7. Registered autonomous body.	Government organisation.

In fact the Study Team on Tribal Development programme, 1966* had this observation to make on the organizational and structural defects. "During its tour in Andhra Pradesh, the team was informed that the Agency areas were not receiving sufficient attention from the district officers and the time had come for

*Report on All India, New Delhi, Planning Commission Committee on Plan Projects.

constituting the extensive tribal belt lying in four different districts, (Srikakulam, Visakhapatnam, East Godavary and West Godavari) into two separate districts for facilitating quick development of the area".[6]

Role of the District Collector

The Collector has a very crucial role to play in tribal welfare and administration of tribal areas. He has many functions namely :

(a) As a Collector of Revenue.

(b) As a District Magistrate he is a court of appeal in judicial and quasi-judicial matters pertaining to the tribal.

(c) As agent to government for the scheduled areas, he is expected to ensure that tribals are protected and their interests properly looked after.

(d) As a Special Officer of the Zilla Parishad, he is expected to ensure that Panchayat Raj institutions in the tribal areas functions properly, and funds are properly utilised, earmarked for tribal development.

(e) As a Chairman of the Girijan Development Agency, he is expected to receive and acknowledge funds of the Government of India and that appropriate and purposeful schemes and programmes are devised and implemented according to the guidelines laid down by the Government of India.

To ensure proper implementation of programmes the Collector coordinates the work of all other departments and it is his chief responsibility to ensure that implementation is carried out smoothly. The important developmental heads working directly under the Collector are made responsible for smooth functioning of their respective departmental staff, and proper implementation of departmental schemes which vary according to local needs. The more important departmental heads at the district level are District Tribal Welfare Officer, District Social Welfare Officer, the District Educational Officer, the Deputy Director of Agriculture and District Agricultural

Officers, Deputy Director of Industries, District Employment Officer, District Veterinary Officer, Secretary, Zilla Parishad, Executive Engineer (Roads and Buildings), Executive Engineer (Irrigation), Divisional Executive Engineer (Electricity) and District Medical and Health Officer.

Prior to the commencement of the monsoon the Collector with the help of the District Agriculture Officer and Deputy Director of Agriculture must assess the resources and prepare the agriculture production plan. This is particularly important because tribals live mostly of their forest produce and their economy is dependent on agriculture. It is important for the Collector to arrange for timely distribution of inputs like seeds, fertilisers, pesticides in the tribal areas. It is necessary that demonstration plots of high yielding varieties are arranged on a wide scale. It is of pivotal importance that the Collector arranges for short-term crop loans through the Cooperative Central Bank of the district, and the District Cooperative Officers has to prepare plans for cooperative credit facilities. Similarly, the Educational Officer and the Tribal Welfare Officer have to arrange for attendance and supply of materials in schools for the new academic session every year. The Collector must also see that hospitals and dispensaries in the tribal areas are adequately staffed and the medicines are readily available throughout the year. The Collector has to ensure that regular vaccination drives for small-pox, cholera, typhoid, T.B. and supply of medicines for prevention of malaria are taken into account. It is also necessary that chlorination of wells and tanks is carried out regularly. The Collector is assisted by the Tahsildars and Revenue Divisional officers and they are required to visit the institutions in the tribal areas and report to him directly whether various services are readily available to the tribals.

Very often the Collector must himself undertake tours of the tribal areas and will mingle with tribals, discuss their problems and try to dispose of as many matters on the spot with the assistance of local revenue and other departmental officers. The Collector must fill the tribals with confidence and it is his responsibility to bring justice to their doorstep and he should pay special attention for the uplift of weaker sections. It is in this context that very often the Collector can make use of certain discretionary grants at his disposal to help poor and needy tribals who have no other means of making out their livelihood. A simple instance would be a child suffering from some malignant disease, the Collector could help him to gain admission at the District headquarters hospital and provide funds for his transport charges and bear the expenses of purchasing costly medicines.

The activities of the Deputy Collectors and Revenue Divisional Officers in the matter of disposing of cases under the land transfer regulation, money-lenders regulation, debt relief regulation are also vigorously reviewed by the District Collector.

Role of Project Officer in G.D.A.

With the setting up of the Girijan Development Agency headed by the Collector as its Chairman and Project Officer as its Chief Executive Officer ; a new pattern of administration was established which had not been tried earlier. The role of the Project Officer in the successful planning and implementation of schemes according to the guidelines laid down by the Government of India is pivotal. The post of Project Officer was to be manned by a senior time-scale IAS Officer since the inception of the agency which was sanctioned by the Government of India. The post was filled up immediately in 1971 itself.

The Project Officer was associated with preparing the plan of action within the parameters prescribed by the Government of India in consultation with the Collector and the Planning Department at the state level. The Project Officer was also made responsible for getting the society registered according to the Societies Act. The Project Officer was also responsible for getting the staff sanctioned and getting the work moving. It can be said that the structure of administration was strong and sound and was oriented towards the needs of the tribals; part of the establishment was located in the tribal areas itself. The Agency actually started functioning from 1972. One of the chief concerns of the Project Officer was to arrange for credit through nationalised banks for financing the programmes as per the subsidy pattern indicated by Government of India. The other important functions of the Project

Officer was that proper identification of tribal beneficiaries of the scheme was ensured who come within the fold. The G.D.A had a massive programme of road construction and irrigation works in the agency areas. Hence, it was necessary that work done was properly reviewed and speedily executed. It was vital that timely payment of wages to the tribal labour employed on road construction was ensured by the Project Officer. The Project Officer also had to be in close touch with the B.D.Os. because all the infrastructure like veterinary institutions, hospitals, schools, agricultural demonstrators and junior engineers were under the control of the B.D.Os.

A special division headed by an Executive Engineer for irrigation works was sanctioned and placed directly under the control of the Project Officer, G.D.A. Another important function of the Project Officer was to coordinate his work with the representatives of nationalised banks so as to arrange finance for tribals in the project areas. The Project Officer has another important function in the absence of any regular D.T.W.Os. to consult the various departmental district heads regarding schemes taken up in the tribal areas. This involves a lot of coordination work and being a junior IAS Officer it was very essential that the Collector threw his entire weight behind the Project Officer so that the departmental heads would ensure their fullest cooperation.

In G.O.Ms. No. 159, Social Weflare (D) Department, dated 21 October 1976 it was said that the Project Officer of the Girijan Development Agency, Srikakulam shall have immediate administrative control of the Agriculture, Horticulture and Livestock Farms, Demonstration units, Ashram schools, Hostels, and so on, which are being financed from the budget of the Tribal Welfare Department in Srikakulam district. The entire special staff sanctioned for tribal welfare work and plan schemes as also the staff employed for implementing the provisions of Andhra Pradesh Land Transfer Regulation, 1960 in Srikakulam district with all vehicles, equipment, etc., with them shall work under the administrative control of the Project Officer, Girijan Development Agency, Srikakulam. The Project Officer, Girijan Development Agency, shall effect such proper redistribution of the work among the staff as is necessary. The

Block Development Officers of all Tribal Development Blocks in Srikakulam district shall also work under the administrative control of the Project Officer, Girijan Development Agency, Srikakulam.

This decision was indeed of momentous proportions as it made a world of difference to the authority of the Project Officer who was until this point of time deriving authority from the Collector. Even though the Project Officer was working under the control of the Collector, the Project Officer was vested with more authority and responsibility. He was made to feel more independent so that programmes could be better implemented and integration of programmes could be carried out. In effect, it meant that the concept of single line agency administration was being introduced. It would also enable the Project Officer to have a closer watch and better control over the functioning of Panchayat Raj institutions. the Project Officer would also be able to keep a close watch over the receipt of funds; preparation of programmes and actual implementation of schemes. Earlier he was not so much a part of the district administration in the sense that he did not have direct control over local institutions while looking after tribal welfare programmes. Now this vacuum which appears to have been a snag earlier was filled and the Project Officer's position became more institutionalised in the sense that he could implement and manage funds both of state and central sector more efficiently. However, one point which cannot be lost sight of is that in district administration authority may be vested in a particular officer or at a particular point in the administrative hierarchy, but nothing can really function smoothly or effectively without the active support and full cooperation of the District Collector. The institution of the District Collector in the development process is unique and ultimately he acts as a catalyst of change in a very subtle way.

The other function which is to be performed by the Project Officer is that regularly once in three months the Governing Body of the G.D.A. is convened so that important administrative and financial decisions involved in the day-to day work of the Agency can be sorted out and executed. During the Governing Body meeting, monthly targets and performances of all the programmes under execution is also reviewed and remedies suggested wherever necessary. Important policy decisions are also taken in the Governing Body meeting with the assistance of non-official members and other dictrict officers. The Governing Body meeting is also a source of good feed-back regarding the needs of the tribal people.

The Project Officer is also required to frequently proceed to state headquarters where release of funds and performance is reviewed. It may be worthwhile to add that even though funds are raleased by the Government of India directly to the District Collector, the state government has an important liaisoning role as it can also project the case for additional allotment of funds directly with the centre. However, the state government does not interfere in the everyday administration of the project. One of the advantages of setting up the G.D.A. is that a great deal of flexibility in devising and implementation of programmes is possible to suit local needs and aspirations. The Project Officer is also expected to proceed to Government of India where the budget allotments are often discussed, and new programmes for the Agency presented before sanctioning committee of the central government

At the close of the financial year as per the articles of association of the G.D.A. the Project Officer is expected to get the accounts audited by Chartered Accountants. This report is presented before the Governing Body for discussion and approval and then transmitted to the Government of India for allocation of further funds before the commencement of the next financial year. The Project Officer is also expected to be in constant touch with the various Head of Departments to hammer out problems of coordination with them. The work of the project is also discussed during the District Development Coordination Meeting convened by the Collector in the Zilla Parishad. Similarly, the Project Officer is also expected to attend all important meetings convened by the ministers when they visit the district to review the work and progress of various developmental programmes.

Staff structure of the G.D.A.

For the performance of implementing the G.D.A. schemes, a skeleton staff structure was sanctioned. The Project Officer was assisted by one Assistant Project Officer of the rank of Deputy

Collector another Assistant Project Officer-cum-subject matter specialist of the rank of District Agricultural Officer, One Assistant. Project Officer-cum-subject matter specialist of the rank of District Veterinary Officer. The subject matter specialists in turn had Extension Officers of their respective departments posted in the block headquarters. In addition, one Executive Engineer (P.W.D.) with the complement of engineering staff was sanctioned for speedy execution of irrigation works. The Project Officer was expected to inspect all the works executed by the engineering division and give guidance wherever necessary in the matter of selection of works, approval of estimates and tenders. As seen from the performance the intensity of irrigation short up very rapidly during the brief span of the G.D.As. existence. Similarly, agricultural programmes also received a shot in arm and tribals started preferring settled cultivatiou instead of shifting cultivation (Podu) which they were traditionally accustomed to as their only means of livelihood.

STRATEGY FOR DEVELOPMENT

In the Revised Action Plan of the Girijan Development Agency from 1972 to 1977, it was mentioned that the low level of production combined with lack of infrastructural facilities has produced a situation where the tribal is helpless. Added to that is the fact of infiltration of political extremists in the tribal areas of Srikakulam which has brought the tribal economy to a stand still. To remedy the situation, and to restore life to normalcy and revival of developmental activity, the pilot project was sanctioned in this area. The following area was identified for the implementation of the pilot project.

However, for the purpose of this study, we are confining ourselves only to the three exclusively tribal development blocks, i.e., Bhadragiri, Pachipenta, and Seethampet. In the remaining areas the blocks are not T.D. Blocks. The economic base which forms the supporting plant from which development activity can take off in case of land owning families is obviously agriculture. For the remaining section of the population, ancillary activities like animal husbandry and cottage industries form the base. It is not easy to compartmantalise

TABLE 6.3 : **Area for implementation of pilot project**

S. No.	Block	Total Population	Tribal Population
1.	Bhadragiri	32,012	26,830
2.	Pachipenta	27,553	18,871
3.	Seethampet	28,369	26,953
4.	Salur	82,846	13,402
5.	Parvatipuram	99,722	13,369
6.	Kurupam	63,160	13,717
7.	Kothuru	1,14,636	19,128
8.	Saravakota	1,17,541	20,893
9.	Mandasa	1,02,955	5,502

the second section of the population according to their occupation as they engaged themselves as agricultural labourers, indulge in shifting cultivation and collection of all or some of the above activities sustains them.

A two-pronged strategy was, therefore, adopted for the development of the above two broad sections. The status of the land owning tribal families would be compared to some extent to that of the sub-marginal farmers and the dry land cultivators of the plains. A family based coverage by providing minimum quantities of inputs of agriculture such as improved varieties of seeds, fertilisers and pesticides, medium term inputs in terms of a pair of draught cattle and basic implements of agricultural production has been envisaged. As a corollary irrigation facilities have been provided. Better facilities of marketing, strengthening of G.C.C. laying link roads to key villages has been suggested.

The limited financial resources both from the state and central sectors have set serious limits to the size of the schemes. One way to obviate this difficulty was to reduce the coverage of families but this would have its own repurcussions. It was, therefore, inevitable that a less attractive proposition from the point of view of the tribal is chosen, that is of linking this programme with loaning programme already under way. This had three distinct advantages : (i) It allows for a larger coverage, (ii) Ensures prevention of misuse of the loans being advanced to the tribals, and (iii) promotes the sense of participation.

Besides this, the extension agency also would be fully involved in the process as it will be their primary responsibility to coordinate the flow of assistance from both the channels, that is, loan and grant.

For the second section of population, land assignment after reclamation was proposed. The area available for assignment was limited to about 25,000 acres of which 8,000 acres had already been assigned. Thus only about one-fourth of the landless tribal families, that is, 3,600 families would have the benefit from the scheme. Suitable outlay on providing minimum facilities to these families to settle on agriculture has been envisaged. For the remaining population, the employment potential generated due to launching of labour intensive projects both under the state and central sectors would provide them a minimum support. Besides the above programme, the investment under the plan on cottage industries and other ancillary activities could be of great support to this section of population if a selective approach was made.

The presence of too many agencies for development poses problems of coordination which results in organisational dysfunction. With the coming of the Girijan Development Agency, the adoption of single line agency of administration was a step in the right direction and helped immensely in proper implementation of programmes and policies. There was better integration of functions and better utilisation of financial allocations available with other departments. It may be seen that all allocations were being properly spent and the system of review and evaluation also improved enormously. Another good effect was that the protective regulations that were being implemented by the Revenue authorities in the agency areas could be brought under the fold of G.D.A. activities in the sense that whenever any land was delivered to the tribals immediate steps were taken by the Project Officer to see that necessary inputs were provided to the new owners of the land. Field problems received quicker attention of the District Collector because of the better coordination that had been achieved. In general, this was a new step and augured well for the future.

REFERENCES

1. Govt. of India, Ministry of Agriculture, "Brochure on Pilot Projects for Tribal Development", p. 1 & 2, Farm Information Unit, Directorate of Extension, Ministry of Agriculture, New Delhi, February, 1974.
2. Ram Reddy, G.; Sharma, B.A.V., *State Government and Politics : Andhra Pradesh*, Sterling Publishers Pvt. Ltd., New Delhi, p. 537, 1979.
3. The Report of the Commissioner for Scheduled Castes and Scheduled Tribes : 1971-72 & 1972-73 (Twenty-first Report)
4. Ibid.
5. Virendra Kumar, *Committees and Commissions in India : 1947-73, Volume VII*, Concept Publishing Company, Delhi :, First published, 1978, p. 384
6. Ibid, p. 385.

7

GIRIJAN DEVELOPMENT AGENCY AT WORK

"It is our duty to see that the backward communities are no more neglected. They are to be made fellow travellers in our way to progress. Their uplift is a must to make our country strong, for disparity is the root of all troubles."

—*Shrimati Indira Gandhi*

IN SRIKAKULAM district, the taluks, viz., Parvatipuram, Salur and Palakonda which constituted our area of study qualified as backward. The State Planning Department used certain indicators to identify backward areas. The following seven indicators were used :

(i) Gross value of agricultural output per acre, 1970-71.
(ii) Gross value of agricultural output per agricultural worker, 1970-71.
(iii) Percentage of gross irrigated area to gross area sown, 1970-71.
(iv) Normal rainfall.
(v) Workers in registered factories per lakh population, 1969.

(vi) Percentage of literates to total population 1971.
(vii) Hospital beds per lakh population, 1970-71.

However, for our purpose we have taken up the evaluation of the following programmes, namely, agriculture and irrigation on the economic development side, education and health on the social sector development side. The importance of institutional finance and road development has also been evaluated.

The eruption of violence due to extremist activities suddenly brought into limelight the inadequacies of the programmes implemented, and the unabated exploitation going on in tribal areas. In order to arrest the dangers of the extremist activities and to wipe out all pervasive regional and group imbalances, the government have launched a number of legislative, administrative and development measures. The establishment of the Girijan Development Agency during the Fourth Plan in Srikakulam district for accelerating the development of tribals of backward region was a major step. Though the Girijan Development Agency was an agriculture-oriented project with emphasis on ancillary programmes like minor irrigation, many other programmes such as special nutrition programme, intensive promotion of ashram schools, etc., have been simultaneously implemented during the Fourth Plan.

The intensive and extensive promotion of development programmes in the tribal areas of Srikakulam district resulted in creation of massive social and economic infrastructure besides modernising the tribals. An attempt is made here to assess the impact of various development programmes in the fields of agriculture, minor irrigation, communications, education and health by way of conducting case studies on purposive sample base. Broadly, a minimum of three villages are selected representing a cross-section of major tribal groups of the three T.D. Blocks, viz., Bhadragiri, Seethampet and Pachipenta. Various social and economic indicators in the fields of agriculture, education, health and institutional finance, have also been worked out to assess the impact of development programmes and to find out the respectivity and response of tribal towards the development activities. Structured questionnaires were used for the purpose of eliciting information from the tribals and the results obtained are encouraging and it could be assessed that the programmes of development in the agency areas of Srikakulam district had a general positive impact on the tribals living in the area. The case studies of development programmes are discussed hereunder:

AGRICULTURE

The Girijan Development Agency, a centrally sponsored scheme was launched in the tribal areas of Srikakulam district in January 1972. The main objective of this Agency was to develop agriculture and allied sectors in tribal areas. The project area of G.D.A. covers both the scheduled and non-scheduled areas of eleven panchayat samitis, viz., Bhadragiri, Seethampet, Pachipenta, Salur, Parvatipuram, Kurupam, Kotruru, Kasi Bugga, Sarvakota, Tekkali and Mandasa.

The tribal population of the composite district of Srikakulam according to the 1971 Census is 2,12,459 constituting 8.2 per cent of the total population of the district. The major tribes inhabiting the tribal areas are Savaras, Jatapu, Konda Dora and Gadaba. The total geographical areas of the district is 3,901 sq. miles with a population of 25,89,999 (1971 Census). The composite district of Srikakulam is situated between 18°21′ and 19°10′ of northern latitude and 83°5′ and 84°5′ eastern longitude. This district is situated in diannual temperature region where summer is hot and winter is fairly severe. The lowest temperature recorded is 13°C, while the highest is 40°C. Most of the rainfall is received during the south-west monsoon period. The rainy season commences from late May or early June and ends in December. The rainfall during the north-east monsoon is moderate and irregular. The average rainfall in this district is 1086.90mm. The rainfall received during the south-west monsoon is utilised for cultivation of major crops during the Kharif season whereas the rainfall during the north-east monsoon is useful for sustaining the crops.

Nature is bountiful with many perennial rivers and several streams. The important rivers like Nagavali Vamsadhara,

Suvarnamukhi, Vegavati, Mahendrathanaya, Gomukhi and Champavathi meander through the tribal areas of the district.

The forests of the Agency area are of mostly deciduous type and important species of the flora are *sal*, *nallamaddi*, Teak etc., The bamboo forests are also widespread in the tribal belt.

The soils in the Agency area belong to red-ferrigeous series, loams and sandy loams of which the former is found in hilly tracts and the later along the river valleys of the tribal areas. The effective utilisation of land indicates economic prosperity of the area. The land utilisation particularly of the tribal areas of the district are given in Table 7.1.

TABLE 7.1 : **Land utilization of tribal areas**

S. No.	Item	Areas in acres (lakhs)	Percentage
1.	Total geographical areas	5.27	—
2.	Forests.	3.28	62.25
3.	Barren and uncultivable land	0.60	11.38
4.	Miscellaneous trees crop grown	0.04	0.76
5.	Cultivable waste	0.25	4.75
6.	Other fallow land	0.17	3.22
7.	Net areas sown	0.93	17.64

The percentage of area under forests works out to 62.25 per cent of the total geographical areas. The net area sown constitutes 17.64 per cent of the total geographical area.

The social and cultural pattern of the tribal groups indicate certain similarities and diversities. Racially Khonds and Savaras belong to the Mongoloid groups while other tribal groups such as Konda Dora, Mooka Dora, etc , exhibited 'proto-Astroloid' strains. Khond, Gadaba and Savara have their own language whereas the other tribes speak Telugu. The similarities are observed in performance of festivals, first fruit eating ceremonies, ancestral worship among all the tribes.

The study area

Twenty tribal households of Donubai in Seethampeta Block, R.K. Bai, Mondukhallu in Bhadragiri Block, and Thonam villages in Pachipenta Block were selected at random to assess the socio-economic conditions, with specific reference to their agro-based economy. These households belong to Jatapu, Savara, and Mooka Dora tribes. The average size of the household is 4.55.

The sex and age group analysis reveals that out of 91 persons, 54.49 per cent are males and the rest are females. Children and adolescents constitute 48.35 per cent to the total surveyed population. The analysis of the marital status indicates that out of the total sample population the percentage of unmarried is 49.45 and that of married is 49.46 while widows constitute 1.09 per cent. Among the unmarried people males are more in number (29.67%) than females, whereas among the married, females (25.29%) outnumber males. This can be attributed to the prevalence of polygamy among the tribal communities.

Occupation

The economy of the tribals of Srikakulam district centres round agriculture and allied sectors. The comparison of the 1961 and the 1971 Census indicates that the total working force among tribals remain static in agricultural sector, while there is a diminishing tendency among cultivators and an increasing tendency among the agricultural labourers. The percentage of cultivators according to the 1971 Census is 34.33 while it was 48.02 per cent during the 1961 Census. Percentage of agricultural labourers is increased from 40.17 per cent in 1961 census to 53.36 per cent in 1971. These figures reveal the dependence of tribals on the agricultural sector.

Agriculture has been the most important occupation of the

tribals in the study area. They thrive on cultivation followed by the collection of minor forest produce (M.F.P.) and engage in forest labour. Agricultural labour and collection of minor forest produce are the major subsidiary occupations of the tribal respondents. The analysis of the occupation pattern shows that 94.5 per cent of the workers are engaged mainly in agriculture. Males and females are in equal number in agriculture; whereas males outnumber females in agriculture labour showing the inability of the weaker sex to undertake strenuous work. Among the subsidiary pursuits, agriculture labour is first in importance. Out of the total population engaged in subsidiary occupations, about 73 per cent and 22.06 per cent are engaged in agricultural labour and collection of minor forest produce respectively. The remaining tribals are found to be engaged in collection of wood for fuel purpose and thread weaving for cots. The collection of minor forest produce stands second in importance among subsidiary occupations. In general, the agricultural sector is sustaining the largest number of tribals.

Economic status

There are 55 earners and 36 non-earners in the sample population. Males constitute 52.72 per cent of the total earners, revealing the economic status of males in the society. Among the non-earners males outnumber the females. The data further reveal that 69.2 per cent of the non-earners belong to age groups of less than 10 years. Hence it can be concluded that the bulk of non-earning dependents comprise of children. Most of the earning population is concentrated in the able-bodied age groups 21 to 50 years.

Land holdings

The possession of land not only adds prestige in society, but also facilitates to obtain loans from financial institutions. Out of 106.56 acres of land cultivated in the sample villages 60.01 per cent and 20.3 per cent and 19.6 per cent of land is under dry, wet, and *podu* cultivation respectively. Thus a large part of the land is under dry cultivation while only a small portion is under *podu* cultivation. The average size of a holding works out to 5.3 acres whereas the man-land ratio is 1.17 acres.

Apart from the usual cultivation, shifting cultivation is also seen in the tribal areas even though the government is discouraging by arranging the anti-*podu* committees in the tribal area.

The average size of *podu*-cultivated area in the selected villages works out to 1.02 acres and it is by and large absent in Thonam village. This type of *podu* cultivation is more practised by the Savara tribe. Almost all the 20 households possess land either wet or dry and are owner cultivators. There are no cases of land leases.

The study reveals that 60 per cent owner cultivators fall under the range of 0.01 to 2.99 acres. Twenty per cent of the cultivators fall under the 3 to 4.99 acres range, and 10 per cent of cultivators fall under 5 to 6 acres range and the rest of 10 per cent cultivators fall under 7 and above acres range. The study also reveals that tribal land is subjected to segmentation and fragmentation.

Cropping pattern

The main ingredient of tribal earnings is agriculture. Hence the discussion on cropping structure gains importance, generally speaking, commercial crops give more income than other crops (like food crops).

The important food crops like paddy, *ragi*, *bajra*, *sama*, *vooda*, *jowar*, etc., and commercial crops like *mesta*, horsegram grams, groundnut are grown in tribal areas. Among all commercial crops *mesta* is the main crop. At a glance it can be stated that 78.95 per cent of area is under food crops and only 21.05 per cent of land is under commercial crops confined to the sample area. Village-wise commercial cropping area is 19.30 per cent, 30.15 per cent, 14.85 per cent and 21.85 per cent in Thonam, R.K. Bai, Donubai and Mondemkhallu respectively. Where the rains are irregular and topography is uneven, the growth of commercial crops increases earnings. Hence it is to say that to boost the earnings of tribals intensive growth in commercial crops may be suggested.

Use of improved technology

Since the inception of the G.D.A. arrangements have been made to supply high-yielding varieties of seeds and improved fertilisers and pesticides to the Girijan farmers. Large-scale demonstration plots were arranged to ensure diffusion of innovations, and timely distribution of seeds and fertilisers was carried out by G.D.A. It was observed that initially tribals were weary of adopting new technology, however, later after watching the results of demonstration plots they readily conceded to it.

Income

Wet, dry and *podu* cultivation are the chief sources of income under agriculture. Relatively speaking, cultivation provides them bread and work throughout the year. So the tribals consider it as a more reliable and stable source of income than other sources like collection of M.F.P., forest labour, etc., which are secondary in nature. Agricultural sector being the main source of income the total income derived from agriculture and agricultural labour is 67.35 per cent of the total income while the respective receipts from collection of M.F.P. and forest labour are 13.26 per cent and 18.67 per cent of the total income. The income derived from these sources constitute 31.93 per cent to the total income. The tribals collect M.F.P. not only for their own consumption but also supplement their major income in agricultural sector by selling them to G.C.C. Next to agriculture, the sale of minor forest produce contributes 33.33 per cent, 27.90 per cent 5.40 per cent and 16.90 per cent of incomes to selected tribal households in the villages of R.K. Bai, Mondamkhallu, Donubai, and Thonam respectively. A small portion of income was contributed by the sale of fruits and vegetables too. The per capita income of the selected households of the villages accounts for Rs. 594.31.

Income and expenditure are two ingredients to indicate the economic position of an individual. The per capita expenditure confined to the selected sample is worked out to 718.51. It is observed that 29.78 per cent, 21.35 per cent, 21.42 per cent and 21.01 per cent of income is spent on food in Thonam, Donubai,

R.K. Bai, and Mondamkhallu villages respectively. In all the selected villages, the tribal household spends, next to food, on alcoholic drinks. It indicates that 19.32 per cent, 19.39 per cent, 21.42 per cent, 20.85 per cent and 18.5 per cent of income was spent on alcoholic drinks in the selected villages. The proportionality of spending on foods and drinks seems equal. Next to drinks the tribal households spend on rites and ceremonies which is worked out to 16.98 per cent, 15.25 per cent, 17.5 per cent and 18.72 per cent in Thonam, R.K. Bai, Mondamkhallu and Donubai villages. The rest of the income was spent on beverages, meat and fish, housing, clothing, medical, recreation and travelling.

Due to opening up of the area, the tribals are habituated to travelling and recreation, which improves their cultural and social status.

MINOR IRRIGATION

Besides the important rivers like Nagavali, Vamsadhara, Suvarnamukhi, Vegavati, Gomukhi and Mahendrathanaya; numerous hill streams, seasonal and perennial flow in tribal areas of Srikakulam district. The uneven topography does not allow sufficient ground-water recharge or help to irrigate the land extensively. Though agriculture is the main occupation fed with low levels of production a cumulative result of low production leads to social and economic backwardness of the tribals. Prior to the inception of G.D.A. in Srikakulam a net area irrigated in scheduled and non-scheduled areas inhabited by tribals was 7,196 hectares of which 2,159 hectares of irrigated area was under minor irrigation (315) sources in T.D. Blocks.

Block	*No. of M.I. works*
Seethampet	175
Bhadragiri	69
Pachipenta	71
	315

The agricultural production plan which aims at initiating sustaining and universalising new agricultural strategy must necessarily aim at optimum exploitation of surface and also ground water. The exploitation of irrigation potential is essential for enhancing agricultural production and for overall development of tribal tracts. Irrigation is the basic input for boosting agricultural production. The other inputs like fertilizers, high-yielding verieties of seeds, improved arts of agriculture etc., depend upon the availability of extension facilities. Prior to inception of G.D.A. no systematic or special efforts were made full utilisation of irrigation facilities due to lack of funds.

In 1972, the Girijan Development Agency came into existence with multi-dimensional schemes for transformation of factor endowments as wall as for optimum utilisation of existing resources between alternative uses. The G.D.A. has undertaken minor irrigation projects as well as lift irrigation projects in tribal areas. The achievements of minor irrigation are as follows :

Sixty-four minor irrigation schemes including seven lift irrigation schemes were taken up at a cost of Rs. 81.97 lakhs bringing an ayacut of 3,667 acres under irrigation. Forty check-dams were constructed at a cost of Rs. 2.83 lakhs benefiting an ayacut of 240 acres. Subsoil water was also tapped by digging 847 irrigation wells, 141 oil engines and electric motors have been installed so as to bring an area about 700 acres under wet with an expenditure of Rs. 1.38 lakhs.

Indicators are worked out to understand the existing situations in Table 7.2.

In order to assess the benefits of irrigation, R.K. Bai, Chappa Gottali and Thonam villages of Bhadragiri and Panchipenta T.D. Blocks were visited and 5 respondents in each village were contacted. The situation is recorded as follows :

Rastakuntu Bai

This village is situated in tribal development block of Bhadragiri where the lift irrigation schemes was introduced with an ayacut of 40 acres and its estimated cost is Rs. 50,000 benefiting 22 tribal beneficiaries.

Commercial crops like sugarcane, gingilly, turmeric, mesta, etc., were also grown in those areas.

TABLE 7.2 : **Existing situation of Srikakulam District**

	Sub-Plan area	Srikakulam district
1. Percentage of workers in agricultural sector to total population	37.09	32.6
2. Per capita cultivable area of tribals (acres)	0.90	N.A.
3. Percentage of net area sown to the total geographical area	14.6	67.1
4. Percentage of area sown more than once to total geographical area	9.3	22.5
5. Percentage of gross irrigated area to gross cropped area	10.6	45.7

Chappa Gottali

10 acres of land is irrigated under lift irrigation scheme confined to the sample. Almost all tribal respondents are of the opinion that the water supplied through the scheme is not sufficient to maintain the crops throughout the year though the water supplied at the time of sowing and transplantation is just sufficient. As a result of this the yield comes down. More than 80 per cent of the tribal respondents are of the opinion that irrigation wells are of better help for them than lift irrigation schemes.

Thonam

This village is situated in Pachipenta Block. 10.53 acres irrigated in kharif season by tank waters through canals. Paddy was the principal crop grown out of the 10.53 acres. Commercial crops like gingilly, kotta and mesta are also grown in dry lands.

With a view to substantiate the general observations and assessment a depth study was conducted on the purposive sample basis taking five households in each village of Mandasa, Seemalaguda, K. Veeraghattam and Rupai villages of tribal development blocks in Srikakulam district.

The objectives of the study are :

(a) To assess the extent of irrigated area.
(b) To know the impact of irrigation facilities in the agricultural income of tribals; and
(c) To know the views of tribals about the operation of schemes.

The village-wise extent of dry and wet lands owned by tribals in the sample villages is shown in Table 7.3.

TABLE 7.3 : **Dry and wet Lands owned by tribals**

Village	Extent of land (acres)	
	Dry	Wet
1. K.Veeraghattam	8.50	9.50
2. Rupai	6.50	8.00
3. Mandasa	5.00	9.00
4. Seemalaguda	8.50	18.00
Total	28.50	44.50

The average irrigated area per tribal household works out to two acres. The sample-wise irrigation facilities are given in Table 7.4.

TABLE 7.4 : **Samplewise irrigation facilities**

Village	Source wise irrigated area (Acres)			
	Canals	Wells	L.I.	Total
1. K.Veeraghattam	—	9.50	—	9.50
2. Rupai	5.50	2.50	—	8.00
3. Mandasa	—	—	9.00	9.00
4. Seemalaguda	11.00	7.00	—	18.00
Total	16.50	19.00	9.00	44.50

Well irrigation is becoming more popular among tribals besides Dams, Anicuts and L.I. Scheme. Only in Manda village L.I. scheme has been in operation.

The impact of irrigation can be measured in terms of income derived by each household prior and after the provision of irrigation facilities.

TABLE 7.5 : **Impact of irrigation**

Village	Average agrl. income of tribal household (in Rs.)		
	Prior to Irrigation	After the provision of M.I.	(+) (—)
K.Veeraghattam	3420	5130	(+) 1710
Rupai	2380	3570	(+) 1190
Manda	2400	3600	(+) 1200
Seemalaguda	3420	5130	(+) 1710
	2905	4357	1451

The foregoing analysis indicates that a slow but steady change is taking place in the land-use pattern in the tribal areas with the expansion of irrigation facilities. The study reveals that there has been a significant increase of about 50 per cent in the income of the tribal households where irrigation facilities are provided.

Government have been putting forth efforts to improve irrigation facilities with a view to increase the agricultural production. The list of proposed minor irrigation sehemes in tribal areas is given in Table 7.6.

EDUCATION

Since independence promotion of tribal education has been receiving the utmost priority and attention during the Plan periods. State and central governments have recognised that education is the pre requisite for any social change. The main objectives in increasing the educational facilities to tribals is to accelerate the pace of change so as to equip them with

TABLE 7.6 : **List of proposed Minor Irrigation Schemes**

Sl. No.	Name of the Scheme proposed	Panchayat Samiti	Proposed Ayacut (*in acres*)	Estimated cost Rs. (*in lakhs*)
(1)	(2)	(3)	(4)	(5)
1.	Construction of anicut across Mandalagadda near Amiti	Bhadragiri	99	2.0
2.	Construction of diversion wire to feed Kirandabatti reservoir	,,	133	2.60
3.	Construction of an anicut across billstream weir Billidi	Kurupam	89	1.80
4.	Construction of an anicut Chimmadigadda near Cheaperbadi	Bhadragiri	99	2.00
5.	Construction of an anicut near Penivasala to feed Kirandabatti near Dommangi	,,	136	2.70
6.	Construction of an anicut across Buddagatta near Karnanda	,,	198	4.00
7.	Formation of tank across Kindra Beoridigadda at J.K.Padu colony	,,	99	2.00
8.	Construction of an anicut across local Vagu near Marriguda	,,	84	1.80
9.	Construction of an anicut near Pattilikana in Geoipala	,,	84	1.70
10.	Formation of reservoir across Nimmalagadda near Mondemkhallu.	,,	79	1.60
11.	Construction of anicut across Panasamandagadda near Udayapuram	,,	99	2.00

TABLE 7.6—*contd.*

1	2	3	4	5
12.	Formation of Tank near Biyyalavalasa	Kurupam	79	1.60
13.	Formation of tank across Gopalagadda near Geoipala	Bhadragiri	79	1.60
14.	Construction of an anicut near Marripala	,,	74	1.50
15.	Construction of Dam across Gomukhi river to irrigate left side lands of Kosipami and Diguvamandangi villages	Pachipenta	350	6.00
16.	Construction of anicut near Salur Amitigadda Nikkilavalasa village.	Salur	30	9.00
17.	Formation of a new tank near Sirikondavalasa	,,	40	1.50
18.	Formation of a new tank near Seethampeta hamlet of Konivalasa.	Pachipenta	45	1.50
19.	Construction of anicut across Innidigadda near Likkidi	Bhadragiri	76	2.00
20.	Formation of a reservoir across Hanumangadda stream.	Pachipenta	34	0.70
21.	Formation of a reservoir Vomiddi near Vanja	Kurupam	120	3.60
22.	Formation of tank across hill streams near Tikka-bai.	Bhadragi-ri.	50	1.50
23.	Formation of a reservoir near Kindangivalasa	Kurupam	80	2.00
24.	[Formation of tank near Gonepadu near Palakonda	Palakonda	76	1.40
25.	Formation of a reservoir across hill streams Tadikonda—Bhadragiri.	Bhadra-giri.	100	3.00

TABLE 7.6— *contd.*

1	2	3	4	5
26.	Construction of an anicut across Tatisee-lagadda.	Bhadragiri	150	3.50
27.	Construction of ani-cut near Baratangi	Seethampet	30	0.80
28.	Formation of a reser-voir near Vunijatti near Veerupadu	Kurupam	68	2.00
29.	Construction of an anicut across local stream near Kondakonam.	Bhadragiri	34	1.50

Source : Medium term Tribal Sub-plan 1978-83 : Srikakulam district.

knowledge, skill and capabilities necessary for competing with materially advanced non-tribals.

Various studies revealed that education in tribal areas mainly suffer from the triple problems of absenteeism, wastage and stagnation. The low literacy rate 5.3 per cent among scheduled tribes in comparison to the level of general literacy rate of 24.6 per cent (1971 Census) is mainly the result of improper coverage on the one hand, and non-utilisation of existing institutions by the tribals on the other. Special steps were taken to raise the level of education by opening Elementary schools; Ashram schools and Hostels in schoolless isolated areas.

As per the new approach Ashram schools are to be opened for the benefit of small and isolated villages. Ashram schools have become the tools for tackling the triple problems mentioned above prevailing in tribal areas.

The education policy in tribal areas has been modified to ensure enrolment of 100 per cent boys and 90 per cent of girls of school age in the age group of 6 to 11 years. Ashram schools have been proposed for clusters of small and isolated villages and primary schools for big villages with more than

300 population. Within these places priority areas were identified for locating the Ashram schools in villages inhabited by backward tribal groups like the Savara in Srikakulam District, Konda Dora, Gadaba, Samantha in Visakha district; Konda Reddi in East and West Godavary district and Khammam district and Kolam and Thoti in Adilabad district as literacy among tribals living in these areas is less than 1 per cent. The educational policy also envisages upgrading of primary schools to upper primary schools and upper primary schools to High schools. Besides providing them necessary infrastructure; construction of schools and hostel buildings were also given priority.

There are 227 primary schools in T.D. Blocks and another 70 primary schools in non-T.D. Blocks of Srikakulam district functioning exclusively for tribal children. There are 21,267 students at primary level, 731 students at Upper primary level and 243 at higher secondary level studying in the institutions.

Methodology and objectives

A study was conducted in Donubai, Rastakuntu Bai, Mondemkhallu and Thonam villages of three T.D. Blocks; Seethampeta, Bhadragiri and Pachipenta respectively taking five respondents in each village on the purposive sample base:

(a) to assess the causes and magnitude of absenteeism, wastage and stagnation in educational institutions.

(b) to assess and suggest the remedial measures for reducing the incidence of the three evils, namely, absenteeism, wastage and stagnation which are the main hindrances for educational promotion.

Definitions

Wastage

The Hartog Committee has defined wastage as the premature withdrawal of children from school at any stage before completion of the primary course. This definition has given room for certain controversies. There is another definition which centres round the concept of incremental gains in learning outcomes.

Stagnation

Stagnation is nothing but retardation or grade repetition. It is defined as the retention of the pupil in a grade for more than one year on account of unsatisfactory progress. Suppose if a student studies more than one year to pass a grade he is the typical example of stagnation. Regarding this definition there is no difference of opinion.

Absenteeism

Irregular attendance of students to schools. Absenteeism is influenced by socio-economic, psychological and educational factors.

The studies of 20 households cover 102 persons. The age-group-wise distribution of literates is given in Table 7.7 The percentage of literacy among sample household works out to 43.13 per cent (Males 27.45 per cent and Females 15.68 per cent). It indicates that more literates are found among males than that of females. It is to say that the degree of tendency towards education is more amongst males than females in tribal areas.

The levels of education reveals that 79.5 per cent, 43.63 per cent and 6.83 per cent were found in primary, upper primary and secondary levels. More percentage of literates in primary standards reveals that education in tribal areas is of recent origin. To support this argument, age-group-wise literacy percentage is given in Table 7.8.

It further reveals that sending females for education is also a recent origin as 29.5 per cent of females were found in 0—10 age-groups and 6.8 per cent in 10—20 age-groups. Moreover, the percentage of educational people, tends to zero as age-group advances. This supports that education in tribal areas is of recent origin. Out of 61 persons who fell under the age-group of 0—20; 36 are found in educational institutions, either at primary, upper primary or secondary and the rest are falling under 20—70 age-group.

TABLE 7.7 : Age group-wise distribution of literates

Age-group	Primary		Upper Primary		Secondary		Total literates		Illiterates		Total		Total
	Males	Females	Males	Females	Males	Females	Males	Females	Males	Females	Males	Females	
1. 0—10	13	13	—	—	—	—	13	13	7	7	20	20	40
2. 10—20	1	3	4	—	2	—	7	3	5	6	12	9	21
3. 20—30	—	—	2	—	1	—	3	—	—	9	3	9	12
4. 30—40	2	—	—	—	—	—	2	—	6	4	8	4	12
5. 40—50	2	—	—	—	—	—	2	—	3	5	5	5	10
6. 50—60	1	—	—	—	—	—	1	—	5	—	6	—	6
7. 60—70	—	—	—	—	—	—	—	—	—	—	—	1	1
8. 70—	—	—	—	—	—	—	—	—	—	—			
Total	19	16	6	—	3	—	28	16	26	32	54	48	102

TABLE 7.8 : Literacy percentage

	Primary	Upper Primary	Secondary
0—10	26 (59.5%)		
10—20	4 (9.05%)	4 (9.05%)	2 (4.54%)
20—30	—	2 (4.54%)	1 (2.25%)
30—40	2 (4.54%)		
40—50	2 (4.54%)		
50—60	1 (2.25%)		
Total	44		

Class-wise studying

The age-group-wise percentage of students studying are as follows :

Less than 5 years	..	11.11%
5 to 10 years	..	75%
10 and above	..	13.89%

The percentage of students studying standard wise are as follows:

1st Class	..	33.33%
2nd Class	..	22.22%
3rd Class	..	16.67%
4th Class	..	8.33%
5th Class	..	5.56%
6th Class	..	8.33%
7th Class	..	2.78%
8th to 10th Class	..	2.78%

The above data lucidly explains that there is abundant wastage in tribal areas as the pupils join in first class are not coming even up to the primary nor to the secondary standards. The percentage rate shows a declining tendency, vividly to see that the first class centres round 33.33 per cent and the second class centres round 22.22 per cent. This difference is due to stagnation and wastage.

This stagnation presents due to irregular attendance which resembles absenteeism. Cent per cent of the tribal students in tribal areas are being benefited by books, slates, clothes, etc. Even with the maximum efforts, stagnation, wastage and absenteeism are prevailing in tribal areas.

Views of the tribal respondents about education

All tribal respondents in Donubai, R.K. Bai, Mondemkhallu and Thonam villlages are of the opinion that educating their children is helpful to their family, and in developing the mass values. 100 per cent of the tribal respondents are of the opinion that vocational education like carpentry, etc., offers immense values in their life. Due to the educational development 9.8 per cent persons were employed.

Reasons for stagnation

Out of 20 respondents expressed that 70 per cent of stagnation prevails as tribals are agro-based one. They are withdrawing their children without completing their education as they are helpful in agricultural sector. Only 30 per cent of the respondents are of the opinion that stagnation prevails due to withdrawal of children to attend domestic works. Irregular attendance of pupils, low intelligence capacity are also attributing factors for stagnation.

Factors influencing wastage are broadly classified as socio-economic, psychological and educational.

Socio-economic

1. Wage-earning : The insufficient incomes of tribal households drags their children to earn a livelihood.

2. Agro-based families : Almost all tribal families are agro-based. They keep their children more than 70 per cent to help them in agricultural sector rather than sending to schools.

3. Migration : Nearly 29 per cent of tribal are nomadic and semi-nomadic in nature, their migration from one place to another stands as a hurdle for schooling their children.

Psychological factors

1. Student indifference : The indifference of the students about the studies is also one of the factors for wastage as education is a null set inherently.

2. Parents indifference : This is the most important factor for wastage. The parents of the tribal students are indifferent to educate their children as it could not be immediate productive one.

3. Educational : Poor progress in education, medium of instruction, poor environment and poor standard of teaching are the factors influencing wastage.

Factors influencing stagnation

Socio-economic :

1. Irregular attendance due to engagement in pursuits and wage earning.

2. Irregular studies at home due to lack of parental guidance and poor educational environment.

Psychological :

(a) low receptivity, (b) indifference of students towards education, and (c) indifference of parents towards children's education.

Educational :

Alien medium of instruction. Equipped schools and poor teaching are the supporting factors.

ASHRAM SCHOOLS

In view of the peculiar socio-economic conditions prevailing in scheduled areas, several committees and commissions like Renuka Ray Committee and Dhebar Commission have suggested the establishment of Ashram schools as an improvement over the existing pattern of education. The concept of

Ashram school combines both functional and literacy based education relieving the tribal parent of the burden of feeding and clothing his school-going children besides providing a congenial school environment. The main objective of establishing Ashram school is to inculcate in the pupil a sense of service to society and link the school learning with household and community activities. Consequently, Ashram schools are expected to reduce the incidence of absenteeism, wastage and stagnation and improve the standard of education at primary level. Besides free boarding and lodging all the facilities such as books, stationery, dress, warm clothing, etc., to the inmates are provided to favourably motivate the tribal children and their parents towards education.

During 1961, the Ashram schools were introduced by the state government and the number of Ashram schools has been increased to 22 by 1968. At present there are 400 Ashram schools in the state. The tribal parents are convinced of the utility of Ashram schools in promotion of education. With this background, a brief study of six Ashram schools were undertaken in tribal areas of Srikakulam district. The main objectives of the study are as follows :

1. To study the structure and functioning of Ashram schools.
2. To study the shortcomings if any in the programme.
3. To assess the real value of the programme from the point of view of tribal parents.

The following Ashram schools are selected for study :

Block	*Selected school*
1. Bhadragiri	1. Kosingi Bhadra Ashram school.
	2. Tikkabai Ashram school.
2. Seethampet	3. Dharmalakshmipuram U.P. Ashram school.
	4. Donubai U.P. Ashram School.
3. Pachipenta	5. Thonam Ashram school.
	6. Badrayakavalase Ashram school.

All these four Ashram schools and two upper primary Ashram schools are located in the sub-plan area of Srikakulam district.

On an average, each primary Ashram school provides facilities to 72 tribal students. The year of establishment of Ashram schools each selected together with its strength is given in Table 7.9.

TABLE 7.9 : **Establishment of selected Ashram schools**

S. No.	Ashram school	Year of establishment	Strength in 1979-80
1.	Kosingi Bhadra	1964	78
2.	Tikkabai	1976	65
3.	Badrakavalasa	1975	67
4.	Thonam	1976	80
5.	Donubai (U.P.A.)	1972	175
6.	Dharmalakshmipuram (U.P.A.)	1968	170

It can be said that most of the Ashram schools are established after the Naxalite movement. The geo-ethnic environment of the sample schools is discussed in brief :

Kosingi Bhadra is situated in Bhadragiri Block. This village is inhabited by Savaras and Jatapus. The Ashram school was started in the year 1964 and the strength of this school during 1979-80 was 78. Among the total inmates, Jatapus constitute about 80 per cent. The physical infrastructure of this shool comprises six acres of land with building and drinking water well is also located in the compound. The staffing pattern of the school is composed of 1 headmaster, 4 teachers, 1 warden, 2 cooks and 2 kamatis. The headmaster has eight years of service and has been working in this school for the past three years.

Tikkabai is in Gumma Panchayat of Bhadragiri block inhabited by Savaras and Jatapus. The Ashram school was established in the year 1976 and it has a strength of 65 (Savaras—11; Jatapus—54). During the years 1977-78 and 1978-79 fourth and fifth standards were introduced. The school covers three villages and the details of inmates tribe-wise and class-wise (1979-80) are given in Table 7.10.

TABLE 7.10 : **Tikkabai Ashram School (inmates)**

Class	Savaras	Jatapus	Total
I	4	12	16
II	4	12	16
III	2	11	13
IV	1	15	16
V	0	4	4
Total	11	54	65

The staff of this school consists of 1 headmaster, 2 teachers, 1 warden, 1 cook and 2 kamatis.

Badnayakavalasa falls under Padmapuram Panchayat of Pachipenta block. It is a multi-tribal village. The tribal groups inhabiting this village are Jatapus, Konda Doras and Mooka Doras. The Ashram school was established in the year 1975 and the year-wise progress of strength is as follows :

Year	*No. of Inmates*
1975	30
1976	40
1977	50
1978	60
1979	67

The headmaster of this school has 18 years of experience and has been staying in this school since three years.

Thonam, a Panchayat village is situated in Pachipenta T.D. Block. The Ashram school was established in this village with a strength of 59 tribal students in the year 1976. At present it has a strength of 80 and its distribution is shown in Table 7.11.

TABLE 7.11 : **Strength and distribution of Thonam Ashram School**

Class	Jatapus		Konda Doras		Total
	B	G	B	G	
I	6	1	11	11	29
II	2	1	8	1	12
III	17	2	—	—	19
IV	8	2	6	4	20
Total :	33	6	25	16	80

The present employees of this school comprises of 1 headmaster, 1 teacher, 2 cooks and 2 kamatis.

Donubai is also a multi-tribal village located in Seethampet T.D. Block. Upper Primary Ashram school has been functioning in this village with a total strength of 175. The tribe-wise break up is as follows :

Savaras	5
Jatapus	152
Konda Doras	2
Scheduled Castes	16
Total	175

In this school, 12 teachers are functioning besides a headmaster who has got 10 years of service. This school serves 15 villages which are around Donubai village. It is located in a *pucca* building which is under repairs.

Another selected upper primary Ashram school in Dharmalakshmipuram which falls in Neelakanthapuram Panchayat of Seethampet block. This school has six acres of land with one building and a drinking water well. It is manned by 1 headmaster, 7 teachers besides 2 cooks and 2 kamatis. It has a strength of 170. It was established in the year 1968. Jatapu, Konda Dora and Savara children are studying in this school.

TABLE 7.12 : Inmates—classwise (1980)

Block Village	1st	2nd	3rd	4th	5th	6th	7th	
Seethampeta								
1. Donubai	25	43	25	33	20	16	13	—
2. Dharmalaxmi-puram	64	36	8	11	07	21	5	152
Bhadragiri								
3. Kosingi Bha-dra	21	13	13	13	9	9		68
4. Tikkabai	16	16	13	16	04	—	—	64
Pahipenta :								
5. Thonam	29	12	9	20	—	—	—	80
6. Badnayaka-valasa	22	16	17	6	5	—	—	67

The strength of this school is increased from 30 in 1968 to 170 in 1979-80.

The Ashram schools have become more popular in tribal areas owing to certain advantages such as reduced economic burden on parents, better enrolment, ensuing reduction in wastage, and stagnation besides promotion of discipline and self-confidence among students. The tribal parents have realised that the Ashram school system provides good quality of education besides removing shyness among students. It is also said that the constant medical checking and regularity of meals in Ashram schools improved the health conditions of students. In view of the advantages of this education system, the tribals consider the location of an Ashram school in their village as prestige symbol.

HEALTH

Health is wealth is an old adage. A war on ill health or disease is essentially a war on poverty and its evil brood. The state and the central government have been undertaking many curative and preventive schemes realising that the development programmes have no meaning if they do not raise the health standards of the people. The emphasis has been on the control of communicable diseases, improvement of environmental sanitation, provision of maternity and child health service, etc., during the five-year Plans.

During the Fifth Plan a review of health services in tribal areas by the Government of India showed that coverage in some of the regions was extremely poor. In pursuance of decision in the Chief Minister's Conference a working group was set up under the aegies of the Health Ministry to have a special look of these problems and to take concrete measures. Effective health coverage is given top priority in tribal areas in view of malnutrition, chronic diseases among tribals and the ecological factors. It is estimated that the effective coverage area is not beyond five to eight miles radius from the medical and health institutions located in the tribal areas. This is due to the impediments caused by topography distance, indifferent attitude, deep routed superstitions, etc., of tribals. However, topography has been recognised as a deciding factor among the other.

During the five-year plan (as on March 1976) the coverage of the medical and health services in sub-plan area is assessed and it is found that the tribal area which constitutes 10.9 per cent of the state area is having only 6.32 per cent of institutions indicating that a medical institution in tribal area has to cover a larger area than the medical institutions in plain area. However, the real needs of the rural and tribal population are met by the Primary Health Centres. In the whole state, there were 416 Primary Health Centres (P.H.C.) at the rate of one P.H.C. per 672 sq. km. while in the tribal sub-plan area, there are 28 P.H.Cs. at the rate of one P.H.C. per 1082 sq. km. Further, some of the indicators in the field of medical and health with allopathic medical institutions with special reference to tribal areas of Srikakulam district are given below :

1.	Medical institution population ratio	1 : 19665
2.	Medical institution in geographical area ratio	1 : 303 sq. km.
3.	Indoor beds and population ratio	1 : 4275
4.	Sub-centres and population ratio	1 : 21850
5.	Doctors and population ratio	1 : 12291

According to the norms prescribed under revised minimum needs programme, there should be a P.H.C. for every thirty thousand population and one community health worker in each hamlet or for a group of hamlets within a radius of three miles.

The norm is not suitable in tribal area, as the thirty thousand population is scattered beyond a radius of twenty-five miles. Hence it is true to state that the strategy to provide the medical and health services should be different from that of the other areas. The suggested approach is : (i) Service through stationary medical institutions for bigger villages, and (ii) services through mobile medical units for sparsely populated areas.

The diseases like T.B., V.D., malaria, mouth cancer which is caused mainly through reverse smoking and other skin diseases are prevalent in some of the tribal areas.

Since inception of G.D.A. to eradicate Malaria, 131 fever depots were started in tribal areas on a monthly honorarium of Rs. 25 for each depot. Eleven checkposts were opened to arrange preventive treatment and sum of Rs. 1.369 lakhs is spent so far. Besides these, ten medical institutions are functioning in the area to cater to the various medical needs of tribals. Special nutrition programme has been under implementation in the tribal area of this district to arrest malnutrition amongst the tribal children and pregnant women and lactating mothers. Efforts were made to provide drinking water supply in tribal villages.

A case study has been taken up with the following objectives in three T.D. Blocks of Srikakulam district to assess the prevalent diseases and availability of medical facilities.

Three villages, viz., Mondemkhallu in Bhadragiri Block, Donubai in Seethampet Block, Thonam in Pachipenta Block were studied through a purposive sample of three tribal households in each village. The health coverage of sample households is shown in Table 7.13.

TABLE 7.13 : Health coverage

Village and Tribe	No. of persons	No. of persons attacked by		
		Cholera	Small-pox	Malaria
Mondemkhallu				
Savara	21	—	1	8
Jatapu	2	—	—	1
Thonam				
Mooka Dora	6	—	—	4
Konda Dora	11	—	—	7
Jatapu	9	—	—	5
Donubai				
Jatapu	17	—	—	12
Total	66	—	1	37

Out of 66 tribals, 37 tribals were attacked by malaria and were treated in out-patients department and a cure was effected. The percentage of the persons attacked by small-pox is very negligible. It is worked out to 0.69 per cent. 51 per cent of respondents are of the opinion that they are getting cured their seasonal as well as other prevalent diseases, through mobile medical units and N.M.E.P. workers. Regarding maternity aid, there are only three cases recorded in Donubai village of Seethampet Block and the ANM has attended them all. However the tribals are of the opinion that the functioning of A.N.M. is satisfactory. No maternity cases were recorded in Mondemkhallu and Thonam villages of Bhadragiri and Pachipenta Blocks.

Health and Hygiene

Household study was conducted on sample basis in Amity village of Bhadragiri block with the following objectives :

(a) to assess the dietary habits of tribals,
(b) to find out the personal hygiene of tribals, and
(c) to assess the awareness and attitude of tribals towards modern and traditional medicines.

Data was collected for five tribal households in Amity village. All the sample households have thatched houses in rectangular shape. The cattle-sheds form part of their houses in the case of two households whereas they are situated by the side of the houses in another two households. One household did not have cattle-shed.

The staple cereals consumed by the tribals are *ragi*, rice and a millet locally known as *vooda samai sorghum* and Italian millet are the other cereals consumed. *Pakali*, which is the cooked rice of the previous night preserved with much *kanji* (gruel) is the common morning food. The mid-day meal generally consists of *ragi* or other millets, cooked in different forms along with vegetable or dal curry. The cereals are cooked in different ways. Some of them are locally known as *topa*, *ambali*, *dappika*, *kanji*, etc. *Puttu* is a cooked stem preparation and is one of the popular dishes.

Pulses like wild redgram, horsegram, cowpea, French beans, etc., are consumed in small quantities. Many varieties of green leafy vegetables, wild as well as cultivated such as pumpkin leaves, *cannabis hibiscus* (congura), *guruju*, *sirikura*, bamboo shoots, etc., and vegetables like pumpkin, brinjal, cucumber, papaya, etc., are eaten.

During times of scarcity, they supplement their diets with a wide variety of wild roots, and tubes, namely, *pindidumpa*, *teegadumpa*, *pandeigu dumpa*, *pulidumpa* and *chedu dumpa*.

Mango and toddy are available abundantly during the summer and form the mainstay for most of the tribal households. The ripe mangoes are eaten during the months of May and June and the seeds are carefully preserved for future consumption. *Tenkupithu* (mango seed powder) is used to prepare *roti* or *ambali*. Most of the tribal families survive only on these seeds for about two to three months in the year.

The tribals are flesh eaters and consume hunted mutton as well as flesh purchased from shandies.

Milk and milk products are not consumed though there is no taboo. However, consumption of tea is becoming popular.

Mohua liquor and toddy are consumed in excess quantities during the season. Indigenous beers from cereals such as rice, ragi and samai are prepared and consumed.

Pakhal (fermented food) forms the breakfast, ragi for lunch and rice is for supper.

The children are breast-fed up to six months and *ragi* or *sama* gruel forms the first weaning food for children. After a few months they are fed with thc same food as their elders.

Usually no special foods are given during pregnancy. After delivery the woman is usually fed with rice and chilly powder or *ragi* gruel for about ten days or so. The lactating women consumes *paladumpa*, i.e., a variety of tuber supposed to increase lactation.

Ordinary diseases like cold, headache, abdominal pain, small wounds are treated by the tribal as a natural phenomena and does not attribute any cause. From times immemorial they used to apply a number of jungle medicines, herbs, roots and barks from which they prepare concotions which are effective. In fact, the tribals know remedies for all common diseases. The situation is different with chronic and epidemic diseases, they do apply natural remedies and if no relief is observed they attribute the disease to black magic or the supernatural. They believe that sickness is caused in most cases by evil spirits. Such beliefs drive them to the soothsayer or magician. A magic cure is, therefore, a matter of right diagnosis.

The aboriginals generally do not have much faith in the modern medicines, surgical operation is unknown to them. However, once they get over their fear and realise the efficiency of the modern medicines they quickly accept drugs available in hospitals.

Epidemic diseases like cholera, small-pox are believed to travel to their village by certain village goddesses or evil spirits. They usually try to avert epidemics by offering animal sacrifices. A goat and a cock will be offered to the deity. Even emaciating diseases such as tuberculosis are believed to be due to the wrath of evil spirits and black magic. It was observed that some patients in interior villages with lesser contacts with modern civilization are still resorting to bark medicines and magical cures, through soothsayers locally called *vijju* or *guru*.

Forty per cent respondents expressed that their health condition is satisfactory and they are not suffering from diseases. Some of them (20%) have expressed that they go in for traditional medicine for small diseases. Most of them are aware of the functioning of medical institutions and they prefer modern medicine for all diseases.

As regards personal hygiene, it is stated that all the five tribal respondents take a bath daily. Three tribals expressed that they change their clothes once in three days, and the other two change their clothes daily after bath.

Tribals have clearly stated that the N.M.E.P. worker, Health visitor and A.N.M. visit their village weekly to take care of their health problems. They have also stated that the Mobile Medical Officer visit their village once in a month.

SPECIAL NUTRITION PROGRAMME

A study was undertaken on S.N.P. centres to elicit information regarding attitude of tribals towards this programme and mode of functioning of the centres. In this study, four S.N.P. centres, two each from Bhadragiri and Pachipenta blocks were selected. These two T.D. Blocks are situated in Kurupam and Salur taluks respectively. A cross-section of the tribals were interviewed in these villages where S.N.P. centres were located about the benefit of the programme. The information was collected through two structured schedules.

Centre-level schedule

This schedule deals with the population of the village, number of beneficiaries, number of lactating and pregnant mothers and the community inhabiting the village, type of food prepared, served, and lastly the attendance of beneficiaries.

Attitude schedule

This schedule incorporates questions relating to the quality of food supplied to them, and their reactions to the programme.

In all the S.N P. centres fortified *upma* is served. Balahar or soya-fortified Bulgir wheat and salad, oil or refined oil is used in the preparation of *upma*. The beneficiaries are served with 80 grams of oil per day per beneficiary irrespective of their age in the form of a local recipe. In addition to this, food items such as jaggery, black gram, bengal gram, ginger, garlic, onions, turmeric, salt, cummin seed, groundnut, dal, etc., are used in seasoning of preparation. This expenditure is met from the funds of tribal welfare.

The following information was elicited through centre level schedule :

In Pachipenta block, Ethamamivalasa and Kunambandavalasa were selected whereas in Bhadragiri block, J.K. Padu Colony and Levidi were chosen. In this study, Kunambandavalasa is having a total population of 206. Except Gadaba there is no other tribal community in this village. In this village, all the 14 lactating and single pregnant mother were covered by S.N.P. centre. No beneficiary under one year age was available in this village as well as in the centre. There are 17 children below 1-3 years, 18 in the age-group of 3-6 years. All the children in the above-mentioned age-group are covered by S.N.P. Out of total of 50 beneficiaries in this centre, 19 are boys, 16 are girls and 1 pregnant and 14 lactating mothers. All are attending this centre regularly without fail.

Ethamanuvalasa village is a predominantly a Konda Dora village. Except Konda Dora no other community is there in this village. The total strength is 320. The total strength of the centre is 50. 18 beneficiaries are in the age-group 1-3 years and 16 in the age group 3-6 years. 20 are boys and 14 are girls. 10 lactating and 6 pregnant mothers came under the benefit of this programme. In this village, like the previously mentioned village, there is no beneficiary in the age-group 0-12 months. This may be due to non-availability of children below one year.

The third S.N.P. centre, Levidi which is situated in Bhadragiri block, is a Jatapu village. The strength of this centre is 50. The beneficiaries include 26 boys, 18 girls, 1 pregnant and 5 lactating mothers. No non-tribals are noticed in this villages. All the eligible beneficiaries were covered by this programme. In this centre, irrespective of other two centres mentioned previously, the organiser has selected the beneficiaries under health and backwardness criteria.

J.K. Padu colony, the fourth S.N.P. centre in this investigation belongs to Bhadragiri block. Unlike the three centres represented in this appraisal, this village is inhabited by both Savaras, Jatapu and scheduled caste people. There are only three scheduled caste families in this village. With this the total strength of this village is 331. The total number of beneficiaries are 61. Out of 61, 27 are in the age-group of 0-12 months belongs to Savara and 12 in the same age-group belong to Jatapu and three belong to scheduled caste community. The extraordinary feature in this centre is that all the eligible beneficiaries are covered by S.N.P., are in the age-group of 0-12 months only. This is showing the malfunction of the organiser. Out of 19 women served by this centre, two pregnant and 13 lactating women belongs to Jatapu community while the remaining are 3 Savara, one S.C. lactating mothers. Judging from the above facts, the study in this centre reveals that this centre is covering only lactating, and pregnant mothers and children below one year leaving the remaining eligible age groups.

The following conclusions are arrived after the visit of these 4 centres. In all the centres, except at J.K. Padu colony, the number of beneficiaries are not more than 50. The total beneficiaries in J.K. Padu colony are sixty-one since it is inhabited by different sections of the people. More number of pregnant and lactating mothers are found in this village. While 0-1 month age-group beneficiaries are not covered under S.N.P., in Ethamanuvalasa and Kunambandavalasa in Pachipenta block, all the age-groups, i.e., 0-12, 1-3, and 3-6 years are engulfed by the benefits of S.N.P. in Levidi of Bhadragiri block. The reversal phenomenon was observed in J.K. Padu colony village in Bhadragiri block as only children below one year are covered. This is an obscure one. In all the centres visited, cent per cent attendance is noticed. A helper prepares food in all the centres. It is observed that irrespective of age, the *upma* is being served equally to all the beneficiaries. The organiser is not facing any difficulties in manning the centre.

It is observed in all the centres that the food distributed at the centre in plates and many children carry them away to homes. In many instances, the food is shared by the family members and there is a lot of dilution to the benefit of feeding.

Attitude of the community

In the 4 S.N.P. centres where the study was undertaken, a cross-section of tribal parents of the beneficiaries and the pregnant and lactating women were interviewed to elicit their views about the programme. The parents informed that food is given on all days without any interruption. There is no complaint about the quality of food and they feel that the quantity of food supplied to each beneficiary may be raised as it is serving as a substitute to breakfast. All the perents interviewed are aware that the feeding is aimed to improve the health of their children. They expressed their satisfaction about the feeding programme as this programme is saving their children from starvation in times of scarcity of food, and also keeps their children from resorting to various sorts of harmful foods available in mess. It was noticed during the interview that the parents are sending their children voluntarily to the feeding centre as soon as the organiser approaches them for enlistment. The present time was convenient for all the areas. Some people have expressed their desire that old people above 60 years may also be covered by this programme. Old members may be fed as the food given by S.N.P. centres will energise the old people. Some sections of people argue that all the family members should be brought under this programme, as they lack good health due to their poor economic conditions. If they are fed with *upma* in the S.N.P. programmes they will also be healthy like their children, without suffering with various sorts of nutrition diseases due to malnutrition.

On the whole it is observed that the programme is functioning well to the satisfaction of tribals. The doctors of Primary Health Centres visit these centres regularly.

COMMUNICATION

Roads and communications are the arteries of economic progress and they are indispensable for successful implementation of developmental programmes in any area. Inaccessibility contributes to chronic backwardness as lack of transport and communication facilities rendered the movement of man and material difficult on one hand and it resulted in isolation of the tribal hamlets on the other. In order to fill up the gap in communications and transport system, to break the partial isolation and ensure quick movement of men and material and services; adequate road network has been proposed by the G.D.A./ITDA of Srikakulam.

During G.D.A. period a realistic need based communication programme for laying of arterial and link roads in tribal areas was taken up. Better communications were provided to market centres. An amount of Rs. 50 lakhs was spent on laying the important arterial roads, viz., Udayapuram to Seethampet, Kurupam to Podi and Santhospuram to Pedagothili. So far 79.49 km. were completed. Besides, an amount of Rs. 30 lakhs was spent for laying 53.45 km. of eight important link roads, viz., Karlimma to Marripadu, Cheepi to Mandasa, Pedapadmapuram to Nelabonthu, Symalapuram to Vondrajola, Kurupam to Muliguda, Kadaripuram to Elwinpet to Ramannaguda, Makhuva to Duggeru and Veeraghattam to Donubai.

The network of roads in these three Samitis fall short of the required needs. In Bhadragiri Panchayat Samiti there is one all-weather road connecting Bhadragiri with Parvatipuram via Kurupam. Another road connecting Bhadragiri and Mondemkhallu and third one Bhadragiri with Kadaripuram. In Seethampet Panchayat Samiti there is one road connecting Mondemkhallu via Donubai and Neelakantapuram. Seethampet is connected with Palakonda by all-weather road. The rest of the places are connected with trucks where no mode of transport can ply. In Panchipenta Panchayt Samiti there is one road connecting Makkuva via Salur—the rest of the places are connected by trains.

The interior-most parts are generally cut off from the main road. The only approach in most of the cases being pathways. In Bhadragiri Panchayat Samiti some of the sorrounding villages lie almost 20 km. away from the nearest motorable road. The approach to the shandy weekly market lies through an area which is primarily hilly and rocky and thickly forested. Likewise in Seethampet Panchayat Samiti Pulla and other interior places are devoid of motorable road. In Pachipenta Samiti bordering Orissa State many places are devoid of pucca roads. On the way many streams have to be waded. Roads have been constructed to interconnect the shandies but their connection to the villages have been neglected. This poses great hardship to the villagers who have to carry their headloads.

SRI VISAKHA GRAMEEN BANK—AN AGENCY FOR INSTITUTIONAL FINANCE

Sri Visakha Grameen Bank came into existence from 1976 onwards under Rural Bank Programme sponsored by Government of India under 20-Point economic programmes. The State Bank of India sponsored and started Sri Visakha Grameen Bank at Srikakulam as its headquarters. It started a number of branches in Srikakulam, Vizianagaram and Visakhapatnam headquarters. To cater to the needs of tribal people Sri Visakha Gremeen Bank branch was started in December 1976 at Gummalaxmipuram. This branch adopted 74 tribal villages and extended its help to the residents of these 74 villages. A second branch was started at Seethampet in April 1977 to cater to the needs of tribals of Palakonda taluk.

The Seethampet branch adopted 22 villages to facilitate the tribals of this particular area. Sri Visakha Grameen Bank adopted almost all interior villages whereas the Andhra Bank adopted mostly roadside villages in Seethampet Panchayat Samiti. In Pachipenta Samiti area Sri Visakha Grameen Bank started in June 1978 at Pachipenta and adopted 31 tribal villages. Very recently another two branches of Sri Visakha Grameen Bank started at Mondemkhallu in Bhadragiri Block area and another at Makkuva in Pachipenta Samiti area to facilitate the tribals to get the credit requirements from these branches.

The performance of these branches have been studied. Regarding the performance of the Pachipenta branch, so far 145 tribals have been provided with Rs. 1,41,000 to purchase plough-bullocks. All these 145 tribals have been identified by the concerned Block Development Officer and part subsidy was paid to Sri Visakha Grameen Bank by I.T.D.A. These tribals used to engage hired plough bullocks to till their lands. They have to incur heavy expenditure towards hiring these plough bullocks. Regarding repayment of loans it is assessed from the Bank Manager that the tribals are enthusiastic to pay the loan amount, and are approaching the Bank for further advances to improve their agriculture. In addition to the above 58 tribal farmers were sanctioned Rs. 31,000 as loan for purchasing the milch animals during 1978-79. Most of them were able to utilise the amount in a proper way and majority of them are supplying the milk to the milk chilling centres. A further, Rs. 51,000 was sanctioned for crop loans. Last year, two irrigation wells were provided to benefit the tribals of Pachipenta Samiti area at Rs. 5,000.

Regarding the performance of Seethampet Samiti branch, so far 317 persons have been issued short term loans to a tune of Rs. 2,11,015 for purchase of plough bullocks. Further 331 persons have been sanctioned crop loan to a tune of Rs. 1,05,150 and 185 persons have been sanctioned to a tune of Rs. 1,48,000 for starting business in the Samiti area.

Gummalaxmipuram branch turned out remarkable business that is so far benefiting 2,324 persons to the tune of Rs. 16,45,000.

It is noticed from the case studies pertaining to the three

tribal development blocks, viz., Bhadragiri, Seethampet and Pachipenta that Sri Visakha Grameen Bank advanced loans not only for agricultural purpose but also to the maintenance of families either as short term or medium term or long term loans on the basis of subsidy, i.e., purchase of milch animals.

Essence of case studies

Bhadragiri

The bank advanced a loan of Rs. 800 to purchase plough bullocks to till 4 acres of wet and 1.50 acres of dry land. Prior to the sanction of subsidy, the tribal respondents had land but used to hire the bullocks. After thes anction of a loan, they not only cultivate the land but are also getting an additional income by carting. In this way, the Grameen Bank is helpful to tribals by advancing loans on subsidy from I.T.D.A./G.D.A.

Seethampet

The Grameen Bank has advanced a loan of Rs. 600 to Mr. Anikadanji to reclaim land of 2 acres on subsidy basis. Prior to the sanction of loan he was striving hard for a means of livelihood. Soon after the sanction of loan, the land was reclaimed and is now under cultivation. Here the loan component acts as a catalyst to improve the economic status of the tribals. On cultivation of land the net income increase of the individual is Rs. 600.

The bank also sanctioned a loan of Rs. 1000 to Mr. Ramaswamy, on subsidy to purchase an oil engine without pump set to cultivate an area of 2 acres of wet and 1 acre of dry. Here the net increase in income due to the sanctioned loan is about Rs. 500. The Bank is granting loans for irrigation purpose also.

In Seethampet, the bank advanced loans for irrigation purpose, i.e., a well and to reclaim land. In this way, Bank acts to boost tribal agricultural and non-agricultural earnings.

Pachipenta

In this block also Sri Visakha Grameen bank has sanctioned loan of Rs. 800 on 50 per cent subsidy basis to Mr. Kothadu

Thorta by caste Konda Dora, aged about 40 years of Gogandavalasa village. He purchased a pair of plough bullocks to cultivate 2 acres of wet and 2 acres of dry land. Prior to the subsidy he was hiring the bullocks with the greatest of difficulty. Now he is tilling his land but is also hiring additional bullocks. He is getting an additional income of Rs. 600.

Mr. K. Narasaiah of Gogandavalsa village, Konda by caste aged about 54 years, cultivating 2 acres of wet and 2 acres of dry in the village has been sanctioned a loan of Rs. 800 to purchase a pair of bullocks on 50 per cent subsidy. Due to sanction of loan he is earning net income of Rs. 1100 out of which the net increase income is about of Rs. 450.

In this way, the Visakha Grameen Bank acts as a catalyst not only to boost tribal earnings, but also helps in adopting modern cultivation practices by tribal farmers.

The above studies represent in fair measure the progress that has been achieved in the tribal areas of Srikakulam district in the recent years. One fact which is pertinent and needs no repetition is that the government and administration will have to strive hard and continue its efforts to achieve social and economic progress. With the increase in population the task is not going to become easier, but will assume more complex proportions. Similarly, the struggle and fight against poverty is ceaseless and efforts with renewed vigour will have to be made to bridge the gap between the poor and the rich. The World Bank Report of August 1980 has highlighted the following facts :

> Political support for human development cannot be taken for granted. The poor frequently are politically weak. They are often too sick, uneducated, geographically dispersed and busy to be politically active. Influential elites, particularly large landowners, may oppose human development programmes if they feel that their power and status might be undermined. They might feel, for example, that educated children are less likely to settle for working in serf-like coditions on haciendas or plantations.
>
> Even if there is no direct opposition, extent and form of human development programmes will generally be influenced

> by keen political competition for limited tax revenues. Because policy makers generally believe in urban areas as do the most politically active of the people who benefit from public services, these programmes tend to suffer from urban bias (though reductions in urban social expenditures do not necessarily lead to increase in rural expenditures). But the health and education facilities available even to urban elites in poor countries are generally inferior to those available to the middle class in rich countries. A major political challenge of the 1980s will be to adapt and extend programmes to the poor, particularly those in rural areas.

However, after all that is said in this study, in Srikakulam, the achievement has been for everyone to see particularly in the fields of agriculture, and minor irrigation. As seen from the results of the Bench Mark Survey household incomes have gone up and literacy levels are also improving. The role of institutional credit has been another major factor in influencing the trend of growth and in this regard the Grameen Banks have done yeoman service. In the field of education and health, Ashram schools are particularly been a great success and have become prestige symbols of the area. In the case of health programmes the very fact that health programmes have become accepted ushered in a new value system.

8

DYNAMICS OF RURAL DEVELOPMENT IN TRIBAL AREAS

All fair-minded persons will have to admit that it is absolutely monstrous that a class of human beings with bodies similar to our own, with brains that can think and with hearts that can feel, should be perpetually condemned to a low life of utter wretchedness and servitude, and mental and moral degradation, and that permanent barriers should be placed in their way so that it should be impossible for them even to overcome them and improve their lot. This is deeply revolting to our sense of justice. I believe one has only to put oneself mentally in their place to realise how grievous this injustice is?

—*Gopal Krishna Gokhale*

THE tribal areas prior to independence were neglected in terms of development because the British rulers followed a policy of isolation with regard to the tribals. The following considerations prevailed in policy-making for tribal areas: (a) administration of tribal areas was difficult and unrewarding; (b) the policy of isolating tribal to keep them from politioal influence; (c) leaving the tribals to live in their own world as they constituted an altogether different economic and cultural entity. This helped the tribals to maintain their identity and cultural traditions but did not help them in terms of economic prosperity. A number of provisions were made in the Indian Constitution to safeguard the interests of tribals. These sections are Article 341 and 342. Article 275 provides special grants-in-aid from the Consolidated Fund of India to states for implementation of special developmental programmes for these areas in order to raise the development of these areas to general level.

Slack progress

The progress of developmental programmes and different approaches after independence have not necessarily resulted in the best possible solution to the problem of development of tribal areas. A number of commissions and reports have pointed out inadequacies in the existing set-up. The chief of these commissions were Shilu Ao Committee, 1969; Verrier Elwin Committee, 1960; Dhebar Committee, 1961 and more recently appraisal reports on tribal development, 1973 by the Planning Commission. Most of these committees had certain common conclusions, namely: (a) in tribal blocks the minimum and specific needs of the tribals have not been met; (b) the programmes adopted did not necessarily conform to their social, economic progress and hence the programmes appeared to be imposed from above; (c) there was a reluctance of personnel to work in tribal areas and lack of understanding of tribal culture and sentiments; and (d) there was no bias in favour of the tribals which should have been the main characteristic of most of the developmental programmes.

Inertia in tribal areas

Tribals as we know keep to themselves and it is no wonder that the tempo of development has been very slack and tardy in these areas. The factors which account for slow development of tribal areas are their isolation, illiteracy, exploitation by various agents and their, socio-economic backwardness. These factors constitute the reasons why tribal development is different from normal development. Added to this fact is that most tribals live in hilly or rocky areas where no proper assessment has been made of the natural resources endowments and to reach them lack of communications and a difficult terrain pose their own problems.

In Srikakulam district most of these problems existed during the 1960s and it is only of late that things have started to change. Till 1973, there was no District Tribal Welfare Officer and all funds were being routed through the Zilla Parishad and the District Social Welfare Officer. From the Fourth Plan onwards funds increased. Till recently no surveys for development of the area had been made except for the Malayappan and Aiyappan Reports which were written in the days of the Madras Presidency. The problem of poor communications existed all along and it is only after the fourth plan period and the coming of the G.D.A. that emphasis have been laid on the construction of roads. Amongst the agencies for administering the area were the District Collector, who is the agent to government for tribal areas. He is assisted by the Sub-Collector who is an Assistant Agent and Civil Criminal Judge of the Area. The Sub-Collector also has to assist the Collector in keeping a watch over the developmental activities initiated by the blocks and reports to the Collector directly what is going on. The other agency is the G.D.A., set up by the Government of India during the Fourth Plan period. Another branch of the administration operating in the Agency area is the G.C.C. which is responsible for purchasing minor forest produce and agricultural produce of the tribals at a fair price. It is also responsible for setting up domestic requirement depots in the deep forest areas and sells consumer items at fair prices to the tribals. For all these agencies except the G.C.C. the District Collector is the kingpin and is the Chief Administrative Officer. The District Collector functions directly under the State Government and is responsible for proper implementation of government policies, programmes and the chief coordinator of all developmental activities at the district level. It will be of interest to note that there are no voluntary agencies functioning in this area except for some activity by the Bharatiya Adimjati Sangh with its head-quarters in New Delhi.

When discussing critically the aims and objectives of the government in ameliorating the conditions of tribals in Srikakulam district the following factors have to be kept in mind: (a) Girijan unrest from 1968 to 1972 and its implications, (b) the institutional framework existing at that time. It is, therefore, quite clear that the environment and mood necessitated the government to achieve rapid economic development in the tribal areas of Srikakulam district and to wean away the tribals from the cult of violence. The government had already sanctioned a post of Special Deputy Collector for Tribal Welfare stationed at Bhadragiri to oversee all developmental avtivities and protection of tribal's land problems. Similarly, the Government of India also sanctioned G.D.A. and thereby introduced a big slice of funds into the tribal areas for ameliorating the economic conditions of the tribals. It can, therefore, be said that there was harmony between the organisational environment and organisational goals and the directives of government were very clear.

New deal for tribals

For the first time since independence a major effort had been made to undo the injustice that has been perpetrated on the tribal people of Srikakulam district. It was required of the project to identify targeted number of families and expenditure had to be incurred within a targeted period of time. Here, it may be mentioned that the funds received from the Government of India and implementation of programmes and policies was not subject to the control of the state government but was the direct responsibility of the Government of India. Regarding the procedures and methods adopted to implement the programmes of the GDA there was lot of responsibility delegated to the Collector and Project Officer and hence the goals of organisational autonomy were given effect. To the greatest extent possible, decentralisation ensured that non-bureaucratic methods of coordination and control were adopted. This to a large extent helped in quick implementation of programmes.

Responsibility of government and administration

In the absence of any other agency other than the government agency functioning in the field it is but natural that the administrator assumed a very important role. It has often been pointed out that rural development of backward areas is solely the responsibility of the administration. Government policies and programmes have necessarily to begin with the effectiveness of the administrative set-up to bring about change in the rural sector. Even those programmes which are designed for people's participation cannot succeed without adequate government support. Therefore, it is very important to lay emphasis on government's commitment, administrative leadership and guidance and the administrator has to act as 'a social entrepreneur'. In this context it may be pointed out that in June 1969, the Agency areas of Srikakulam district had been declared as disturbed areas and so there was no question of any other agency participating in developmental work in these areas except the government. Hence the responsibility of the government was not only to obliterate memories of the past bitterness, but also to draw the Girijan away from a stance of positive hostility. It was in this environment that the G.D.A. was set up and, it was therefore heavily dependent on the strength and support of the government for fulfilling the hopes and aspirations of the tribal people.

Institutional bottlenecks

Administration in this sense serves two purposes that is it has to frame a strategy for rapid development, and has to solve the day-to-day problems of the tribals. Even though the G.D.A. had its own subject matter specialists to assist the Project Officer it was, however, heavily dependant on the district administration for giving full effect to its avowed policies and the one problem was that of personnel because institutions belonging to different departments located in the project area owed their loyalties to the respective departmental heads. It has often been pointed out that officers are posted to serve in agency areas when it is a question of "probation, promotion and punishment". With this kind of approach it is doubly difficult to make programmes a success. To augment the efforts of the G.D.A. a special engineering wing was sanctioned for expediting irrigation and road works. However, in other departments for instance, health, there was a usual constraint of non-availability of medicines and non-placement of doctors in charge of the public health centres.

Similarly with regard to schools the constraints faced were lack of proper accommodation, teaching equipment and non-availability of teachers. Most of the teachers were unwilling to work in the tribal areas owing to non-availabilty of accommodation and distance from the home town. Similarly, in the field of irrigation and agriculture, weaning away the tribals from *Podu* cultivation posed a big problem and to bring about 'acculturisation' of tribals was difficult. It is a known fact that tribals are used to subsisting on primitive type of agricultural practices like eating fruits and leaves, and the idea of growing commercial crops like paddy, wheat were quite foreign to them. To this extent the block staff helped in providing the extension methods for financing the tribals to change their past practices. As a matter of fact, the Girijan Development Agency was specifically oriented towards bringing about change in agriculture and irrigation.

An administrative landmark

The setting up of the G.D.A. is a landmark in the concept of approaches to tribal development. It was a clean break from the earlier factors of relying on the Panchayat Raj institutions. Any administrative reforms have to have a professed goal here namely, rapid development of the tribal areas of Srikakulam district. Three broad categories of goals can be identified: improved order, improved method, improved performance. Let us consider each of these objectives and examine the type of reform which they imply.

Improved order

The tribal unrest in Srikakulam district was against the old order and authority that prevailed during the time. Therefore, a new set of values was substituted for old ones to bring about rapid change. This meant bringing about a change in the entire approach to development of tribal areas. So, procedural reforms were carried out and the district administration was not dependant on the state government for massive injection of funds which entailed cumbersome procedures and time wasting remedies.

Improved Methods—structural reforms

In bureaucracies there is always a tendency to adhere to established procedures and methods of work. However, to induce rapid development and to make the administrator assume the role of a change agent, it is necessary to bring about improved method and technical reforms. To this extent the G.D.A. brought about immense amount of financial delegation and it was free from the normal budget control. One of the features of the scheme was that programmes could be designed to suit local needs and hence a considerable amount of flexibility of method was ensured. There was no difficulty about flow of funds because the government gave a completely free hand to the district administration to plan and execute schemes which brought about relief to the tribal people. Major goals were very clear and well articulated and effectively translated into various action programmes. Improvement in methods, increased efficiency and better implementation of programmes resulted in greater degree of realisation of basic goals.

Improved performance

Improved performance was an equally important task because the impact of schemes had to be made speedily to wean away the tribals from violence . . . One of the features of the G.D.A. was that in its governing body non-officials were also members, and hence, the degree of popular participation in programmes was ensured. The governing body which was headed by the Collector thus acted as a watchdog and also was a good source of feedback for correcting and improving the scope and content of programmes. The unrest in the tribal areas widened the distance that had developed between the tribals and the administration. The needs of the tribals required urgent attention. To bridge the gap between the people and the administration was the need of the hour. Therefore, it can be said that to suit the new environment and milieu a certain degree of administrative reforms was necessary and that was carried out in the case of the Srikakulam tribal administration.[1]

It would be necessary here to clarify what is meant by growth. 'Growth' denotes increase in production or output. It implies an increase in income manifested over a given period of time. It also applies to other spheres, for example, educational growth in terms of more graduates at various levels in different frameworks. Growth also means process or accumulation of wealth and is quantitative in nature.

'Development' is different from growth in the sense that it implies change in institutional structure and activities rather than in output. Development constitutes institutional unfolding, restructuring and consolidation and specifically (a) diversification and broadening of the basis of activities, (b) specialisation and rationalisation, (c) institutionalisation and coordination of behaviour. Generally, it would mean for instance setting up of new and specialised type of schools, better method of allocation and utilisation of resources, providing more opportunities for employment, emergence of specialised frameworks of mobilisation and decision-making, rationalisation in the process of government and administration and stratificational development, which would imply more mobility amongst groups.

'Transformation' on the other hand is a process in which the changes transcend and reshape existing values and institutional terms of reference and which forms new patterns of behaviour.

'Modernisation' by contrast, is specifically a process of increasing societal (and individual) openness and flexibility; of purposive exposure to and ability to solve problems of growing complexity, of 'absorbing' difficulties and reversal and of creation of novel opportunities. It is essentially, in other words, a legitimation of a potential for a contiuous rearrangement of existing commitments and for an untrammelled flow; exchange and mobilisation of all social 'goods'.[2]

Financing

By 31 March, 1978, Rs. 231.50 lakhs were released to Srikakulam G.D.A. During 1978-79 a sum of Rs. 250 lakhs was provided. Statement indicating releases/expenditure since the inception of G.D.A, up to 1977-78 (April-March) is shown in Table 8.1.

It was initially envisaged that about 10,000 tribal families and 50,000 tribal participants would be covered under various

TABLE 8.1 : **Statement indicating releases/expenditure since the inception of G.D.A. up to 1977-78**

(*Rs. in lakhs*)

State/T.D. Project	IV Plan up to 1973-74		1974-75		1975-76		1976-77		1977-78		Total releases	Expenditure
	Releases	Expenditure	Releases	Expenditure	Releases	Expenditure	Releases	Expenditure	Releases	Expenditure		
1	2	3	4	5	6	7	8	9	10	11	12	13
Srikakulam (13-7-72)	78.00	71.25	32.50	32.20	33.36	29.82	44.64	55.23	43.00	43.00	231.50	231.50

economic development programmes in a period of five years. Because of the extended period of its operation the target of the coverage of tribal families was raised to 70,000 in case of G.D.A. Srikakulam. The core programme of economic development relates to tribal agriculture, horticulture, land reclamation, land development, soil conservation measures, control of shifting cultivation, minor irrigation, development of animal husbandry, encouragement of forest-based industries, debt redemption, land restoration, land records and survey. Ordinarily the Agency will subsidise 50 per cent to 75 per cent of the requirements on each programme and the balance 25 per cent to 50 per cent is expected to be met by the tribal beneficiaries from institutional and other resources. The cost on communications (rural as well as arterial) is to be borne cent per cent by the Tribal Development Agency.

Fifth Plan approach

After the completion of the G.D.A. which was designed for a specific purpose to achieve quick rapid growth in agriculture and irrigation, a new approach to tribal development has been envisaged by the Government of India. The new successor organisation is known as the Integrated Tribal Development Agency. In the beginning of the Fifth Plan a new approach was adopted for tribal development where all areas with more than 50 per cent tribal concentration would clearly identify and special plans were prepared. The basic objectives of the new task in the Sixth Plan can be defined as follows :

(i) the entire tribal population, whether living in 'areas of tribal concentration' or outside, will be covered by suitable developmental programmes during the Sixth Plan period;

(ii) the gulf between the level of development in the tribal areas and the surrounding areas will be generally bridged by the end of the Sixth Plan, and in the case of more backward tribal areas, in the course of another five years, i.e., by the end of the Seventh Plan; and

(iii) the tribal communities outside the tribal areas will be helped to attain the general level of development in the area by the end of the Sixth Plan or latest by the end of the Seventh Plan in the case of more deprived communities.

The socio-economic situation of tribal communities varies considerably from one area to another. Therefore, it is not possible or even desirable to have uniform prescriptions for all of them. The Constitution already provides for adequate flexibility in legal, procedural and administrative framework so that the problems of each specific area can be attended to effectively through suitably administrative action and developmental programmes. However, the broad approach to tribal development will have to depend on the pattern of distribution of tribals in area and the level of their economy. In predominantly tribal areas, area approach with focus on the development of the tribal communities will be suitable for dispersed tribals, community-oriented programmes will have to be evolved, and in the case of primitive groups, which are facing special problems and are small in size, a very cautious individualised approach will have to be adopted lest their precarious balance is irretrievably lost. Thus, the problem of tribal communities will continue to be tackled in terms of the following three categories, namely—

(a) Areas of tribal concentration,
(b) Dispersed tribals in other areas, and
(c) Primitive tribal communities.

Thus, raising of economic conditions of tribals in the immediate future and enabling them to come up to the general level in a period of twelve years will require:

(i) consolidation of protective measures initiated in the Fifth Plan;
(ii) major thrust in educational and health services; and
(ii) full employment economy in tribal areas by the end of the Sixth Plan.

While the above priority frame will be valid for the tribal development efforts at the national level, it will have to be flexible in its application to specific regions. It may be recalled that the first premise in tribal development is that there cannot be a formula for all situations and all territories. The central problem of the area will determine the priority schedule for the new efforts. The national policy frame will provide the broad guidelines within which the details have to be worked out in the regional context.

Methodology of financing the programmes

It will be necessary to arrive at a first order projection with regard to the level of investment from various sources in the tribal region during the Fifth Plan period. All sectors including the financing institutions and autonomous organisations will have to give a higher priority for programmes of these areas. The resources for the sub-plan will comprise: State Plan outlay; sectoral outlays in the Central Ministries for tribal areas; special central sector allocation for tribal areas; and institutional finance.

With a view to ensure that a dent is made in the basic problems facing those regions during the Fifth Five Year Plan the programmes may be categorised into core and other programmes. The core programmes will comprise the following:

(i) credit and marketing including regulation of tribal markets and money lending:
(ii) preparation of land records including restoration of land alienated;
(iii) crop husbandry, agricultural extension, training of farmers and horticulture;
(iv) minor and medium irrigation programmes;
(v) forest based programmes, problems of forest villagers and forest labourers;
(vi) the problem of special groups including shifting cultivators, extremely backward communities and those effected by major projects;
(vii) primary road network linking important markets and growth centres;
(viii) problems of tribal artisans facing competition from organised sector;

(ix) elementary education including citizen education ;
(x) medical and Health Programmes;
(xi) rationalisation of administrative structure and personnel policies;
(xii) strengthening of traditional panchayats and voluntary organisations; and
(xiii) techno-economic survey and evaluation studies.

A comparative approach

It would be perhaps necessary at this point to compare and contrast the two organisations, namely, the G.D.A. and the I.T.D.A. whereas in the G.D.A. the approach was to cover a targeted number of families in the tribal areas; the I.T.D.A. is more area flexible. The following will illustrate the points of contrast between the two programmes.

TABLE 8.2 : **Compare and contrast of the two organisations, GDA and ITDA**

G.D.A. & Prior to G.D.A.	*I.T.D.A.*
1. Lack of Area approach	1. Area approach adopted
2. Meagre investments from general sector.	2. Flow of general sector funds ensured.
3. Absence of integrated approach in programme formulation and execution and persistence with systematic budget and isolated sectoral approach.	3. Integrated approach was adopted. Integration of area, programmes and finances.
4. Absence of special programmes for primitive and backward tribal groups.	4. Special programmes for primitive groups were taken up.
5. Lack of perspective plan.	5. Perspective plans were prepared
6. Lack of coordination.	6. Coordination of different departments achieved.
7. Mainly agriculture oriented project with emphasis on irrigation Other sectors like education and health were neglected.	7. Integrated approach for uniform development of all the sectors was adopted.
8. Regulatory aspect was not kept under the control of the G.D.A.	8. Regulatory and development aspects were combined.
9. Single line of administration was not ensured.	9. Single line of administration is ensured.
10. Meagre staff.	10. Subject matter specialists posts were created in ITDA and all the Institutions were kept under the control of the Project Officer.

Social inputs Vs. economic development

The founding fathers of the Constitution were aware of the contradictions in Indian society. Swami Vivekananda, Mahatma Gandhi, Pandit Nehru and Dr. Ambedkar constantly stressed the aspect of caste and society and the social hierarchy which resulted in discrimination against the poor and weaker sections. India had to catch up with the Western world in as short a span of time as possible within the democratic framework as laid down by the Constitution. The Constitution is particularly articulate in respect of equality, liberty, and fraternity. As a result fundamental rights are the most important part of our Constitution and certain guidelines in the shape of the directive principles of state policy have been stressed. No government can afford to ignore these directives laid down in the Constitution. Added to this is the special reference and provision for protection and upliftment of weaker sections like Scheduled Castes and Scheduled Tribes. All these ideas are closely linked with the foundation of a welfare state in India. It may be remembered that our Constitution has by and large been designed on the British parliamentary model, and hence, it was inevitable that the concept of a welfare state would also seep into the minds of the Constitution makers. Most leaders after independence have stressed the aspect of not only ensuring political democracy but also economic democracy in India. It is towards this end that planning was adopted as the most rational method for increasing production and proper allocation of resources and removing imbalances in Indian society.

We have seen how the successive plans has stressed the removal of poverty and the most significant were the Fourth and Fifth plans. This has already been discussed in our earlier chapters. It would be relevant to discuss the progress to be achieved in the Sixth Plan. The Sixth Plan aims at a growth rate of 5.2 per cent per annum in gross domestic product and of 3.3 per cent per annum in the per capita income.

A major aim of the Plan is to achieve self-reliance by ensuring speedy development of the economy, reduction in the dependence on foreign aid, diversification of domestic production and a consequential reduction in imports for certain critical commodities and the promotion of exports.

With a view to ensuring speedy development, emphasis has been laid on the core and critical sectors of the economy with power getting a substantial outlay. In the agricultural sector, an outlay of Rs. 5,695 crores has been provided, the outlay for the rural development being Rs. 5,346 crores; special area programme Rs. 1,480 crores; irrigation and flood control Rs. 13,160 crores; energy Rs. 26,535 crores; industry and minerals Rs. 15,018 crores; transport Rs. 12,412 crores.

The development strategy visualises accelerated progress towards removal of poverty, generation of gainful employment, technological and economic self-reliance, and strengthening the agricultural and industrial base.

Also, consistent with the overall social and economic objectives sustained efforts will be made to have sharper redistribution raising the share of the poor section in national income, consumption and in the utilisation of public services.

Thus, specific action programmes like the national rural employment programme and other anti-poverty schemes meant for selected target groups have been made an essential component of the Plan strategy.

The percentage of the people below the poverty line is postulated to decline from 48.44 per cent at the beginning of the Plan to 30 by the end of the Plan. The Plan programmes aim at increasing employment from 151 million standard person years to 185 million standard person years. The monthly per capita consumption of foodgrains will go up from 12.95 kg to 14.32 kg and life expectancy will increase from 52.6 to 55.1 for males and 51.6 to 54.3 for females by the end of the Plan.

The Plan gives high priority to the minimum needs programme with a provision of Rs. 5,808 crores as against Rs. 2,607 crores in the Fifth Plan provision of free or subsidised services through public agencies will improve the consumption levels of those living below the poverty line and thereby improve the productivity efficiency of the poor, especially in the rural areas.

Under the minimum needs programme, the plan aims at enrolling 95 per cent of children in age-group 6-11 in the first stage and 50 per cent in the age-group 11-14 by the end of the

Plan and universal enrolment in the age-group 6-14 by 1980.

Rural health infrastructure would be further strengthened, the ultimate objective being to have one community health volunteer for every village or a population of one thousand; one sub-centre for a population of 5,000 in the plains and 3,000 for hilly and tribal areas; one P.H.C. for 30,000 population in the plains; and 20,000 hilly and tribal areas and one community health centre for a population of one lakh or one community development block. The Plan aims at providing safe drinking water to all the 1.90 lakh problem villages.

Administration

An empirical study was conducted in some tribal villages of Srikakulam to assess the perception of tribals towards administration and to assess the impact of administration on Tribals and Tribal areas.

In each selected village, 15 tribal households are selected to assess the perception and impact of administration. Altogether 90 cases were studied. The distribution of sample, village and tribal-wise is shown in Table 8.3.

The selected 90 tribal households are represented by different tribal groups, namely, Jatapu-55, Savaras-20; Konda Dora-11 and Mukha Dora-4. Jatapu tribe is found in all the selected villages, whereas Mukha Dora is only in two villages, viz., M. Dandigam and Mondemkhallu. The status-wise distribution (TL=8, PL=19, C=41, L=22) indicates that cultivators (45.55) and Panchayat leaders (21.11) constitute 66.66 per cent to the total sample.

Perception

It is said that the tribals, who are shy and illiterate, are not able to participate effectively in the decision-making process in Panchayat Raj administration. The respondents belonging to different tribal groups are able to converse with officials, 47.7 per cent of the tribals expressed that they are aware of administration and all of them emphasised that administration is indispensable for the development of their community and area.

TABLE 8.3 : **Sample villages : Tribal-wise distribution**

Village	Jatapu				Savaras				Konda Dora				Mukha Dora				Total
	TL	PL	C	L	TL	PL	C	L	TL	PL	C	L	TL	PL	C	L	
Donubai	—	4	7	4	—	—	—	—	—	—	—	—	—	—	—	—	15
Seethampet	2	4	4	1	1	1	—	2	—	—	—	—	—	—	—	—	15
Thonam	—	1	5	2	—	1	2	1	—	1	2	—	—	—	—	—	15
M. Dandigam	—	2	3	1	—	—	—	—	2	—	1	2	—	1	1	2	15
R.K. Bai	1	2	6	—	—	—	2	4	—	—	—	—	—	—	—	—	15
Mondemkhallu	—	—	5	1	—	1	3	2	2	1	—	—	—	—	—	—	15
Total	3	13	30	9	1	3	7	9	4	2	3	2	—	1	1	2	90

TL = Tradition Leader PL = Panchayat Leader
C = Cultivator L = Labourer

With the introduction of multi-faceted development programmes, the tribals have been coming into contact slowly with different departments especially the officers like Police, Tehsil, Excise, Forest, Agriculture and G.D.A. in tribal areas. The distribution of respondents who are in contact with different offices is given in Table 8.4.

TABLE 8.4. : **Tribals' contact with administration**

Department/Office	Yes	No	Total
1. Tahsil	76	14	90
2. Police	47	43	90
3. Excise	5	85	90
4. Forest	22	68	90
5. Agriculture	86	4	90
6. G.D.A.	77	13	90

The above situation reveals that most of the respondents are not in close contact with offices like Excise, Forest and Police. These three departments are regulatory departments and it is generally observed that most of the tribals are afraid of these departments. Most of the tribals are in constant touch with development departments such as agriculture and Girijan Development Agency.

In order to assess the perception of tribals about administration, respondents were asked to state the officers known to them at village, samiti, division, project and district levels and their relationship with them. Most of them have expressed that their relationship with officials at village and samiti levels is both official and friendly. At division, project and district levels. the officers known to them are less in number and their relationship with them is purely official.

Kula Panchayat, a traditional institution is still playing a vital role in settling the disputes like family maladjustment, quarrels and riotings. A noteworthy feature of the tribal society is that the cases of dacoits are brought to the notice of statutory panchayats but not *kula* panchayats. In the case of health troubles, out of 90 respondents, 82.2 per cent of them approached the doctors. The major change noticed among tribals is in the case of institutional finance. Out of 90 respondents, 61 of them (67.75%) have expressed that they approach banks to meet their financial requirements.

Impact of administration

Benefits accrued to villagers

The opinion of the respondents was ascertained whether certain community area benefits accrued to them are due to government or Panchayat Raj administration. The opinions recorded with regard to community area benefits are as given in Table 8.5.

TABLE 8.5 : **Impact of administration : Community area benefits**

S. No.	Benefit	No. of tribals benefitted due to			
		Government	P.R.	Don't know	Total
1.	Approach road	21	38	31	90
2.	Irrigation Project	22	38	31	90
3.	Internal roads	—	61	29	90
4.	School	35	27	28	90
5.	Hospital	60	3	27	90
6.	Drinking water well	13	44	33	90
7.	Panchayat Ghar	4	39	47	90
8.	Bus f.cility	50	2	30	90
9.	Crop society	12	28	50	90
10.	Radio	44	4	42	90

The opinions of respondents differ from activity to activity. With regard to each activity, some of the respondents expressed "Don't know". A disquieting feature as regards 'Panchayat Ghar' is that 52.2 per cent of the respondents expressed "Don't know". Another unique feature as regards internal roads is that 67.7 per cent of respondents expressed that this specific activity accrued to them only due to Panchayat Raj administration. Most of the respondents are of the opinion that hospital and bus facilities are accrued to them due to government.

Besides the above benefits; respondents have also expressed that they are benefited by Grameen Banks and G.C.C. Out of 90 respondents, 88 and 89 respondents are of the opinion that G.C.C. and Grameen Banks are most useful institution to them respectively. As regards Milk chilling plant, only 7.77% of the respondents have expressed a favourable opinion. This indicates that Milk chilling centre did not gain momentum in the tribal areas.

As regards the direct (individual) benefits derived by them from governments/Panchayat Raj administration, the number of respondents together with frequency are recorded as given in Table 8.6.

Social amenities are provided to certain respondent households more than 4 times. As regards economic benefits most of the respondents are not benefited more than three times. In the case of scheme like improved implements, irrigation wells and milch cattle, more than 50 per cent of the respondents are not benefited. More than 83 per cent of respondents are benefited under high-yielding varieties scheme, health and education schemes.

Tribals are more aware of local administration than government administration. The oldest regulatory Revenue Department and Traditional Administration is more popular among them. It is gratifying to note that 37.78 per cent of respondents are aware of democratic administration. (see Table 8.7).

The impact of administration on tribals can be fundamentally known by interviewing the respondents whether the local leaders like Panchayat President, Panchayat Member, Cooperative Society President, Kula Pedda, Samiti President, M.L.A. and M.P. are connected with local administration. The response of interviewers is recorded as given in Table 8.8.

This situation indicates that the tribals are in a position to distinguish Kula Pedda from other local leaders. They are well aware of the duties of Kula Pedda and they are able to differentiate statutory leaders from traditional leaders. Further most of the tribal respondents expressed that the Panchayat Member President and Samiti President are more well connected with local administration when compared to other leaders like Cooperative President, M.L.A. and M.P.

TABLE 8.6 : **Impact of administration : Individual benefits**

S. No.	Benefits	Frequency (No. of respondents)		
		Less than 3	4+	Nil
1.	High yielding varieties	75	—	15
2.	Fertilisers	63	—	27
3.	Improved implements	1	—	89
4.	Plough bullocks	50	—	40
5.	I.M.S. Loans	66	—	24
6.	Milch cattle	30	—	60
7.	Veterinary aid	26	31	33
8.	Irrigation well	11	9	70
9.	Education to children	51	21	18
10.	Education facilities	54	19	17
11.	Health facilities	6	80	4

TABLE 8.7 : **Awareness of administration of tribals about different types of administration**

Type of administration	Yes	No	% awareness
1. Local	44	46	48.88
2. Government	14	76	15.55
3. Revenue	44	46	48.88
4. Development Admn.	17	73	18.88
5. Traditional	67	23	74.45
6. Statutory	10	80	1.12
7. British	20	70	22.23
8. Democratic	34	56	37.78

TABLE 8.8 : **Impact of administration : Respondents' awareness**

S. No.	Local leaders	Connected with local Admn : No. of respondents	
		Yes	No
1.	Panchayat President	79	11
2.	Panchayat Member	73	17
3.	Coop. Society President	34	56
4.	Kula Pedda	—	90
5.	Samiti President	59	31
6.	M.L.A.	43	47
7.	M.P.	44	46

SOCIAL STRATIFICATION

An empirical study was conducted in the tribal areas of Bhadragiri and Seethampet T.D. Blocks of Srikakulam district with a view to find out the social stratification of different tribal groups. For this purpose, data is collected through an open-ended questionnaire by contacting the tribal respondents belonging to Savara, Jatapu, Konda Dora and Gadaba communities residing in and around Bhadragiri and Seethampet Block Headquarters. Altogether empirical and qualitative information is collected for 25 tribals. Besides the collection of primary data, secondary sources and literature is also referred.

The objectives of this study are :

1. to study the social distance of different tribal groups,
2. to assess the awareness of tribals towards different development programmes,
3. to study the leadership pattern in traditional and modern institutions, and
4. to find out whether social stratification results in emerging elites.

The results of the empirical data are discussed hereunder :

The existence of multiple tribes in the areas of Bhadragiri and Seethampet gave rise to a broad cultural configuration with undercurrent of racial, linguistic and occupational diversity. The tribes inhabiting this area are the Savara, Jatapu, Konda Dora, Gadaba, Manne Dora, Mukha Dora and the Khonds. In ethnic, linguistic, social, economic and cultural diversity, these tribes reflect a miniature of tribal Andhra Pradesh. The social structure of these tribes is also marked with diversity. The Savaras social organisation is peculiar due to the conspicuous absence of a clan system, while the Khond and Gadaba social structure is characterised by a loose phratry organisation which is a product of the proscribed and prescribed marital relations and in between these two extremes exist the tribes like Konda Dora, Manne Dora, Mukha Dora and Jatapu who have non-totemistic *inteperulu* or surnames which assume the role of clans. Besides horizontal stratification in each tribe, the various tribes of the belt have been vertically stratified to form social hierarchy with Mukha Doras occupying the highest rung, the Savaras along with Gadabas, the lowest rung with Manne Doras, Konda Doras, Jatapus and Khonds in the intermediary rungs according to the status criteria decreed by tradition and reflected in the behavioural patterns.

Every tribe has a powerful tribal council presided over by a head called *Naidu* or *Naik* or *Padda* to safeguard the norms of the tribe and prescribe its social and ethnic identity. In the tradition-bound tribal society, authority is still vested in traditional leaders who in most cases became statutory leaders. Every tribe has a 'head' in each village who acts as liaison between village and government. The powers of these authoritarian leaders are all pervasive. With the extension of democratic decentralisation to the tribal areas, the tribals have been involved in various stages of development. They are now represented on various standing committees of the Panchayat Samiti as well as the Zilla Parishad to draw up various schemes for the planned development of the tribal areas. As members of the policy-making bodies the tribals are participating in the programmes of development of tribals and tribal areas even at the grass-root levels as members of Gram Panchayats.

Agriculture

Most of the tribal families own land. The landless tribals work as agricultural as well as ordinary labour. With the introduction of ryotwari system, the tribals now possess individual *pattas* and thereby they are able to get loans from banks and government agencies. Loans are also advanced to these landowners for purchase of fertilisers and inputs. The government is making every effort to improve their agricultural practice by introducing modern methods of cultivation and supplying improved variety of seeds, etc. With the efforts of the government more tribals are taking to modern cultivation in individual lands as community owned joint farms. In view of these facilities, the tribals who are able to avail these, distinguish themselves from the other tribals. Further, the tribal beneficiaries are of the opinion that their economic status is comparatively improved.

Animal husbandry

Animal husbandry is one of the programmes which has generated a lot of economic activity in the tribal areas. The milch cattle distribution has been so well organised that it started providing gainful supplementary employment to the landless tribals who formed the majority of the beneficiaries. The milch cattle distribution on 50 per cent subsidy is done on identified milk routes and tribals sold the surplus milk after consumption at the milk collection points to repay the loan component to the satisfaction of commercial banks. Even the Savaras who do not have milch cattle due to traditional taboos, started milching cattle because of immediate and encouraging economic returns. This proves that once the tribal is convinced of the utility of the programme, he does not hesitate to adapt himself to new occupations brushing aside even taboos.

Prior to launching of these schemes in tribal areas, the tribals had no idea of the economic benefit. With the result, they never bothered to feed and manage the livestock properly. Now the tribals are deriving the benefits of these programmes by selling milk and other livestock products such as eggs, etc. Motivation in respect of animal health care has also undergone changes. Now the tribals are taking interest and initiative for the health coverage of their livestock. Whenever they find their animals ailing, they approach the veterinary institution for treatment.

Education

Promotion of tribal education has been receiving the top most priority and attention of the government. In spite of efforts, the desired results could not be achieved and the literacy level among the tribals remained less than expected. This is due to the low economic standard of the tribals and their lack of motivation to send their children to schools. Most of the tribals who pass class fifth or below are struggling for jobs as contingent workers, or class four employees, or getting themselves in their traditional occupations. To avoid this type of situation, the government gave incentives like free textbooks, notebooks, stationery and a pair of dresses, free boarding and scholarship amount to the tribal students. With these, the level of literacy has increased from 8.02 per cent in 1971 to 10.4 per cent recently. In view of the liberal educational incentives and establishment of Ashram schools in every nook and corner of tribal areas, the tribal parents are now well motivated to send their children to schools and they are not complaining that their children are any kind of burden. It is evident that now-a-days many tribal children are admitted in reputed institutions and public schools. It is observed that tribal parents are proud of their educated and employed children. Tribals distinguish the educated ones as superiors to them.

Medical and health

Tribal respondents expressed that they are making use of the modern medicine and they are in the habit of going to P.H.Cs. and other allopathic centres. They have almost completely departed from the practice of treating the diseased with magico-religious rituals. Due to the use of milk and milk products, eggs, etc., their health is considerably improved.

Leadership pattern

In every stage of socio-economic evolution, nature has been man's most dependable ally. Land stands for all natural resources which field an income or which have exchange value. The utility of land is obvious in the agricultural stage. The Zamindari system was in vogue in most of the villages of Bhadragiri agency. The villages formed part of Kurupam estate and Jaipur Kumarika estate. The Kurupam estate was abolished in 1954 under the provision of the Estates Abolition and Conversion into Ryotwari Act, 1948. Under the present ryotwari system, every registered holder of land is recognised as its proprietor and pays revenue. The tribals expressed that the old system of unconditional supremacy has been done away with and now-a-days they insist that the people should work for the benefit and development of the community, irrespective of their wealth and traditional status. When once the tribals are convinced of leadership qualities of a particular person, they choose him as their leader and follow him. This situation reveals that one cannot claims a supreme position in tribal society, even though he gives feasts and drink parties. Further, the acquisition of skills like hunting will not help one to become a leader. However, knowledge, education and skilled persons are respected and highly regarded.

Tribal respondents expressed that they attach importance to the positions like Sarpanchs, Village head-man, etc. Such persons wield a lot of influence and power and their word carries more weight than any other person in the village. With the introduction of panchayat raj system, the tribals prefer to have the election system, to elect their leaders for a position in Samitis and even for a traditional institution. This indicates that the democratic principles have struck roots both for nourishing panchayat raj and traditional institutions.

Social values

It is observed that social distance is found among the different sects of tribes and other tribal groups in respect of marriage, food habits and traditional institutions. Traditional institutions are set up separately for each community. For example, a savara cannot become the head of Jatapu community or a Gadaba cannot become the committee member of Savara community. In the case of marriages social distance is strictly maintained. Marriages are possible within the community only. Inter-caste marriages are strictly prohibited. resulting in social distance. In cases, where a higher tribeman marries a low tribe woman, the low tribe admit them to their community if he desires, and after excommunicated by his tribe and this is vice-versa in respect of sex. In marriage functions, it is observed that the economically, socially and politically advanced tribals are looked after in a better way compared to other relations and friends. In respect of drinking, rituals, festivals and jatras, social distance is not observed among the different tribes and they move freely.

Material values

The material culture of major tribal groups of Bhadragiri and Seethampet Blocks is undergoing changes. It is seen that tribal people are fond of possessing transistors, radios, furniture, cosmetics, mirror and combs, etc., Dress pattern among males and females is undergoing fast changes like the use of coloured banians, brassiers, etc. Tea stalls, fancy shops and touring cinemas are popular in tribal areas. The quality of life of tribals has changed a lot.

With the implementation of multifarious development programmes, coupled with constitutional sefeguards privileges and concessions, the economic and social status of different tribal groups has improved resulting in the emergence of new classes, such as petty business men, traders, political and social leaders, educated and employed tribals.

Development of tribal areas requires a totally different approach and orientation. We have seen how tribal areas differ from the rest of the country. People in these areas have lived in ignorance over centuries with their usual rituals and customs. There are other difficulties like bad communications and unhealthy tracts which make it difficult for the administrator to visualise the problem. For this purpose, it is imperative that initiative must come from the tribals themselves and voluntary efforts should be encouraged. For new methods of administration to succeed in these areas, the personnel should be very carefully selected and should be committed to government programmes and policies. What we require is a band of dedicated workers who can live and think in the same way as the tribals. The administration should be willing to share their grievances and difficulties, and prove that the state is sympathetic to them, and is ever ready to help them. In the tribal areas, there are numerous kinds of field problems which have to be attended with an air of urgency failing which matters deteriorate. The tribals are usually very sensitive and any feeling of neglect turns into hostility and animosity towards the government. Poverty in its multi-faceted dimensions has to be tackled very urgently or else it may create irreparable damage to the efforts already made.

REFERENCES

1. Bann Been Lee, *Bureaucratic Models and Administrative Reforms: Development and Change*, Institute of Social Studies, The Hague, Vol. II, 1970-71, p. 53.
2. Dov Weintraub, *Developmental Change Towards a Generalised Conceptualization of Its Basic Dimensions and of the Relations among Them*, Institute of Social Studies, The Hague, Vol. III, 1971-72, p. 7.

9

CONCLUSIONS

> On the 26th January, 1950, we are going to enter into a life of contradictions. In politics we will have equality and in social and economic life we will have inequality. In politics we will be recognising the principle of one man one vote one value. In our social and economic life, we shall, by reason of our social and economic structure, continue to deny the principle of one man one value. How long shall we continue to live this life of contradictions ? How long shall we continue to deny equality in our social and economic life ? If we continue to deny it for long, we will do so only by putting our political democracy in peril. We must remove this contradiction at the earliest possible moment or else those who suffer from inequality will blow up the structure of political democracy which this Assembly has so laboriously built up.
>
> —*Dr. B.R. Ambedkar*

THE CHALLENGE of constructing a new secular social order with equality of opportunity to all irrespective of caste, creed, race, sex or place of birth needs to be achieved in the shortest possible time span. The Constitution-makers kept in their minds the socio-economic conditions of tribal communities and hence made special provisions to protect their rights and make them useful members of society. In recent times the planners also accepted a wider definition of growth which should be „growth with social justice".

The events leading to the Girijan revolt in Srikakulam and the subsequent developmental activities are in itself a microcosm of inertia, trauma and revival in the field of tribal development. We are familiar with the isolistic policy adopted by the British towards the tribals and the efforts of the founding fathers of the Constitution to bring about social, political and economic justice to the weaker sections of this country. A vast set of provisions were made in the Constitution which have been given effect to by the representatives of the people, and those who are ultimately concerned with the administration of such goals and ideals. However, many of the promises that were spelt out in the Constitution were never given full shape as a consequence of which there was lethargy and apathy. The upshot was that Communist elements who derived inspiration from the cult of violence took the law into their hands. The Communists and Marxists adopted the Maoist slogan, "political power flows from the barrel of the gun". The methods adopted were inconsistent with democratic means and many of their violent acts are unjustified and condemnable in the eyes of law. But at the same time they achieved a limited success in the sense that the entire nation focussed its attention on Srikakulum to try to come to grips with the problems of rural reconstruction and administering these areas as effectively as possible so that justice would be done. The government was concerned and faced a challenge-response situation.

The time had come for replacing the old rusty approach of administering and developing tribal areas. Even though panchayat raj brought about democratic decentralisation in decision-making at the grass-roots level, there was no corresponding change in the quality of life in these areas. The ruling elites were unable to bring about social and economic change in the lives of the poorest of the poor. The kaleidoscopic aspects of development of tribals needed to be studied more diligently and a new orientation in the outlook of personnel serving in these areas was the necessity of the hour. The government and the administration had to fight a race against time and telescope as much of dynamism and change in as short a time-frame as possible. In short, the government faced a hostile population who had lost all faith in its exhortations and actions. The task was complex and the path littered with bitter and explosive memories.

The problem is thus a complex amalgam of several factors like policy, approach, coordination, strategy, planning, constitutional safeguards, protective regulations, quality of personnel, attitudes, ecological harmony, and, macro and micro level understanding of issues and possible remedies. It is increasingly realised that the key to accelerated development is the quality of development administration which is as much a scarce resource as other economic inputs. Thus, institutions governing tribal development with special reference to those controlled by the government, should be seen as critical inputs for effective administration of rural development programmes in tribal areas. An attempt will be made to analyse these factors in the following pages.

Towards a new tribal policy

A study of the dynamics of development in tribal areas in its multi-dimensional aspects brings us face-to-face with the future. It is clear that tribal development is different from ordinary development. The conflict that is ever present is whether to bring the tribals into the mainstream of life or whether they are to be left isolated and their development takes place in the normal course. Owing to centuries of long neglect and exploitation by landed interests and deprivation of forest rights and increasing awareness as in the case of Srikakulam, it led to an explosion of emotions and pent up anger which resulted in a major Girijan revolt. In this respect there is not so much lack of policy, but the lack of political and administrative will, to implement the policy. Therefore, a study of the frequency and major causes of tribal unrest at comparative level would help to take measures for effective administration.

One argument is that the vast maze of rules and procedures has a dampening effect on developmental activity. Full consideration will have to be given to decentralise authority, reshape priorities and streamline procedures at the state and district level.

Closely related to decentralisation is another snag of major importance and that is the lack of tribal participation in development programmes. In spite of the constitutional safeguards, this has not received serious thought and attention. In tribal areas. Panchayat Raj institutions did not help in fulfilling local hopes and aspirations. Traditional leadership amongst tribals is a force to reckon with and could be utilised more effectively for implementation of developmental programmes. Hence if development of tribal areas is to become more meaningful it must depend upon the active and voluntary participation of the people themselves.

Even in relation to constitutional provisions themselves, there are some important provisions which have to be reviewed and the full purpose and scope behind them should be fully realised. Article 275 (1) of the Constitution provides for grants for raising the level of administration of the scheduled areas. It appears as though full advantage has not been taken of this provision and the scope that it provides is not realised. How often has this provision been invoked by the state governments nobody really knows. As we have seen in Srikakulam, and other parts of the country as well, administration of tribal areas has to be geared up to high level of efficiency and full advantage should be taken of this constitutional provision. Again the 5th Schedule of the Constitution which deals primarily with thea dministration of the scheduled areas has not been fully studied and made use of. For instance, the governor of the state is supposed to take a direct interest in the administration of scheduled areas. But in reality, what happens is that the governor's reports are merely a review of the departmental activities and tribal welfare department's activities in tribal areas. Again, is the governor supposed to act in his personal capacity while reporting to the centre about the administration of the scheduled areas, or is it supposed to be a review of proper implementation of laws in these areas ? Or is he expected to act on the advice of his Council of Ministers before such report is sent to the centre ? Is the report of the governor merely a description of the events of the year or is it a critical judgment of the progress achieved by the state government in scheduled areas ? This aspect needs to be viewed very seriously and in future some positive thinking must be done in this direction.

The role of the Commissioner of Scheduled Castes and

Scheduled Tribes is also not very clear. It does not appear as though the Commissioner of Scheduled Castes and Scheduled Tribes is responsible for any field functions, but is to act as a mere observer. In his present capacity he cannot give any specific directions or carry out evaluation of a situation on the spot. As such the functions of the Commissioner of Scheduled Castes and Scheduled Tribes, are merely to submit a review report. There is no scope for malady-remedy analysis.

As a matter of fact a controversy is raging whether the centre is competent to deal with injustices and atrocities committed on members of Scheduled Castes and Scheduled Tribes. Recently the Commissioner of Scheduled Castes and Scheduled Tribes in his report has maintained that the centre is empowered in case of failure of the state government to act on its own. It bases itself on Article 256 and 257 which envisages issue of directions to the state governments to ensure compliance with the laws made by Parliament. Even otherwise, the Commissioner finds ample justification for central initiatives. It cites Article 46 which casts upon the union and states alike an imperative obligation "to protect the members of the Scheduled Castes and Scheduled Tribes from social injustice and all forms of exploitation". The fact that this is one of the Directive Principles, and as such not enforceable in courts of law, according to the report, does not detract from its value as guidelines for action by the centre.

The other arguments could be summed up as follows: If "protection of the members of the Scheduled Castes and Scheduled Tribes from social injustices and all forms of exploitation" is an imperative obligation on the union and the states constitutes a fundamental tenet in the governance of the country, there can be no doubt that their subjection to atrocities would constitute the worst kind of social injustice and exploitation and should, therefore, obviously be a matter of the greatest concern both for the union and the states.

The responsibility resting on the shoulders of the union government cannot be passed on to the states with a feeling of helplessness in the matter of taking adequate and effective steps. Such a feeling would only be based on a misconception.

The question is whether the power to legislate on matters

relating to social injustice and exploitation are outside the purview of the union on account of any entry in the state list. It is necessary to determine the proper meaning of the expressions "social injustice and exploitation".

Injustice, of course, means negation of justice. The Preamble of the Constitution speaks of "justice, social, economic and political". The last three words should not, however, be interpreted as meaning that social, economic and political justice are quite separate and exclusive spheres of justice. They are clearly overlapping concepts, and in fact social justice is itself comprehensive enough to include economic and political justice. The expression "exploitation" too connotes everything that hampers or retards the full growth of an individual for the benefit of somebody else and denies to him the dignity of human personality. It does not necessarily imply physical oppression, and the mere use of another human being for one's own purposes and benefits may legitimately be said to amount to exploitation. If these two expressions are given their due and proper meaning, it can, undoubtedly, be said that the worst sufferers from social injustice and éxploitation have been the members of the Scheduled Castes and Scheduled Tribes.

The power to legislate on these matters is not to be found in any of the lists, central, state or concurrent. The centre is, therefore, competent to act by virtue of Article 248 which gives it residuary powers.

The only provision in the Constitution which is pleaded by the states, for appropriating to themselves the exclusive right to deal with these matters is entry 1 of the state list which speaks of "public order". The argument is that social injustice and exploitation may, and often, do lead to public disorder and the states alone have, therefore, the right to legislate and necessarily also to take executive action in respect of them.

According to the observations in an Allahabad High Court's judgment "while public order is included and is a part of order, it does not cover the entire area of order." The Constitution restricts the powers of the states for dealing with public disorders out of their scope which are to be dealt with by the centre under its residuary powers.

New focus

For accelerating rural development programmes it is necessary to involve and activate local institutions. The introduction of Panchayat Raj institutions enabled power to be decentralised and planning from below which meant that decisions could be taken by the local village-level leaders. Panchayat Raj institutions also helped in creating awareness among and motivating the rural masses about their rights and duties in the matter of developmental priorities, functions and process. However, one of the ill-effects of Panchayat Raj was also to let in more of casteism and political factions. In this context, it is essential to lay stress on the role of voluntary agencies in rural development. Rural development is a total national effort, of all agencies governmental, industrial, banks and voluntary agencies should be partners in development. All agencies should accept the new concept of rural development with focus on people and reaching the poorest of the poor, so that people want perceptions of their own problems and their own priorities are given due recognition.

A study of the foregoing chapters it is evident that in Srikakulam corrective action was resorted to by the government to restore a certain amount of balance and justice in the tribal society of the area. It must be remembered that because of the violence that erupted from 1968 to 1972, these steps became all the more necessary. Because of the stagnation and frustration of the society around them and the sense of deprivation and injustice that overcame them, the tribals resorted to violence. It was reaction against a new system's inability to deliver the goods in spite of the provisions made under the Constitution for promoting tribal welfare. For instance, even though the *muttadari* system had been abolished, yet the system remained in all its evil form and must have contributed to the discomfiture of the tribals. Even though land was supposed to have been restored to them in 1959 Act, there does not seem to have prevailed any sense of urgency to effect justice in this direction. As a consequence there was a lack of commitment and this is precisely what added to the mounting frustration which resulted in violence creating a serious law and order situation. As a consequence of this the Girijan Development Agency was set up with a limited objective of benefiting targeted number of families within a stipulated period of time. In order to achieve this a more flexible framework was necessary and this is precisely what was done.

The main grievance of the tribals was that they have been deprived of their rightful land and property. The tribals felt that their traditional rights or natural rights were being interfered and encroached upon. There was no security of life and the law and order machinery seem to be laid in favour of the elites and rich landlords. On the one hand, they felt insecure about their lands, and on the other, the forest officers also resorted to preventing the tribals from entering new areas and hence they felt completely ill at ease and frustrated. It is significant to note that during the period of rebellion the two main targets were the rich landlords and supposedly corrupt forest officers. The tribal as we know is traditionally accustomed to live in harmony with the forests and this constitutes the very core and fundamental fact of his life. His natural environment was threatened by the presence of outsiders and this led to threatening his own stability and peaceful and harmonious life. In effect, with the advantage of hindsight it seems that what was lacking was a human touch in the situation.

It may be worthwhile at this point to digress a bit and discuss Banfield's theory of amoral familism. Banfield tries to answer the question: Why do peasants not take initiative—which they can—to get for their community facilities and advantages which they are badly in need of. His answer is in the form of the concept of amoral familism. That is, the objective of security for one's family is the primary objective for the head of a household in any backward peasant situation. To provide this one would even go to the extent of stealing and killing. The immorality of these actions is justified on the basis of the security needs. In this way the nucleus family seeks to and succeeds in maximising short-term material advantage.[1]

In Srikakulam, however, one of the most unique features of the situation was that the tribals revolted. This means that they were prepared to get rid of the poverty and backwardness that had shackled their society for centuries. They even defied the law and order machinery of government to carve a new society where the rights of all the oppressed would be given a new shape and meaning. To this extent, it can be said that Banfield's theory is contradicted and must be seen in a new light.

Critical inputs of tribal development

Socio-economic factors

To achieve a minimum standard of living and improve the quality of life in tribal areas it is essential to give a boost to programmes of socio-economic significance. The investment pattern on socio-economic inputs in the tribal areas of India in comparison with the State of Andhra Pradesh is furnished in Appendices I to VI. It is relevant to note that per capita expenditure on tribals has multiplied from the First Plan to the end of the Fifth Plan in Andhra Pradesh (Appendix I).

Since the majority of tribals depend on land and agriculture, it is necessary to streamline agriculture and its allied activities. They are agriculture and irrigation, forests and the land problem. Similarly, education and health play a significant role in overcoming poverty and increasing incomes. Education imparts specific knowledge and develops general reasoning skills, it also induces change in beliefs and values and in attitudes towards work and society. Health improvement increases life expectancy, income earning capacity, family planning and understanding of nutrition and sanitation.

Education

To bring the tribals into contact with the world outside and to enable them to mingle with the mainstream of life, it is essential that the spread of education is given top priority. With the increasing awareness of opportunities elsewhere and the massive efforts of rural development, it is essential that employment opportunities should be made available. This can only be done through education.

It has been observed that up to the primary level most tribals are willing to send their children to Ashram schools, but the dropout rate is high as the student moves on to upper primary and high school levels. It is perhaps necessary to study the environment and ecological factors which lead to this situation. Keeping in view the environment and ecological factors a programme of vocational and need-based educational training can be set up in tribal areas where dropouts will automatically be absorbed into this other line. There is also a necessity to set up polytechnics which encourage training in forest-based industries so that tribals can take advantage of their environment and evolve new avocations suiting their genius and serve their community. It is also necessary that special employment exchanges be set up for tribal areas which will provide employment to the tribals nearer to tribal areas rather than sending them to city areas. It is also necessary that some arrangement should be made for encouraging higher education amongst the tribals and it would be ideal if a university is set up in tribal areas. The Government of Andhra Pradesh is already studying the setting up of such a university at Salur which is a predominantly tribal area in Vizianagaram district.

Regarding the activities at schools more tribal teachers should be trained and employed as teachers and headmasters in educational institutions of the tribal areas. There is also a need to give an incentive to teachers who are non-tribals for living and working in those areas. An incentive may also be provided for learning tribal languages and using these as a medium of instruction at the primary school level. It is difficult for a tribal child to understand foreign languages. It is also essential that the nutritional needs of children should be properly attended to and teaching aids and equipment are readily available in schools of tribal areas. It happens so often that because of lack of proper communication tribal schools do not have the bare necessities like text-books and other teaching aids necessary at the primary level. Tribal youth should also be encouraged to participate in sports because they are naturally endowed with good physique and good health. More avenues of employment should be provided for them.

Voluntary agencies like the Ramakrishna Mission or Bharatiya Adimjati Sangh should be encouraged to set up schools with sufficient state support. Another suggestion is that an Agricultural University for tribal areas may be set up. One polytechnic institute for training tribal students which will help generate employment may be set up.

Health

For proper mental and physical development it is essential that health programmes are given a boost in tribal areas. With the disappearance of forests tribals are gradually being deprived of the flora and fauna and their nutritional needs are also receiving a setback. It is, therefore, very essential that nutrition programmes in tribal areas are carefully and properly administered. In this regard child development programmes should be given a special place of importance. Pregnant mothers should be given all the consideration and sympathy which is essential. At the primary school level also it is essential that young children are regularly vaccinated against hazardous diseases and a regular medical check-up is conducted periodically. In tribal areas, particularly in view of the fact that communications are not well developed, Indian systems ayurvedic of medicine which are mainly based on forest products could be encouraged. Again hospitals should be properly staffed and there should be no shortage of medicines. Regular sanitation work should be carried out in the tribal areas to help in checking the spread of infectious diseases like cholera, smallpox, chicken-pox, etc., Another big killer in the tribal areas is malaria, anti-malaria campaigns should be properly administered in tribal areas. In Srikakulam district, checkposts have been set up in the tribal areas to check the influx of malaria from bordering districts of Orissa State. The doctors working in tribal areas should be given added incentives like special family allowance and family quarters to live in. In tribal areas because of lack of communication barefoot doctors should be encouraged so that they can cover difficult distances on foot. Similarly, mobile health clinics should also be encouraged. There should be an automatic follow-up of complicated cases and all facilities should be made available for referring such cases to district headquarters, hospitals or nearby medical colleges. This facility is sadly lacking in tribal areas.

Agriculture and irrigation

In view of the dependence on land, there is a necessity to introduce innovation in agricultural methods and practices. To a great extent success has been achieved and the first signs of change are already visible. The tribals are found to be receptive to change in the field of agriculture. However, apart from introducing them to use of fertilisers and high yielding varieties, it is also essential that they be encouraged to adopt new cropping patterns which will be remunerative financially. At Rastakuntubai in Bhadragiri Block a Girijan Krishi Kendra has been set up and it is responsible for carrying out research and extension in tribal areas in the field of agriculture. The Krishi Kendra also has propagated the spread of cash crops and the tribals are responding favourably. It is also necessary that income be supplemented by encouraging animal husbandry, horticulture, sericulture and fisheries programmes. Steps must also be taken to discourage *podu* cultivation through extension methods. As a matter of fact, in Srikakulam district in 1977, anti-podu committees were formed consisting of tribals, local head-men and the extension staff of the block and spectacular results were achieved in a brief spell which got down a great extent of *podu* cultivation. Horticulture programmes should be encouraged and they may as well act as a break and prevent *podu* practice. As regards irrigation, it is found in some areas that tribals have to be properly motivated regarding the usage of irrigation wells. It would be appropriate to encourage setting up of community irrigation wells which would benefit a cluster of farmers.

Another problem identified with irrigation practices is the problem of energy. It is not infrequent that there are power cuts during the peak cultivation season and shortage of diesel supply for energising the pump sets. Very often the farmer gets angry and feels frustrated regarding the supply of diesel. There is also cost of transportation of these items which requires urgent attention and perhaps the cost of transporting diesel to the tribal farmer field should be subsidised by the government. Similarly, at the time of the cultivation season, inputs like fertilisers and seeds should be provided at the appropriate moment when the necessity arises. It is necessary that the agricultural administration at the village and block level is geared up.

Forests

In tribal life forests are an important part of his daily chore.

Over the years there has been control by government on forest areas and exploitation by contractors who may be regarded as outsiders. The first and foremost task facing administration in forest areas is that the problem of shifting cultivation and its harmful effects should be explained to the tribals and adequate propaganda and extension methods should be employed. As mentioned earlier, anti-*podu* committees which were set up in Srikakulam district may be tried on a wide scale. The exact area of shifting cultivation should be assessed from the data obtained from pre-investment survey, aerial photography and ground-water survey methods. The diverse agricultural practices by different types of *podu* cultivating tribals may be studied and appropriate cultivation techniques and cropping patterns for different agro-climatic zones may be recommended after proper research.

Diversification of welfare activities touching upon special agencies like S.F.D.A./M.F.A.L/C.A.D.A/D.D.A.P. selecting suitable beneficiaries are to be carried out in those areas for their speedy progressive and sustained economic development.

The development structure in the tribal areas may be suitably designed on the basis of available technology best suited to the area and to the liking of the tribals.

For efficient marketing of the commodities collected by the tribal cooperative, an inter-state marketing corporation should function as an apex body to coordinate marketing efforts and thus eliminate the stronghold of merchant's monopoly in such trade.

Traditional leadership should be created and voluntary agencies may come forward for the implementation of developmental policies and programmes for the benefit of the tribals.

Control of shifting cultivation should be kept as a core sector in the Sixth Five Year Plan to tackle the problem effectively specifically through a centrally sponsored scheme for which adequate funding may be made.

The forest policy should be suitably amended so as to serve the interests of tribals better. Edible and commercial fruits and oilseeds bearing trees and fodder species may be planted as mixtures in all plantation programmes in the vicinity of villages. In traditionally *tussar* rearing areas, plantation of *Assan* and *Arjun* trees may be taken up to serve tribal interests for promoting sericulture.

To guard against exploitation of tribals at the hands of unscrupulous, traders a legislation on the Madhya Pradesh pattern should be adopted by other states so that traders may not purchase timber from tribal holdings at throw-away prices.

Integrated development of the tribal areas should be carried out in an intensive manner studying the structure of the soil, terrain, agro-practice, agro-botany, socio-economic and political structure of the particular areas. Its planning and implementation should be carried out at a faster rate with a multi-disciplinary approach.

Land problem

Land ownership and means of cultivation forms an important facet of the tribals way of thinking and living. As has been seen in earlier chapters, the land problem in tribal areas is vexatious and has very often led to discontentment and uprising. It is, therefore, necessary to review the existing land regulations from time to time so that most vital interests of the tribals life will be protected.

It was very often found that the tribal to whom land was restored was not in a position to cultivate land owing to lack of credit facilities. In such cases there should be a scheme for provision of inputs free of cost for a period of two to three years. The enforcement of legislation regarding money-lenders and scaling of debts should receive serious attention for preventing land alienation since indebtedness was the root cause of alienation of lands by tribals. It is necessary to have a regular machinery for detection of cases and for processing them till they are finally disposed of. Frequent surveys should be carried out to determine whether the position is secure after ownership rights have been passed over to the tribals. Adequate arrangements should be made for provision of legal aid to tribals for defending their ownership rights. Lawyers in tribal area should be specially employed for defending cases for involving tribals relating to protective legislation; they will be paid permanent rates or daily fees based on the actual work done. It is a common experience that tribals' suits get prolonged and delayed both in the Revenue as well as Judicial courts. It may be examined whether a summary procedure can be evolved for disposal of such cases as justice is difficult to obtain for those who are poor. Deterrent penalty is necessary in cases involving illegal transfer of lands and this matter should be reviewed. There should also be provision for the second appeal. The state government should have *suo-moto* powers to set aside transfers within a period of 30 years if the consent from the competent authority for transfer of land is found to have been obtained fraudulently. Such provision exists in the laws of Bihar State. In Maharashtra, a law has been enacted in 1974, under which even legally transferred lands can be given back to tribals on payment of compensation. Such a provision will be helpful in any place where no land is available or where the more fertile lands belonging to tribals have gone into the hands of non-tribals. Such an amendment to the existing laws will introduce a greater element of flexibility and easier implementation of laws in favour of tribals.

While effective implementation of the legislations may help, the permanent solution to the problem will lie in building up of the necessary economic infrastructure which will reduce the compulsions in respect of alienation of land by tribals. The strengthening of the cooperative structure, liberalisation of loan procedures, provision of consumption credit and liberal financial support for land development schemes under tribal sub-plans are some of the measures which need urgent consideration.

ADMINISTRATION AS AN AGENCY FOR CHANGE

Personnel policy

In keeping with the objective of helping and developing tribal areas which constitute the poorest of the poor in our society, certain preferences have to be expressed when it comes to selecting the personnel responsible for bringing about change in these areas. Earlier, we discussed that there was a necessity to provide certain incentives to attract young and capable people to work in tribal areas. In addition to the incentives there is need to buttress with other requirement necessary for development of tribal areas. When we think of tribal development, we think of not only growth and productivity in the areas but also total development of the human being in relation to his environment and the values which are cherished by the Constitution. In doing so, we are trying to achieve social change which includes changes in the institutions, values, attitudes and the future of the community at large. For achieving these ends, the personnel have to be specially trained for the purpose. It is important that those who work in tribal areas, or are in any way associated with tribal development are imbued with the sense of commitment and a bias in favour of tribal development. Another important aspect is that once such a personnel has been located and identified he should be allowed to perform his function for a reasonable length of time so that he can get the sense of achieving what is expected of him. He should also be able to endear himself to the people in whose areas he is working. A deep sense of commitment coupled with a sympathy for tribal problems and combined with the human touch will go a long way in successfully implementing development programmes. This prescription does not apply to the elitist bureaucrat alone but is also meant for the low bureaucracy which consists of V.L.Ws., B.D.Os., *Tashildars*, Revenue Inspectors, Agriculture demonstrators and Forest Officers. It is also essential that people working in the tribal areas are encouraged to freely mingle with the tribals so that they can understand their beliefs, customs, rituals, language and way of living. It is not merely enough to tinker with the problems but to be fully involved in the process of day-to-day life and get a feel of the problems faced by the tribals. One great disadvantage is that these days an officer can come in a jeep, tour a few villages and go away after ascertaining the needs of the people. However, this does not help in narrowing the gap between the tribal and officialdom. As a matter of fact during the British times, officers used to live in the tribal areas for days together right in the midst of the jungle in a camping tent and share the life of the tribal in its minutest details. Such a practice is necessary. In Srikakulam, it is obvious that after the British left there was a gap between the administrators and the people which resulted in giving an expression to their pent-up feelings in the shape of violence. It would indeed be a great thing if educated tribals themselves could work in the tribal areas. This would also help in solving the problem of unemployment in tribal areas as those who are dropouts could be given employment in their own natural habitat and nearer to their homes.

An administrative structure, however, perfect it may be, cannot deliver the goods unless it is properly manned. Experience all over the country has shown that a large number of posts are lying vacant particularly in the tribal areas thereby jeopardising the developmental efforts. Time has come when serious thought has to be given to remedy the situation. It has to be admitted that tribal areas suffer from certain disabilities like lack of housing, educational and medical facilities, etc. Consequently, there is strong disinclination on the part of government officials to serve in these areas. Therefore, to attract suitable personnel to serve in the tribal areas, the following measures are recommended :

(i) the places of posting in tribal areas should be graded on the basis of accessibility, availability of social services, etc., and suitable special pay should be given to persons posted there.

(ii) scholarships and priority in admissions to enable children of such persons as are posted in places without a Middle School or a High School should be given subject to a maximum of two children.

(iii) free-housing may be provided to all personnel working in the tribal areas. In case residential accommodation is not available suitable compensatory allowance should be given.

(iv) long term benefit could also be given to persons rendering satisfactory service of 5 years or more in the tribal areas in the shape of higher pension and gratuity on retirement.

(v) preference may be given to the personnel who have worked in the tribal areas in the selections for foreign assignment/training abroad and awards of fellowships, etc.

(vi) all personnel of the state and the all-India services

may be channelled to serve in the tribal areas within three years of their initial entry into service.

(vii) personnel serving in the tribal areas should be encouraged to learn recognised tribal dialects for which training facilities should be provided. Those who undergo such training and attain required proficiency could be given lump-sum monetary rewards.

(viii) special care should be taken for selecting the right type of personnel for serving in the tribal areas particularly at the level of Block Development officers, Project technical heads, and Project Directors. Their tenure in a project should be for a minimum period of 3 years and it would be fair to give them postings at good places on completion of such tenure in tribal areas.

(ix) the central government should provide special funds under Article 275 (i) of the Constitution for raising the level of administration in the tribal areas and the measures suggested above should qualify for such assistance.

(x) in order to give a correct orientation to personnel working in tribal areas they should have a rudimentary knowledge of such disciplines like social anthropology, rural sociology, social psychology.

Towards a new administrative culture

The District administration is sometimes referred to as the 'cutting edge' of government as it is at this level that policies are ultimately translated from paper into action. Therefore, it is at this level, that the rationality of all programmes and schemes is tested. The result of implementation of schemes and plans serves as a source of direct feedback through state level to central authorities. It is equally important that administrators serve in the districts before they occupy higher positions of authority as the experience gained at the district level is of everlasting value. It will not be enough to post an officer in the tribal areas who is young, alert and energetic but should have a vision of a bright future for the poor and depressed classes.

In Andhra Pradesh, the Collector is vested with vast

powers and is the supreme authority in the district set-up. According to M.T. Raju Committee report, the Collector is the Chairman of all the Standing Committees of the Zilla Parishad. After the dissolving of Zilla Parishad in 1975, Collectors have been designated as Special Officers of the superseded Zilla Parishads and hence are all powerful in developmental matters. Similarly with regard to revenue administration and law and order, even though there is a District Revenue Officer and the Superintendent of Police looks after law and order, the final authority is the District Collector under whose supervision all officers are expected to function. Dr. Muttalib has said that the chief merit of the Andhra Pradesh pattern is that the line of command is clear and there is no room for ambiguity.[2] In implementing developmental programmes and policies, it can also be said that decentralisation is maximum in Andhra Pradesh, because of the vast powers and authority that the Collector enjoys in Andhra Pradesh. All developmental departmental heads at the district are designated as P.As. to Collectors and hence at the district level all of them owe their allegiance to the Collector. In short, there are no major problems of coordination because all power and authority is concentrated at one point. By way of criticism it can be said that non-officials have a lesser say in developmental matters in Andhra Pradesh. It can also be said that too much of concentration of authority at one point tends to be harmful as sometimes the whims and fancies of an individual may affect developmental programmes.

It would be useful if tribal districts of about the size of sub-division is created and each Firka area supervised by a Senior Deputy Collector or young IAS Officer. If the districts for tribal areas are small it will be easier to plan from below as the administrators will have more time to be in touch with the needs of the people. A few pre-requisites for rural development in tribal areas are necessary. These are (1) assessment and development of natural resources in the rural areas, land, water, etc; (2) development of infrastructure (social overheads); (3) promotion and strengthening of leadership arising from the weaker sections and reorientation of the outlook of the existing rural elites; (4) regulation and redistribution of private property rights in land; and proper control and regulation of the use of public domain; (5) development of viable technology which will be accessible to the weaker sections and promote modernisation and productivity of their occupations and not just for their survival.

Another fact which should be kept in mind by the administrator in tribal areas is to be in touch with the elders of a tribal group as their authority is still accepted amongst the tribals. The Panchayat Raj system did not exactly serve the purpose of helping the tribals as very often non-tribals also benefited in the tribal areas. Administrators should also be encouraged to learn the folklore, customs and language of the tribals. For instance, a lot can be learned about the condition of tribals if the administrators were to present himself at the weekly shandies. The shandy is not only an arena for commercial activity but also a place for social interaction. Here it may be mentioned that the first necessary step for ensuring success in administering the area is ensuring posting of selected persons in the tribal areas. Another drawback to implementation is that many posts remain unfilled and the average tenures are very brief; and there has been no systematic appraisal of personnel already posted in these areas.

As far back as 1966 the Study Team of Tribal Development Programmes observed: "The lack of rapport between the District officers and the tribal population has facilitated the propagation of subversive propaganda amongst the tribals by interested parties out to foment trouble in the Agency areas of Srikakulam district".[3]

Lastly, it is important that officers working in tribal areas should feel confident while taking decisions that the whole government is behind them and they need not run a risk if some minor mistake is committed. To improve the quality of decision-making it is essential that delegation of financial powers is effected immediately. The Project Officer should be authorised to take decisions up to Rs. 5 lakhs for executing works, etc. If such a delegation is made remedies can be hastened and unnecessary procedures and rules can be sidetracked.

A NEW MODEL FOR DEVELOPMENT ADMINISTRATION

For the success of any plan of development it is necessary that all previous approaches are properly evaluated and the deficiencies and loopholes plugged in so as to improve performance and aim for better results. Since all plans and programmes are implemented at the district level a certain amount of careful planning should be initiated at the block level and the block plan should be integrated into the plan prepared at the district level. In view of increasing specialisation in all fields of activity, and greater demand for services in as little time as possible, it is necessary that a multi-disciplinary approach is adopted. At the district level the authority overall incharge of executing plans and programmes may be assisted by a group of specialists from all major disciplines which touch upon the environment and everyday affairs of rural life in tribal areas. For instance, the Collector and the Project Officer should be assisted by experts and subject matter specialists from the ground water, animal husbandry, rural credit, agricultural, engineering and statistical disciplines and sectors who can always feed the authority with latest facts and figures and also help in evaluating plans and priorities.

The entire process of planning will have to be centered around the concept of (a) area development, and (b) the development of tribal communities; in which the block will play a crucial role and successfully implement all programmes. The administrative structure below the project level should be as simple as possible and over-specialisation should be avoided. For instance, there need not be too many subordinate officers from various departments working directly under the Project Authority as it would tend to create a dysfunction, the reason being that the existing special staff in the block should be fully utilised. All technical staff should work under the leadership of the District Collector and extend full support to Project Authority. The District Collector has overall charge to coordinate all the district programmes; and the Project Authority could be vested with sufficient powers, but would work under the direct control of the District Collector. The Collector should also be given specific responsibility for planning, implementation, monitoring and evaluation all programmes in the project area falling within his district. Adequate staff support should be provided to the Collector for effective discharge of the above responsibilities for the project areas.

Tribal participation in decision-making and developmental processes

After independence two types of administration have emerged, namely, regulatory administration which includes maintenance of law and order, and revenue collections.

In the tribal areas of Srikakulam we have observed earlier how developmental activities were carried on throughout the fifties and the early and the later half of the sixties. The Panchayat Raj institutions unfortunately did not deliver the goods that were expected of them, but instead power at the village level became centred in the hands of important caste leaders, landlords and elitist groups. As a matter of fact, *muttadari* system, though it was supposed to have been abolished, existed in its most virulent and rabid form in the agency areas of Srikakulam district. Coupled with this was the fact that there was no committed involvement of the administration in tribal welfare programmes and, as such, there was administrative apathy towards the tribals. Because the area was backward and there were no communications, voluntary agencies did not venture to take the initiative in these areas. As seen earlier, the Communists seeing the opportunity jumped into the fray and started anti-government propaganda. Their main plank of demands was the wages, problem of land, employment and forest rights.

As a matter of fact, the Girijans were in the clutches of non-tribal money-lenders and contractors who choked them into a position of utter helplessness. They mortgaged the properties of the tribals and reduced them to a status of slavery and serfdom. There were a large number of cases of bonded labour which were also detected subsequently. The landlords employed the Girijans on their farms for such meagre wages that they were reduced to a state of starvation and subsistence living. The Communists organised Girijan Sanghams at the village level and commenced the political education of the

Girijans by forming a cadre of Girijan Sangham workers. The Girijans under Communist guidance raised the banner of "new democratic revolution" and formation of a Girijan "autonomous region". The Marxist carried out propaganda against the landlords on a war-footing and demonstrations and processions were launched against the landlords. This action forced the landlords to flee from the area. Thereby Girijans were enabled to take possession of their lands and also successfully persuaded the landlords to raise wages substantially. The next stage was actual seizure of standing crops and possible occupation of land from the landlords. The result was that the landlords started to organise resistance for restoration of land which ultimately resulted in violence and conflict. It may be recalled that the Girijans who had formed Girijan Sanghams, made the Sangham function like village communes or soviets.[4] The Sanghams indulged in seizing land and grains which were redistributed amongst the inhabitants of the "liberated areas". Here it must be mentioned that there was a total collapse of law and order and a new parallel economy and system came into existence. The administration had virtually no control over the areas held under the sway of Sanghams.

All these events occurred as a reaction against the existing system. When we talk of participation we refer to participation in decision-making in a democratic manner. In Srikakulam the extremists organised their own system without the assistance of government, and it serves as an eye opener of what can be done when popular passions and discontent is aroused.

Although a state of anarchy prevailed, yet it was demonstrated that tribals are capable of fighting against injustice and oppression of the elitist groups. There is also a high level of political consciousness amongst the tribals and they have come a long way from their supposedly 'state of nature' and the museum specimen image that the tribal was identified by outsiders. It is, therefore, essential to encourage tribals to participate in the decision making process of developmental activities.

There are two diametrically opposite views about the direction in which developmental programmes in tribal areas should proceed. One is the paternalistic view, where it is presumed that the Central Government is strong and all initiatives are vertical that is from top to bottom. The other view is that the people know best what is good for them and that all the initiatives must come from the bottom to the top. In India, however, because of the vast variations in local conditions from one region to another, it is absolutely necessary that there should be a certain degree of flexibility and originality in the approach from one area to another respectively. Indeed in a welfare state the government is under heavy moral and constitutional obligation to enter the field of tribal development in a big way. Government machinery, however, has its limitations. Since independence the emergence of Panchayat Raj institutions created a certain amount of awareness and the tribal was made aware of his rights and share in the developmental process and his expectations were also raised.

As seen from the political set-up in this country, the elites possess power and the masses do not. In order to alter the situation it is necessary that people's participation in developmental programmes should be stepped up. One way out is to make block level planning more effective and all local people and traditional leaders and important individuals interested in uplift of the poor should be taken into confidence when a plan is prepared. This need not necessarily include those who are *sarpanches*. In tribal areas strong community links is an accepted fact and there are always some representatives of the community who are regarded as important by them. Such elders should be involved more closely in the process of development. It may also be necessary to build up an organisation which can be used as a forum of expression of popular feelings and local aspirations. The traditional *Gram Sabha* should be utilised more effectively. It would be necessary to introduce adult education in the tribal areas as it would definitely help in creating awareness amongst the tribals. It is in this context that voluntary agencies could play a very important role. For instance, in the north-eastern states Christian Missionaries have won the hearts of tribals living in the area and their programmes of socio-economic uplift have gone a long way in helping the tribals. The literacy rate in this area is very high and this can be attributed mainly to the efforts of the Christian Missionaries.

The voluntary agencies should not have any political party affiliation and they should be registered agencies. Their services should be available to all people irrespective of caste and creed. Its accounts should also be audited and published. Only such voluntary agencies should be encouraged whose character and integrity is unquestionable and they should not be allowed to play with the lives of innocent people.

Another important aspect is that an effort should be made to train up a cadre of workers especially young people, who are enthusiastic and dedicated and are specially interested in working for the rural masses. A body of such people or corps of rural areas could be created and utilised whenever there is need. It could also be possible to encourage more village adoption schemes for the total development of the people living in the area. A start has already been made by certain industrial houses in this direction and this trend should be further encouraged and promoted. Another possibility is to create a body of experts who could give counselling and consultancy services to individual ryots and farmers for organisation. It would be perhaps necessary that a directory of voluntary organisations and social workers block-wise should be prepared for ready reference.

A voluntary effort will, however, require the support and sympathy of government. A very interesting fact which has not been brought to light is that under the Constitution, Governors of states are vested with overriding powers in respect of tribal areas. There is no such single instance in the history of free India where any Governor has made use of these powers. The Governor has powers under the Fifth Schedule to make special Regulations with the prior approval of the President. This power is almost unlimited. In these provisions, the Governor can suspend enforcement of any law passed by the State Legislature or even by the Parliament; or he can direct that these laws will be applied in a modified form; or if he considers necessary an entirely new law, in the form of a Regulation, can be promulgated for these areas. Since the entire administrative system functions within a legal frame, therefore, the Constitution has authorised the Governor to adapt the entire administrative system according to the local situation.[5]

For proper implementation of the various programmes relating to the development of tribal areas and the welfare of the tribals in our country, effective and constant review would be necessary. While we have Advisory Committees and such other agencies for monitoring the progress of the various schemes it is felt that a High Power Review Committee should be established at the state level with the Governor of the state as the Chairman, the Chief Minister and the Minister in charge of tribal development as Deputy Chairman, with concerned Head of Departments, and representatives of voluntary organisations to review the progress of work every quarter, and identify shortfalls and issue directions for the full implementation of the Plan programmes. Such a committee would help to remove administrative bottlenecks and inter-departmental procedural hurdles.

REFERENCES

1. Edward C. Banfield, *The Moral Basis of A Backward Society*, The Free Press Research Centre in Economic Development and Cultural Change, The University of Chicago, Dec. 1963, p. 85.
2. Prof. Muttalib, M. A., *Development Administration in Rural Government for Agricultural Production: An Approach in Comparative Administration*, Dept. of Publication and Press, Osmania University, Hyderabad, 1973, p. 198.
3. Kumar, Virendra, *Committees and Commissions in India 1947-73, Vol. VII. 1966*, Concept Publishing Company, Delhi, 1978, p. 343.
4. Frankelf, Francine, R., *India's Political Economy, 1947-1977: The Gradual Revolution*, Princeton University Press 1978. p. 377.
5. Sharma, S.K. (ed.), *Dynamics of Development: An International Perspective*, (Vol. II), Article by Sharma, B.D., Concept Publishing Company, Delhi, 1978, p. 638.

APPENDICES

APPENDIX I

PER CAPITA EXPENDITURE ON TRIBAL DEVELOPMENT

Plan	Expenditure (In Rupees)
First Plan	15.05
Second Plan	18.89
Third Plan	13.56
Fourth Plan	45.60
Fifth Plan	266.00

APPENDIX II

TRIBAL DEVELOPMENT PLAN-WISE INVESTMENT (GOVERNMENT OF INDIA AND GOVERNMENT OF ANDHRA PRADESH)

Plan	India	Andhra Pradesh (Rupees in crores)
First Plan	19.03	1.19
Second Plan	42.92	2.50
Third Plan	51.05	1.79
Annual Plans (1966-69)		
Fourth Plan	34.54	0.72
Fifth Plan	1390.00	59.35

APPENDIX III

STATE SECTOR TO THE TRIBAL SUB-PLAN

(*Rs. in lakhs*)

State	1975-76		1976-77		1977-78		1978-79	
	State Sub-Plan	Spl. Central Assistance	State Sub-Plan	Spl. Central Assistance	State Sub-Plan	Spl. Central Assistance	State Sub-Plan	Spl. Central Assistance
(1)	(2)	(3)	(4)	(5)	(6)	(7)	(8)	(9)
1. Andhra Pradesh	665.00	123.00	960.00	194.75	1192.52	285.25	1473.00	263.00
2. Assam	66.00	100.00	570.00	203.00	734.00	257.00	1000.00	325.00
3. Bihar	1742.00	281.00	4115.00	614.00	5378.00	807.50	6225.00	985.00
4. Gujarat	800.00	200.00	1600.00	326.00	2350.00	473.10	3350.14	606.00
5. Himachal Pradesh	140.00	31.00	250.00	68.00	372.09	90.00	5690.35	130.00
6. Karnataka	N.Q*	10 00	100.00	20.00	128.50	24 00	203.00	28.00
7. Kerala	N.Q*	15.00	N.A.	26.00	51.00	25.00	91.00	26.00
8. Madhya Pradesh	2300.00	506.00	4000.00	1097.00	5324.00	1554.25	6354.00	1846.00
9. Maharashtra	1350.00	104.00	2155.00	231.00	3278.79	378.25	4851.81	398.00

APPENDIX III *contd*

(1)	(2)	(3)	(4)	(5)	(6)	(7)	(8)	(9)
10. Manipur	472.00	43.00	700.00	90.00	869.00	128.00	1434.00	177.00
11. Orissa	2125.00	292.00	2617.00	587·00	3360.35	770.15	4751.60	970.00
12. Rajasthan	629.00	150.00	963.00	246.25	622.25	288.10	1374.00	337.00
13. Tamilnadu	N.Q.*	12.00	117.00	44.00	153.27	45.00	159.00	54.00
14. Tripura	234.00	36.C0	408.00	68.00	460.00	96.40	722.50	115.00
15. Uttar Pradesh	N.Q.*	5.00	50.00	11.00	25.00	15.00	58.00	18.00
16. W. Bengal	377.00	72.00	823.00	149.00	1352.00	225.00	1354.60	268.00
17. A.N. Islands	N.Q.*	20.00	—	17.00	41.60	17.00	75.00	43.00
18. Goa, Daman & Diu.	N.Q.*	Nil	20.00	8.00	29.07	11.00	45 00	22.00
Total	10911.00	2000.00	19178.00	4000.00	5721.74	5500.00	34412.00	6611.00

*Not qualified.

APPENDIX IV

STATEMENT SHOWING OUTLAYS IN FIFTH PLAN (1974-78)—HEAD OF DEVELOPMENT-WISE

(*Rs. in lakhs*)

Head of Development Head of department	Total Fifth Plan 1974-78
(1)	(2)
1. Agriculture	1845.22
(a) A.P. Agricultural University	255.62
(b) Director of Agriculture	309.78
(c) Director of Marketing	18.72
(d) A.P. State Werehousing Corporation	32.00
(e) Forests and Rural Development Department	
(i) D.P.A.P.	1143.79
(ii) S.F.D.A. and MAFALDA	60.31
(iii) I.R.D.P.	—
(f) Agro Industries Corporation	25.00
2. Land Reforms Director of Survey & Settlements (Agency staff)	
3. Minor Irrigation	2236.79
(a) Ground Water Department	206.24
(b) Chief Engineer (M.I.)	1700.40
(c) A.P. Irrigation Dev. Corporn.	230.15
(d) Chief Engineer (P.R.)	100.00
4. Soil & Water Conservation	177.39
(a) Director of Agriculture	150.74
(b) Chief Conservator of Forests	26.65
5. Area Development Command Area Development	751.25
6. Animal Husbandry Director of Animal Husbandry including A.P. (Meat & Poultry Development Corporation)	323.73

APPENDIX IV—*contd.*

1	2
7. Dairy Development A.P. Dairy Development Corpn.	489.00
8. Fisheries (Director of Fisheries including Fisheries Development Corporation)	308.66
9. Forests Chief Conservator of Forests (including Forest Development Corporation)	382.45
10. Investment in Agricultural Financial Institutions (Debentures) Registrar of Co-operative Societies.	812.84
11. Community Development and Panchayats (Panchayat Raj Department)	238.51
I. Agriculture and Allied Services	7700.42
II. Co-operation	1898.59
III. Water & Power Development	68457.99
IV. Industries and Minerals	3612.74
V. Transport & Communications	9257.79
1. General Education	1666.33
(a) Director of School Education	1192.74
(b) Director of Higher Education	451.85
(c) Director of Youth Services	21.74
2. Art and Culture	33.67
(a) Director of State Archives	7.14
(b) Director of Public Libraries	6.25
(c) Director of Archaeology & Museums	16.29
(d) Director of Oriental Manuscripts Library and Research Institute	3.39
3. Technical Education Director of Technical Education	123.67
4. Medical	565.39
(a) Director of Medical Services	522.99
(b) Deputy Director of Medical Services (ESI)	17.06
(c) Director of Indian Medicines and Homeopathy	25.34
(d) Controller of Drugs	—
5. Public Health	558.12
(a) Director of Medical Services	

APPENDIX IV—*contd.*

1	2
(i) Normal P.H. Schemes	116.29
(ii) Minimum Needs Programme	415.83
(b) A.P. State Board for Prevention and Control of Water Pollution	26.00
6. Urban Water Supply and Drainages Chief Engineer (Public Health)	3513.95
(a) Schemes in Municipalities	
(i) State Share	470.00
(ii) L.I.C. Funds	752.00
(b) Manjira and Hyderabad Water Works	1957.00
(c) Mahedrigedda Water Supply Scheme	323.00
(d) Revalidated Funds S.T.D.	11.95
7. Rural Water Supply and Sanitation	1275.00
(i) State Share	1082.00
(ii) L.I.C. Funds	193.00
8. Housing	2257.91
(a) A.P. Housing Board	708.39
(b) A.P. Police Housing Corporation	155.C0
(c) Director of Town Planning	7.12
(d) A.P.S.Cs. and S.Ts. Co-operative Housing Societies Federation	29.23
(e) Commissioner of Labour	34.37
(f) Chief Engineer (Roads & Buildings)	68.66
(g) Chief Engineer (P.H.)	2.81
(h) Registrar of Co-operative Societies	4.28
(i) Town Planning Trust, Visakhapatnam	25.00
(j) Director af Harijan Welfare	1187.25
(k) Director of Municipal Administration	35.80
(l) Spl. Officer, Municipal Corporation of Hyderabad	—
(m) Grant-in-aid at Rs. 150 per individual for construction of houses	—
9. Urban Development	684.91
10. Information and Publicity Director of Information & Public Relations	38.08
(i) Publicity	34.41
(ii) Broadcasting	3.67

APPENDIX IV—*contd.*

1	2
11. Labour and Labour Welfare	116.93
12. Welfare of Backward Classes	1769.24
(a) Director of Harijan Welfare	744.37
(b) Director of Backward Classes	366.62
(c) Director of Tribal Welfare	658.25
13. Social Welfare	124.80
(a) Director of Harijan Welfare	6.00
(b) Director of Women & Child Welfare	108.99
(c) Inspector-General of Prisons	9 81
14. Nutrition	483.43
(a) Director of Municipal Administration	110.00
(b) Director of Tribal Welfare	246.35
(c) Director of School Education	34.00
(d) L.E. & T.E. Department	48.08
(e) Director of Women & Child Welfare	—
15. Other Social and Community Services	30.95
Zoological Park, C.C.F.	—
VI. Social and Community Services	13197.38
1. Secretariat Economic Services	
(a) Finance & Planning (Plg. Wing) Department	20.71
(b) Block level planning for employment	—
2. Regulation of Weights and Measures Controller of Weights and Measures	24.27
3. Statistics Director Bureau of Economics & Statistics	39.12
VII. Economic Services	84.10
VIII. General Services Public Works (Buildings), Chief Engineer	254.26
Grand Total	1,04,463.27

APPENDIX V

THE CUMULATIVE EXPENDITURE (1974-80)

(Rs. in lakhs)

Year	State Plan	C.A.	C.S.S.	I.F.	Total
1974-80	4748.55	1051.02	224.24	383.51	6407.32

The Cumulative /Physical Achievements

(In rupees)

Sl. No.	Scheme	Unit	Achievement (1974-80)
1	2	3	4
I. *Education*			
1.	Supply of dresses, note books, text books, etc.	Nos.	3,20,000
2.	Pre-Matric Scholarships	Nos.	68,000
3.	Hostels	Nos.	327
4.	Ashram Schools	Nos.	410
5.	Construction of buildings for educational institutions		197
6.	Residential Schools	Nos.	2
7.	Industrial training Institute		1
II. *Economic Uplift*			
1.	Area covered by soil conservation measures	Hects	1,45,000
2.	Area covered by HYV Seeds	Acs.	1,36,502
3.	Supply of Plough bullocks	Nos.	11,070
4.	Supply of oil engines, electric motors	Nos.	849
5.	Horticulture on large extents	Acs.	33,471
6.	Land development	Acs.	1,51,712
7.	Coffee Plantation	Acs.	1,650
8.	Irrigation Wells	Nos.	1,216

APPENDIX IV *contd.*

1	2	3
9. Lift Irrigation Schemes	Nos.	52
10. Milch animals	Nos.	7,455
11. Sheep Units	Nos.	2,593
12. Milk chilling centres	Nos.	12
13. Beneficiaries under TRICOR	Nos.	29,511
Other Schemes		
1. Electrification of villages	Nos.	733
2. Villages provided with drinking water wells	Nos.	324

Key

C.A : Central Assistance

C.S.S. : Centrally Sponsored Schemes

I.F : Institutional Finance.

APPENDIX VI (a)

SRIKAKULAM : PLAN 1974-75

Scheme	Releases	Expenditure
1	2	3
1. Minor Irrigation	1,47,000	3,07,000
2. Land Acquisition (Sch. Tribes)	25,300	25,176
3. Land Acquisition (D.N. Tribes)	8,100	—
4. Scholarships	22,500	10,793
5. Upgrading of Ashram Schools	43,065	17,559
6. Ashram Schools	30,960	30,960
7. Agriculture	20,060	30,000
8. Horticulture	9,000	9,000
9. Plant Protection	4,000	4,000
10. Minor Irrigation	2,95,000	15,000
11. Subsidy to share capital	30,000	30,000
12. Schemes for landless	22,000	22,000
13. Short term inputs	9,000	9,000
14. M.T.I.	30,000	30,000
15. Trade Assistance	4,000	40,000
16. Animal Husbandry	5,000	5,000
17. Educcated unemployed tribals	17,670	17,805

APPENDIX IV (a)—*contd.*

1	2	3
18. Special Nutrition Programme	13,02,300	19,31,163
C.S.S.		
1. Girls Hostels	93,000	—
2. T.D. Blocks	3,05,000	2,16,748

APPENDIX VI (b)

SRIKAKULAM : NON-PLAN 1974-75

Scheme	Releases	Expenditure
1. Animal Husbandry	88,700	51,812
2. Agriculture	42,500	26,189
3. Publicity	8,320	6,732
4. Primary Health	47,630	7,958
5. Hospitals & Dispensaries	1,70,950	1,70,683
6. Administration	52,880	—
7. Govt. Secondary Schools	18,000	—
8. Girls Hostels	1,59,961	—
9. Ashram Schools	5,11,036	5,05,367
10. Ashram Schools	2,14,173	1,03,535
11. Primary Schools (Non-Govt.)	3,40,000	—
12. Primary Health Centres (GIA)	2,25,630	—
13. Hostels	2,98,348	—
14. Supply of Books, etc.	51,000	51,000
15. Post-Matric	6,000	4,461
16. Construction of Hostel Buildings	6,650	—
17. Special Nutrition Programmes	3,00,000	—
18. Non-residential scholarships	5,000	

APPENDIX VI (c)

SRIKAKULAM : PLAN 1975-76

(In rupees)

Schemes	Releases	Expenditure
1	2	3
1. Scholarships	11,500	22,650
2. Ashram schools	35,450	—
3. Pre-Matric	1,70,000	1,79,299
4. Land Reclamation	15,000	15,000
5. Tractor Ploughing	12,000	12,000
6. Short term inputs	24,000	24,000
7. Plough Bullocks	14,000	14,000
8. Agricultural implements	15,000	15,000
9. Electric Motors	23,000	23,000
10. Horticulture	6,000	6,000
11. Plant protection	3,000	3,000
12. Minor Irrigation	6,22,000	6,22,000
13. Share Capital Contribution	21,000	21,000
14. Land Assignment	20,000	20,000
15. Seeds & Fertilisers	6,000	6,000
16. Schemes for landless	25,000	25,000
17. Trade Assistance	3,000	3,000
18. Land Acquisition (House sites)	25,000	—
19. Special Nutrition Programme	6,29,710	5,30,000
20. Training programmes	9,380	7,085
C.S.S.		
1. Post-matric	46,250	—
2. Girls Hostels	75,000	—
3. T.D. Blocks	1,41,600	—

APPENDIX VI (d)

SRIKAKULAM : NON-PLAN (1975-76)

(in rupees)

Schemes	Releases	Expenditure
1. Hospitals & Dispensaries	3,72,395	3,11,626
2. Post-Matric (Sch. Tribes)	3,500	—
3. Post-Matric (D.N. Tribes)	25,000	—
4. Pre-Matric (Sch. Tribes)	4,400	5,703
5. Pre-Matric (D.N. Tribes)	4,400	5,703
6. Hostels (S.Ts.)	4,63,240	—
7. Public Health	62,088	65,935
8. Supply of Books, etc.	300	300
9. Ashram Schools	10,22,475	11,51,534
10. Administration	2,49,408	3,14,455
11. Co-operatives	4,213	—
12. Spl. Nutrition Programme	28,400	49,075
13. Animal Husbandry	1,50,300	1,30,805
14. Supply of Books (Sch. Tribes)	56,000	—
15. Panchayat Samiti (D.N. Tribes)	3,336	2,824
16. Agriculture	48,800	38,452
17. Aided Schools	4,03,434	3,40,901
18. Schools (Panchayat Samiti)	4,15,870	2,59,600

APPENDIX VI (e)

SRIKAKULAM : PLAN 1976-77

(In rupees)

Schemes	Releases	Expenditure
1	2	3
1. Pre-Matric Scholarships	1,86,000	68,834
2. Ashram Schools	3,52,080	3,50,305
3. Hostels	31,125	28,162
4. Supply of Books, slates, etc.	75,000	74,999

APPENDIX VI (e)—*contd.*

1	2	3
5. Minor irrigation	1,50,000	1,50,000
6. Agriculture 14 M.W.	17,000	17,000
7. Agriculture 19 M & S	35,000	35,000
8. Supply of livestock	50,000	50,000
9. Share Capital contribution	24,000	24,000
10. Trade Assistance	6,000	6,000
11. Training Programmes	3,000	3,000
12. Spl. Nutrition programme	2,40,506	2,40,506
13. Land Acquisition	1,00,000	1,00,000
Denotified Tribes		
14. Post-Matric scholarships	1,84,006	1,84,006
15. Land Acquisition	7,500	7,500

APPENDIX VI (f)

SRIKAKULAM : NON-PLAN 1976-77

Schemes	Releases	Expenditure
1. Administration	3,60,274	3,85,391
2. Maintenance of C.R. Sets	17,801	17,171
3. Aided schools	5,39,700	4,84,305
4. Primary schools	4,20,740	4,20,740
5. Ashram Schools	12,05,659	13,41,972
6. Govt. Hostels	5,78,215	6,28,408
7. Supply of books, slates, clothes, etc.	60,900	60,900
8. Post-Matric scholarships	3,500	3,651
9. Hospitals & Dispensaries	3,04,800	3,16,815
10. Public Health	71,000	68,681
11. Irrigation	5,84,000	5,84,000
12. Agriculture	39,000	42,953
13. Animal Husbandry	76,560	1,10,464
Denotified Tribes		
14. Primary Schools	2,520	3,636
15. Supply of Books, slates, etc.	300	600
16. Per-Matric scholarships	4,400	4,400
17. Govt. Hostels	32,285	36,474

APPENDIX VI (g)

SRIKAKULAM : PLAN—1977-78

(In Rupees)

Scheme	Releases	Expenditure
Scheduled Tribes		
1. Pre-Matric scholarships	48,500	2,89,811
2. Ashram Schools	6,17,430	4,85,402
3. Hostels	1,74,150	1,61,438
4. Supply of books, slates, etc.	66,400	1,43,868
5. Minor Irrigation	4,60,000	4,60,000
6. Agriculture 100 M.W.	54,400	54,000
7. Agriculture 190 M&S	34,200	34,200
8. Supply of livestock	1,00,000	1,00,000
9. Share capital contribution	3,200	2,988
10. Trade Assistance	2,000	2,000
11. Training programmes	12,310	12,310
12. Special Nutrition Programme	3,06,998	2,50,000
Denotified Tribes		
Post-Matric scholarships	1,91,957	2,11,468
C.S.S.		
Post-Matric scholarships	1,000	4,524

APPENDIX VI (h)

SRIKAKULAM : NON-PLAN 1977-78

(In Rupees)

Schemes	Releases	Expenditure
1	2	3
1. Administration	4,02,773	4,14,324
2. Maintenance of C.R. sets	9,448	8,983
3. Aided schools	5,42,[illegible]10	5,29,231
4. Secondary schools	2,410	2,410
5. Primary schools	5,19,700	5,19,700
6. Pre-Matric scholarships	40,000	—
7. Ashram schools	18,26,175	17,24,013

APPENDIX VI (h)—*contd.*

1	2	3
8. Govt. Hostels	8,42,185	8,27,977
9. Supply of books	79,000	—
10. Post-matric scholarships	3,400	5,375
11. Hospitals & Dispensaries	5,68,000	4,74,669
12. Public Health	83,490	75,866
13. Land Acquisition	33,000	—
14. Family & Child Welfare	60,000	60,000
15. Irrigation	7,95,000	7,95,000
16. D.T.W.	40,000	40,000
17. Agriculture M.W.	50,000	49,250
18. Animal Husbandry	1,15,700	1,33,180
19. Intercaste marriages	12,000	12,000
20. Special Nutrition Programme	3,20,310	3,39,721
Denotified Tribes		
21. Govt. Primary Schools	4,790	5,720
22. Supply of books, slates	400	400
23. Pre-Matric scholarships	43,400	43,400
24. Govt. Hostels	39,715	40,524
25. Post-Matric	30,500	39,502
26. Land Acquisition	3,500	—

D.T.W. : District Tribal Welfare Officer

APPENDIX VI (i)

SRIKAKULAM : PLAN 1978-79

(In Rupees)

Schemes	Releases	Expenditure
1. Pre-Matric scholarships	2,00,000	4,65,905
2. Ashram Schools	6,80,760	6,42,944
3. Govt. Hostels	11,080	14,513
4. Mid-day meals	23,800	—
5. Supply of books, slates, etc.	1,44,150	1,43,669
6. Post-Matric	500	10,903
7. Minor Irrigation	53,000	53,000
8. Agriculture M.W.	5,000	5,000

APPENDIX VI (i)—*contd.*

1	2	3
9. Agriculture M & S	8,200	8,200
10. Livestock	33,500	33,500
11. Training programmes	68,500	68,500
12. Civic amenities	30,000	30,000
13. Special Nutrition Programme	6,75,525	6,75,525
Denotified Tribes		
Post-matric	1,32,700	1,32,696

APPENDIX VI (j)

SRIKAKULAM : NON-PLAN 1978-79

Schemes	Releases	Expenditure
1. Administration	4,74,269	4,54,312
2. Govt. Primary Schools	7,500	7,500
3. Aided Schools	6,17,820	6,19,985
4. Pre-matric	15,500	18,819
5. Primary schools	4,26,350	4,26,350
6. Ashram schools	22,59,076	22,11,012
7. Girls Hostels	10,94,650	10,72,525
8. Supply of books, slates	2,00,000	1,99,237
9. Post-matric	5,400	7,349
10. Minor Irrigation	7,95,000	7,95,000
11. Agriculture—M.W.	73,850	54,377
12. Agriculture M &S	28,000	—
13. Animal Husbandry	1,13,100	1,52,202
14. D.D.W.	40,000	—
15. Hospitals & Dispensaries	6,49,920	5,61,216
16. Primary Health Centres	42,000	42,392
17. Family and Child Welfare	86,000	86,000
18. Land Acquisition	49,628	—
19. Intercaste marriages	17,000	17,000
20. Special Nutrition Programme	1,63,428	43,936
Denotified Tribes		
21. Govt. Primary Schools	6,280	5,280
22. Hostels	43,468	46,006
23. Post-matric	30,360	2,21,589

APPENDIX VI (k)

SRIKAKULAM : PLAN 1979-80

(In Rupees)

Schemes	Cumulative Expenditure
1	2
1. Special Nutrition Programme	5,96,360
2. Supply of Livestock	10,500
3. Agriculture 142 — M.E.	4,660
190 — MSS	6,440
4. Pre-Matric scholarships	2,00,000
5. Hostels	82,111
6. Construction of staff quarters in taluks.	83,300
7. Supply of books, slates, clothes, etc.	18,130
8. Ashram Schools	30,500
C.S.S.	
1. Post-Matric Scholarships	10,000
2. I.T D.A. (G.I.A.)*	21,98,300

Srikakulam : Non-plan 1979-80

Scheduled Tribes	
1. Administration	5,22,100
2. Maintenance of C.R. Sets, etc.	10,170
3. Aided Schools (G.I.A.)	6,17,840
4. Primary Schools (P.S.) (GIA)	4,24,340
5. Mid-day Meals (Schools)	17,800
6. Hostels	13,96,800
7. Ashram Schools	27,09,950
8. IADP Ashram Schools (GIA)	14,58,850
9. Supply of books, slates, etc.	3,53,913
10. Agriculture	86,150
11. Hospitals & Dispensaries	5,47,480
12. Family and Child Welfare (GIA)	99,300
13. Public Health	75,800
14. Land Acquisition	23,000
15. Animal Husbandry	1,20,200

APPENDIX VI (k)—*contd*

1	2
16. Incentive awards to intercaste marriages	13,000
17. S.T. Pre-Matric scholarships	19,000
18. Monetary relief & legal aid to the victims of atrocities on Scheduled Tribes	1,575
19. Post-Matric scholarships	7,500
20. Special Nutrition Programme	3,42,310
21. Irrigation (G.I.A.)	1,32,600
Denotified Tribes	
1. Primary Schools (Supply of books, slates, etc.)	5,740
2. Hostels	57,900
3. Post-Matric Scholarships	1,45,000
4. Pre-Matric Scholarships	2,52,822

*I.T.D.A. : Integrated Tribal Development Agency

G.I.A. : Grants-in-aid.

Key :

C.R. Sets : Community Radio Sets

G.I.A. : Grants-in-aid

P.S. : Panchayat Samiti

Bibliography

Banfield, C. Edward, *The Moral Basis of A Backward Society*, The Free Press Research Cantre in Economic Development and Cultural Change, The University of Chicago, December 1963.

Banfield, C. Edward, *Political Influence*, The Free Press of Glencoe, INC Cowell-Collier Publishing Company, New York, 1961.

Benfield, C. Edward (Ed), *Urban Government*, The Free Press of Glencoe, INC, Cowell-Collier Publishing Company, New York, 1961.

Das Gupta, Biplab, *The Naxalite Movement*, Allied Publishers Pvt. Ltd, Bombay, 1974.

Elwin, Varrier (Ed) *India's North-East Frontier in the Nineteenth Century*, Oxford University Press, 1959.

Frankel, Francine R., *India's Political Economy—1974-1977: The Gradual Revolution*. Princeton University Press, 1978.

Gafoor, Khaja Abdul, *Social Service among the Tribes and Backward Classes in Hyderabad*, Krishnavan International Printers & Publishers, Malakpet, Hyderabad-Deccan.

Greenstein, I. Fred (Ed), *Policies and Policy Making*, Addision Wesley Publishing Company.

Haragopal, G., *Administrative Leadership and Rural Development in India*, Light & Life Publishers, New Delhi, 1980

Heydebrand, Wolf (Ed), *Comparative Organisations—The Result of Empirical Research*, Prentice-Hall, INC Engle Wood, Cliffs, New Jersey, 1973.

Khan, Waheeduddin, *Papers and Proceedings of the Workshop-cum-Seminar on Rural Institutions and Agricultural Development*, National Institute of Community Development, Hyderabad, 1972.

Kumar, Virendra, *Committess and Commissions in India: 1947-73*, Vol. VII, Concept Publishing Company, Delhi, 1978.

Lee, Bann Baan, *Bureaucratic Models and Administrative Reforms: Development* and *Change*, Institute of Social Studies. The Hague, Vol II, 1970-71.

Mason, A.H. and Paget, W.H., *Tribes of the North-West Frontier*, Gian Publications, Delhi, 198C.

Mathur, Harimohan, *Development Administration in Tribal Areas*, The HCM State Institute of Public Administration, Jaipur, 1976.

Mayerson, Martin, and Banfield, C. Edward, *Politics, Planning and the Public Interest*, The Free Press, New York, 1955.

Minhas, B. S , *Planning for the Poor*, S. Chand & Company, New Delhi, 1974.

Misra, R. P.; Sundaram, K. V.; and Prakasa Rao. V. L. S., *Regional Development Planning in India—A New Strategy*, Vikas Publishing House Pvt. Ltd., Delhi, 1974.

Muttalib, M. A., *Development Administration in Rural Government for Agriculture Production: An Approach in Comparative Administration*, Department of Publication & Press, Osmania University, Hyderabad, 1973.

Muttalib, M. A., *Democracy, Bureaucracy and Technocracy*, Concept Publishing Company, Delhi, 1980

Nigro, Felix and Nigro, Lyod, *Modern Public Administration*, Harpar & Row Publishers.

Palmer, Monte and Thomson, R. William, *The Comparative Analysis of Politics*, F. E. Peacock Publishers, INC Iasca-Illinois, 1978.

Patnaik, Nityanand & Bose, Saradindu, *An Integrated Tribal Development Plan for Keonjhar (Orissa)*, National Institute of Community Development, Hyderabad, December, 1976.

Ram Reddy, G and Sharma, B.A.V. (Ed), *State Government*

and Politics : Andhra Pradesh, Sterling Publishers, Pvt. Ltd., Delhi, 1979.

Rao, S. K. (Ed) *Rural Development in India—Some Facets*, National Institute of Rural Development, Hyderabad, 1979.

Reddy, T. Nagi, *India Mortgaged—A Marxist-Leninist Appraisal*, Tarimela Nagi Reddy Memorial Trust, Anantapur, 1975.

Sahay, B.N., *Pragmatism in Development : Application of Anthropology*, Booklive Publishers, New Delhi.

Sen, K. Lalit, *Readings on Micro Level Planning and Rural Growth Centres*, National Institute of Community Development, Hyderabad, 1972.

Sen, Samar (Ed); Panda, Debabrata; Lahiri, Ashish, *Naxalbari and After : A Frontier Anthology*, Vol. I, Abani Ranjan Roy, 19, Shyama Charan Street, Calcutta, June, 1978.

Sen, Samar (Ed); Panda, Debabrata; Lahiri, Ashish, *Naxalbari and After : A Frontier Anthology*, Abani Ranjan Roy, 19, Shyama Charan Street, Calcutta, December, 1978.

Shah, P. G., *Tribal Life in Gujarat*, Gujarat Research Society, Bombay, 1964.

Shakdher, S.L., *The Constitution and the Parliament in India—The 25 Years of the Republic*, The Lok Sabha Secretariat, New Delhi, National Publishing House, New Delhi, 1976.

Sharkansky, IRA, *Public Administration : Policy Making in Government Agencies* : Rand McNally College Publishing Company, Delhi, 1969.

Sharma, S.K. (Ed), *Dynamics of Development : An International Perspective*, Vol. II, Concept Publishing Company, Delhi, 1978,

Taylor C. Carl, *A Critical Analysis of India's Community Development Programme*, The Community Projects Administration, Govt. of India, 1956.

Tripathy, R.N.; Pradhan, F.M. and Lakshmaiah, T., *Tribal Development Programme in Keonjhar (Orissa)—An evaluation*, National Institute of Rural Development, Hyderabad, August, 1979.

Vidyarthi, L.P. (Ed), *Gandhi and Social Sciences*, *Booklive* Publishers, New Delhi.

Vidyarthi, L.P. and Rai, B.N., *Tribal Culture in India*, Concept Publishing Company, New Delhi, 1977.

Vyas, N.N.; and Mann, R.S., *Indian Tribes in Transition*, Rawat Publications, Jaipur-Delhi, 1980.

Weintraub, Dov, *Developmental Change towards a Generalised Conceptualisation of its Basic Dimensions and of the Relations Among Them*, Vol. III, Institute of Social Studies, The Hague, 1971-72.

Reports

Administration Report of Srikakulam Agency, 1955.

Administration Report of Srikakulam Agency, 1957.

Administration Report of Srikakulam Agency, 1962-63.

Administration Report : 1972-73 : Girijan Development Agency, Srikakulam : Andhra Pradesh.

Anantaraman Committee Report, 1961.

Annual Administration Report, 1973-74 : Girijan Development Agency, Srikakulam : Andhra Pradesh.

Annual Report of Girijan Development Agency, Srikakulam 1974-75.

Annual Report of Girijan Development Agency, Srikakulam, 1975-76.

Annual Report of Girijan Development Agency, Srikakulam, 1976-77.

Annual Administration Report : 1977-78, Girijan Development Agency, Srikakulam.

Ayyappan Committee Report, 1946.

Brochure on Pilot Projects for Tribal Development, Farm Information Unit, Directorate of Extension, Ministry of Agriculture, New Delhi, February, 1974.

Hill and Tribal Area Development : Govt. of India, Ministry of Home Affairs, New Delhi, 1978.

Integrated Tribal Development Plant for Tribal Areas of Srikakulam District, TCR&TI, T. W. D., Govt. of A.P., Hyderabad, 1977.

Malayappan Committee Report, 1952.

Preparation of Tribal Sub-plan 1978-83 and Project-wise Annual Sub-plan 1979-80 : Ministry of Home Affairs, Govt. of India, New Delhi, 1978.

Report on the Bench Mark Survey in the tribal areas of

Srikakulam District : TCR & T.I., Govt. of A.P., Hyderabad, 1975.

Report of the Committee on Special Multipurpose Tribal Block, Ministry of Home Affairs, New Delhi, 1960.

Report of S.C. Areas and Scheduled Tribes Commission, Govt. of India, New Delhi, 1961.

Report of the Study Team on Tribal Development Programmes, Committee on the Plan Projects, Planning Commission, Govt. of India, New Delhi, 1969.

Report of the Commissioner for Scheduled Castes and Scheduled Tribes Commission, 1971-72 and 1972-73 : (Twenty First Report).

Report of the Task Force on Development of the Tribal Areas, Planning Commission, Govt. of India, New Delhi, 1972.

Report of the House Committee on Deficits and Misappropriations in the Girijan Cooperative Corporation, A.P. Legislative Assembly, 1976.

Report on the Study of Girijan Development Agency, Srikakulam District, Agro-economic Research Centre, Andhra University, Waltair, April 1977.

Report of the Administrative Staff College of India, 1977-78.

Report of the Working Group on Tribal Development during Medium Term Plan, 1978-83, Ministry of Home Affairs, New Delhi, July 1978.

Report of the Working Group on Monitoring and Evaluation on Tribal Development and Development of Backward Classes, Govt. of India, Ministry of Home Affairs, New Delhi, 1979.

Shilu Ao Committee Report, 1969.

Study of T.D. Block—Bhadragiri—Srikakulam District, T.C.R, and T.I., TWD, Govt. of AP., Hyderabad, 1969.

Study of Aided Elementary Schools, Srikakulam, Visakhapatnam, East and West Godavari districts, T.C.R. and T.I. T.W.D., Pratap D.R. and Others, 1973.

World Development Report, 1980 : The World Bank, Washington DC, August 1980.

World Bank Annual Report, 1980 : The World Bank, Washington DC, August 1980.

Occasional Papers

Administrative Aspects of Marketing in Tribal Areas, Govt. of India, Ministry of Home Affairs, New Delhi, 1976.

Administration for Tribal Development, Govt. of India, Ministry of Home Affairs, New Delhi, 1977.

Agricultural Land Settlement : A World Bank Issues Paper, January 1978.

Approach to Tribal Development in the Sixth Plan, A Preliminary Perspective, Govt. of India, Ministry of Home Affairs, New Delhi, 1977.

Background Papers on Tribal Sub-plan-1 : Annual Tribal Sub-Plan for 1977-78 : A Resume, Govt. of India, Ministry of Home Affairs, New Delhi, 1977.

Background Paper on Tribal Development—3 : Provisions in the Constitution of India for Scheduled Tribes, Govt. of India, Ministry of Home Affairs, New Delhi, 1978.

Background Paper on Tribal Development—4 : Scheduled Tribes and Scheduled Areas in India : Govt. of India, Ministry of Home Affairs, New Delhi : 1978.

Background Paper on Tribal Development—5 : Classification of Selected Scheduled Tribes by Literacy : Govt. of India, Ministry of Home Affairs, New Delhi : 1977.

Bonded Labour—The Problem and The Prospect, Govt. of India, Ministry of Home Affairs, New Delhi, 1978.

Bonded Labour in Tribal Areas—A Historical Perspective with Special Reference to Bastar : Govt. of India, Ministry of Home Affairs, New Delhi, 1978.

Colonial Transformation of the Tribal Society in Modern India, Govt. of India, Ministry of Home Affairs, New Delhi, 1978.

Development of Small Tribal Communities—A Theoretical Frame, Govt. of India, Ministry of Home Affairs, New Delhi, 1978.

Education for Scheduled Castes and Scheduled Tribes, Govt. of India, Ministry of Home Affairs, New Delhi 1976.

Education : Sector policy paper : World Bank, April 1980.

Forestry : Sector policy paper, World Bank, Feb. 1978.

Growth Centres in Tribal Areas, Govt. of India, Ministry of Home Affairs, New Delhi, 1978.

Health : Sector policy paper : World Bank, Feb. 1980.
Industrial Complexes and their Tribal Hinterlands—A conceptual frame of their problems and prospects, Govt. of India, Ministry of Home Affairs, New Delhi, 1977.
Land Reform : Sector policy paper, World Bank, May 1975.
Legislative powers about tribal areas : Govt. of India, Ministry of Home Affairs, New Delhi, 1978.
Micro-Level Planning for Full Employment in Tribal Areas, Govt. of India, Ministry of Home Affairs, New Delhi, 1978.
Perspective on Tribal Development, Govt. of India, Ministry of Home Affairs, New Delhi, 1976.
Planning for Industrial Development of the Tribal Areas, Govt. of India, Ministry of Home Affairs, New Delhi, 1978.
Planning from Below with Special Reference to Tribal Areas, Govt. of India, Ministry of Home Affairs, New Delhi, 1977.
Planning for Educational Development in Tribal Areas, Govt. of India, Ministry of Home Affairs, New Delhi, 1977.
Proceedings of Conference of Tribal Commissioners held on 14th and 15th July, 1977, Govt. of India, Ministry of Home Affairs, New Delhi, 1977.
Role of Education in Tribal Development, Govt. of India, Ministry of Home Affairs, New Delhi, 1977.
Role of Voluntary Organisations in Tribal Development, Govt. of India, Ministry of Home Affairs, New Delhi, 1976.
Rural Electrification : A World Bank Paper : October, 1975.
Rural Development : Sector Policy Paper, World Bank, February, 1975.
Tenth International Congress of Anthropological and Ethnological Sciences and Tribal Development, Govt. of India, Ministry of Home Affairs, New Delhi, 1979.
University and Tribal Development, Govt. of India, Ministry of Home Affairs, New Delhi, 1978.
Urbanization : Sector Policy Paper, World Bank, June 1972.

Constitution, Acts, Regulations, etc.

Seerwai, H.M., Constitutional Law of India : Second Edition : Volume—I : N.M. Tripathi Private Limited, Bombay, 1975.

Seervai. H.M., Constitutional Law of India : A Critical Commentary : Second Edition : Vol. II. N.M. Tripathi Pvt. Ltd., Bombay, 1976.

The Agency Tracts Interests and Land Transfer Act, 1917.

The Ganjam and Vizagapatnam Act, 1839.

The Scheduled Districts Act, XIV of 1874.

The Andhra Pradesh Scheduled Areas Land Transfer Regulation, 1959.

The Andhra Pradesh (Scheduled Areas) Money Lenders Regulation, 1960.

The Andhra Pradesh (Scheduled Tribes) Debt Relief Regulation, 1960.

The Andhra Pradesh Scheduled Tribes Debt Relief Regulation, 1970.

The A.P. Muttas (Abolition and Conversion into Ryotwari) Regulation, 1969.

The A.P. Scheduled Areas Ryotwari Settlement Regulation, 1970.

The Madras Scheduled Areas Estates (Abolition and Conversion into Ryotwari) (A.P. Amendment) Regulation, 1960.

Articles/Periodicals

Approach to Tribal Development in the Sixth Plan—A Preliminary Perspective, Govt. of India, Ministry of Home Affairs, New Delhi, 1977.

Govt. Orders, Instructions and Guidelines on Implementation of Integrated Tribal Development Projects in Andhra Pradesh, Govt. of Andhra Pradesh, Social Welfare Department, Hyderabad, 1976.

Tribal Development in the Fifth Plan, Some Basic Policy Papers, Vol. II, Ministry of Home Affairs, Govt. of India, New Delhi, 1975.

Tribal Souvenir published by the Bharatiya Adimjati Sangh, New Delhi.

Index